Comics Above Ground
How Sequential Art Affects Mainstream Media

By Durwin S. Talon

Edited by Karen Hankala & John Morrow
Proofreading by Eric Nolen-Weathington
Original Transcriptions by Steven Tice
Design Assistance by Markus Creasy

DEDICATED TO MARK KNEECE AND BOB PENDARVIS

Teaching is a challenging job. Teaching the art of comics even more so. Mark and Bob not only teach how to create comics, they also teach how to love, enjoy and communicate through comics.

It is my honor to have taught beside them.

I would also like to thank all the talented individuals interviewed in this book for their vision and their stories. I would also like to thank Brian Ludwick, Dan Baldwin, Clint Koch, Scott Hampton, Mark Chiarello, Bob Shreck, Markus Creasy, John Morrow, Steven Tice, and especially Karen Hankala for their support in this process.

I would finally like to thank my students for being the inspiration to make this book happen.

Copyright © 2004 by TwoMorrows Publishing
10407 Bedfordtown Drive, Raleigh, NC 27614
(919) 449-0344 • fax: (919) 449-0327
e-mail: twomorrow@aol.com • web: www.twomorrows.com

Table of Contents

Comics & Storytelling

Words define our culture and images reflect our sensibilities. Because words and pictures working together are at the heart of comics, there are those who invalidate the art form as a medium suitable only for kids. The fact that even a child can understand a comic book is exactly why comics *are* a valid medium–it takes great skill to craft words and pictures as one, and it takes an accomplished communicator to tell comics stories for an audience young and old alike.

Comic books *are* worthy of pursuit, study, and dissection. Oftentimes, comics are referred to as a gutter art form, suitable only for adolescents and geeks–like jazz in a world of hip hop and rock and roll. Comic books share similar truths with jazz: both are relatively newer art forms invented in America and both are extremely difficult fields in which to succeed. And yet, there will always be those who want to tell their stories though comics.

A story must be worth telling to make a good comic book. Comic book writers are still writers; they deal with plot, character development, detail, and environment. As with any artist, comic book artists must understand the foundations of illustration including composition, perspective, color theory, and technique, and they must be able to draw from both reality and imagination. However, because comic book stories unfold over time, there are other skills that must come into play: pacing, consistency, and direction.

Creators are attracted to comics because they can tell any kind of story, without limited budget, casting constraints, or defined length. As a comics creator, you are only limited by imagination and by time. Having your stories published by a publisher is extremely difficult. The comic book *industry*, like any industry, answers to sales, is driven by marketing, and is sustained by popularity. Breaking in at any level of comics publishing takes conviction and passion.

Having been in education for more than a decade, I noticed that my favorite students were the ones who exhibit both conviction and passion. As a former professor of Sequential Art at the Savannah College of Art and Design, I was amazed by the ferocity my sequential art students tackled comic book storytelling. To them comics were not just a passive hobby; comics were a noble endeavor to undertake, with a Xerox machine, if need be.

I am proud to say that several of my students broke into comics as writers, pencilers, inkers, and colorists. To a person, they would attribute their "pro" status to timing or luck, though they indeed had the talent to back it up. My other students, just as driven and just as talented, applied their sequential art skills and flourished in other fields, including illustration, storyboarding, Web and graphic design.

Fast forward to the School of Informatics at Indiana University, IUPUI. Within the New Media Program, I am surrounded by students who are interested in integrated media, video games, animation, video and sound production. And yes, I have more than a few students who have been inspired by or are inspired to create comic books. So what is the common thread that ties new media and sequential art? *A story worth telling.*

How the story is told is as unique as the individual. Marshall McLuhan, the great communicator, once said that the "medium is the message." But the creator determines the vehicle in which the message is delivered. The keys needed to drive the vehicle will always be vision, communication, and clarity. However, the story must *always* dictate the medium, never the other way around. A good idea succeeds in its medium, but a great idea takes advantage of its medium shortcomings and strengths. What makes a great comic book rarely makes a great movie adaptation. Problem solving in video game creation is different than in illustration. More complex? No, just different. And these differences are the heart of the communication problem.

A strong concept should be an interchangeable one. A comic book can inspire a video game, a novel, or a movie. But true interchangability means that the idea must fully utilize and integrate its vehicle of delivery. If sound is crucial to a story, then the Web, animation, or motion picture might be possible avenues. If the story demands a more active participation from the audience, then novels or video games might be a possibility. A comic is both an interactive and intimate experience. The reader reads the character's balloons to hear the dialogue and ties multiple images together to create a narrative flow. The rate and speed of reading is determined by the reader. Comics are a unique art form with vast potential, but other mediums can be just as compelling and comics creators are finding more avenues to tell their stories. A creator must have the courage to recognize when a medium is not the right fit for their concept. Moreover, a comics creator knows when a story can only be told in the comics medium, and these stories (like *The Watchmen*, *Dark Knight Returns*, or *Maus*) become transcendent.

Comics Above Ground delves into mainstream storytelling media including, cover art, novels, illustration, children's books, video games, motion pictures, storyboards, concept art, visual special effects, and animation. And as diverse as these fields are, one common thread binds Adam Hughes, Greg Rucka, Dave Dorman, Louise Simonson, David Guertin, Jeph Loeb, Chuck Woitkevicz, Bernie Wrightson, Jon Van Vliet, and Bruce Timm together–a healthy respect for comics and storytelling. They also understand the differences between comics and their current profession of choice. And though many of these creators started off in comics, by concentrating on the business of storytelling, they have been able to diversify.

The undeniable impact of comics books can be felt beyond mainstream media. Comics can also be felt in history, fine art, design, and in education. Even though it is still considered a sleeper art form, comics are coming of age. Hollywood is looking to comics as self-contained storyboards complete with script, dialogue, and casting directions. Traditional writers find themselves moonlighting in comics and becoming rock stars at conventions. Animators are attracted to designing pages with weird shapes and balloons. And if other creative individuals can find a home in comics, then certainly comics creators can test themselves outside of the field.

Words and pictures bind mainstream media together. As long as a creator has a story to tell, with a unique voice and a singular vision, the story itself will demand the form it takes, be it through comic books or through other means.

A good story is a good story, no matter what form it takes.

Adam Hughes
on Comics & Comics Book Covers

The first thing that captivates a comic book reader is the cover. A good illustration clues the reader into the narrative, style, and excitement within the pages of the book. A good cover demands the reader to pick up and buy the comic. Many comic book illustrators take care of the nuts and bolts narrative that unfolds over many pages. Few of these illustrators also illustrate the cover, and even fewer specialize in this.

Adam Hughes is a renowned comic book cover artist. Fans will buy comics solely because his art graces the cover. He blends traditional comic book production techniques with tried and true illustration concepts—all on the computer. His artistic journey began growing up in New Jersey reading Marvel Comics.

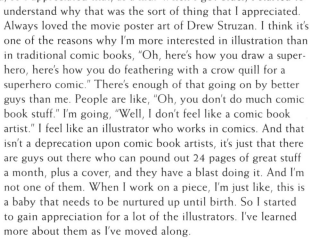

ADAM HUGHES: In my formative years, I read Jack Kirby's *Fantastic Four*, since there wasn't a lot of that being produced, just reprinted. I got into George Pérez. From George Pérez, I got into John Byrne. These were the comic book guys, the superhero guys that I was—sort of the guardians of my childhood. When I got a little older, I discovered a couple comic book artists who were a little different, not your usual Marvel/DC type of approach to drawing comics. In a perfect world, you're going to get to a point where you go, "Hey, there's more out there than just mainstream superheroes." There comes a day when you discover your first Will Eisner and you go, "Oh my goodness! This doesn't look like Spider-Man, but this is amazing!" There comes a point where you appreciate a wider scope of things, and at the right time in a young man's life, I discovered other artists. Guys like Steve Rude, Jaime Hernandez, those are the ones who opened new doors for me. All along the way, I did not and still don't have much of an art education. Or a regular one, now that I think about it. Damn, am I ignorant!

I loved Rockwell, because my mom was into Rockwell and had Rockwell books floating around, so I appreciated that, as a kid. When I got older, I started to understand why that was the sort of thing that I appreciated. Always loved the movie poster art of Drew Struzan. I think it's one of the reasons why I'm more interested in illustration than in traditional comic books, "Oh, here's how you draw a superhero, here's how you do feathering with a crow quill for a superhero comic." There's enough of that going on by better guys than me. People are like, "Oh, you don't do much comic book stuff." I'm going, "Well, I don't feel like a comic book artist." I feel like an illustrator who works in comics. And that isn't a deprecation upon comic book artists, it's just that there are guys out there who can pound out 24 pages of great stuff a month, plus a cover, and they have a blast doing it. And I'm not one of them. When I work on a piece, I'm just like, this is a baby that needs to be nurtured up until birth. So I started to gain appreciation for a lot of the illustrators. I've learned more about them as I've moved along.

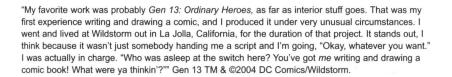

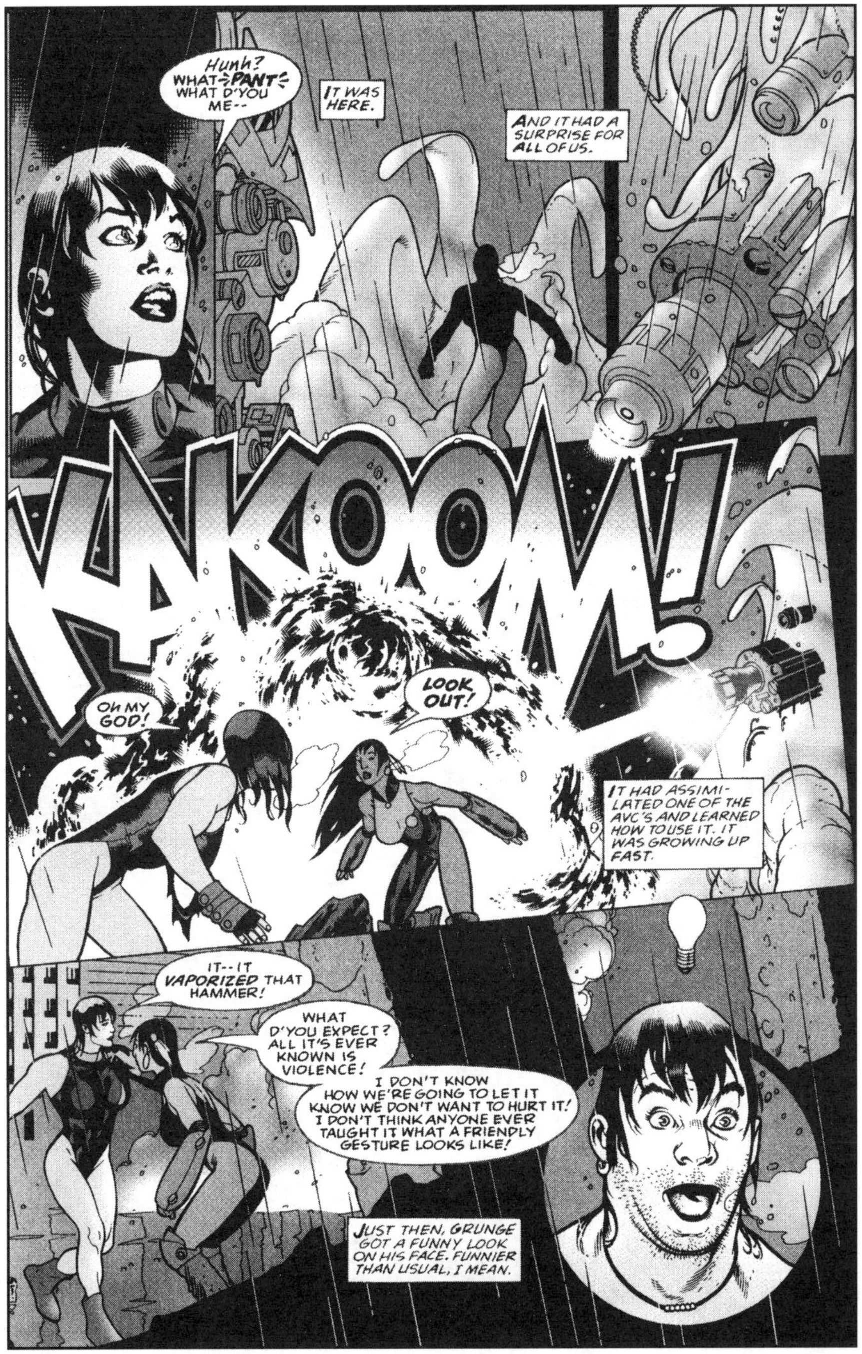
Hunh? WHAT-PANT-WHAT D'YOU ME--
IT WAS HERE.
AND IT HAD A SURPRISE FOR ALL OF US.
KAKOOM!
Oh MY GOD!
LOOK OUT!
IT HAD ASSIMILATED ONE OF THE AVC'S AND LEARNED HOW TO USE IT. IT WAS GROWING UP FAST.
IT-- IT VAPORIZED THAT HAMMER!
WHAT D'YOU EXPECT? ALL IT'S EVER KNOWN IS VIOLENCE!
I DON'T KNOW HOW WE'RE GOING TO LET IT KNOW WE DON'T WANT TO HURT IT! I DON'T THINK ANYONE EVER TAUGHT IT WHAT A FRIENDLY GESTURE LOOKS LIKE!
JUST THEN, GRUNGE GOT A FUNNY LOOK ON HIS FACE. FUNNIER THAN USUAL, I MEAN.

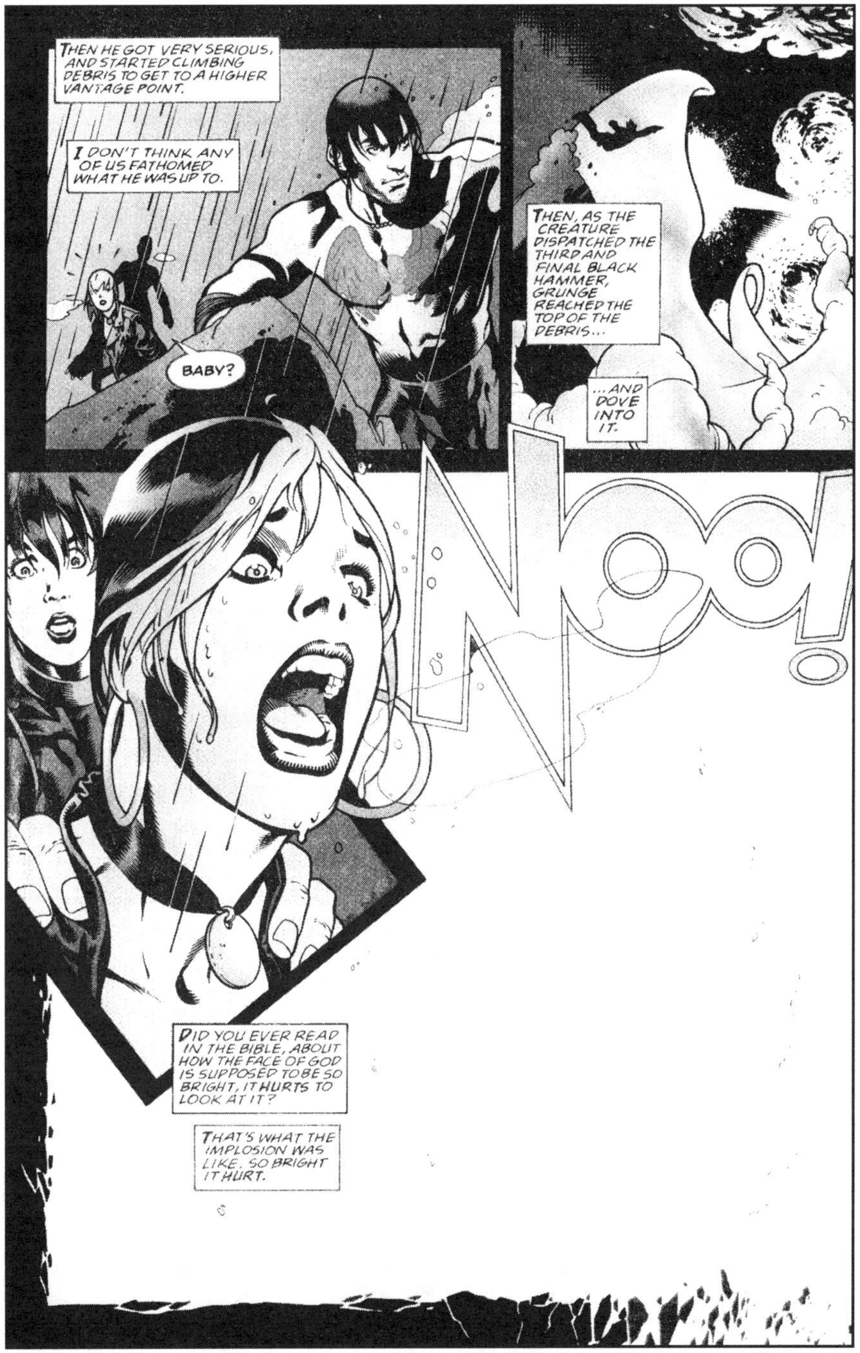
THEN HE GOT VERY SERIOUS, AND STARTED CLIMBING DEBRIS TO GET TO A HIGHER VANTAGE POINT.
I DON'T THINK ANY OF US FATHOMED WHAT HE WAS UP TO.
BABY?
THEN, AS THE CREATURE DISPATCHED THE THIRD AND FINAL BLACK HAMMER, GRUNGE REACHED THE TOP OF THE DEBRIS...
...AND DOVE INTO IT.
NOO!
DID YOU EVER READ IN THE BIBLE, ABOUT HOW THE FACE OF GOD IS SUPPOSED TO BE SO BRIGHT, IT HURTS TO LOOK AT IT?
THAT'S WHAT THE IMPLOSION WAS LIKE. SO BRIGHT IT HURT.

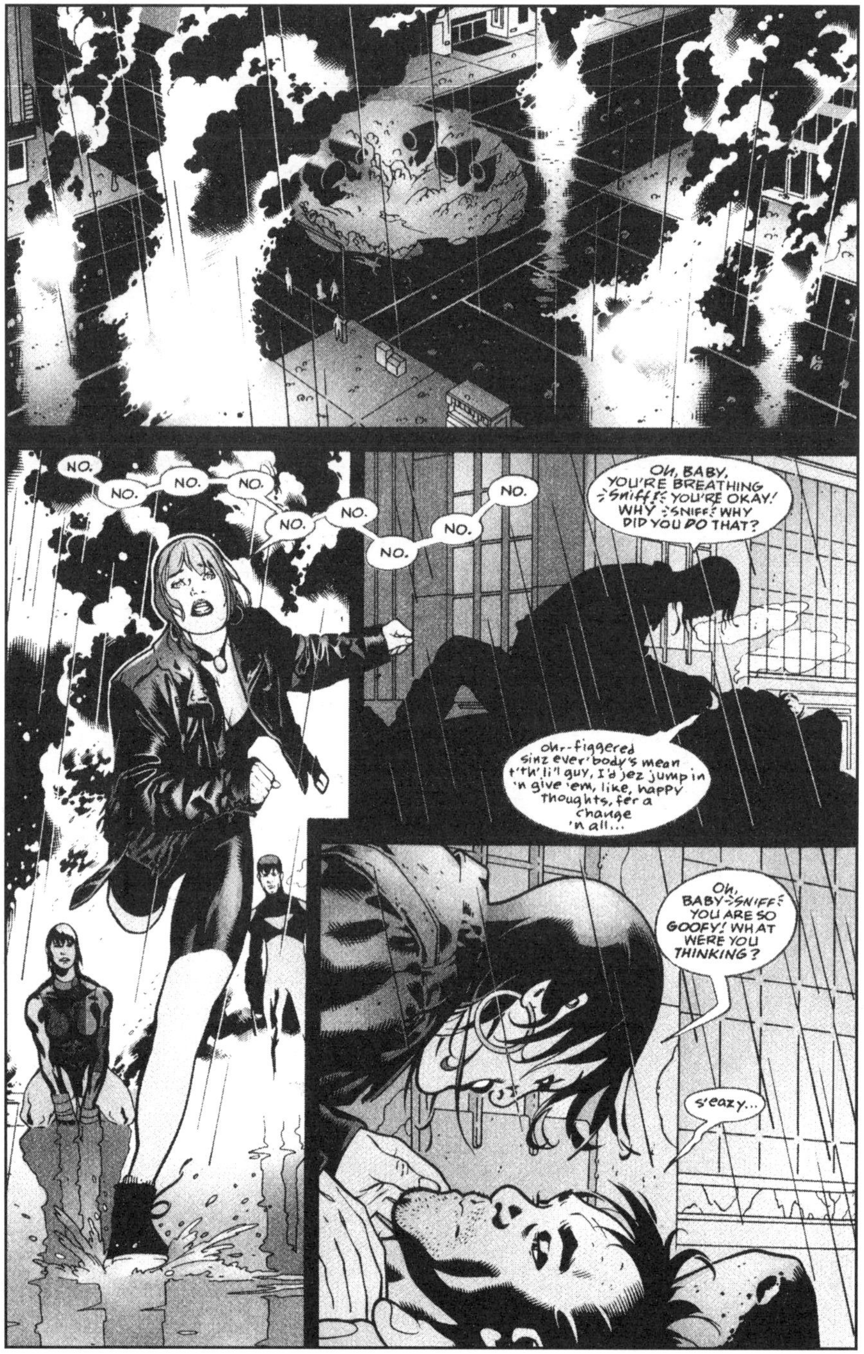
NO.
NO.
NO.
NO.
NO.
NO.
NO.
NO.
NO.
Oh, BABY, YOU'RE BREATHING -SNIFF!- YOU'RE OKAY! WHY -SNIFF- WHY DID YOU DO THAT?
oh--figgered sinz ever'body's mean t'th' li'l guy, I'd jez jump in 'n give 'em, like, happy thoughts, fer a change 'n all...
Oh, BABY -SNIFF- YOU ARE SO GOOFY! WHAT WERE YOU THINKING?
s'eazy...

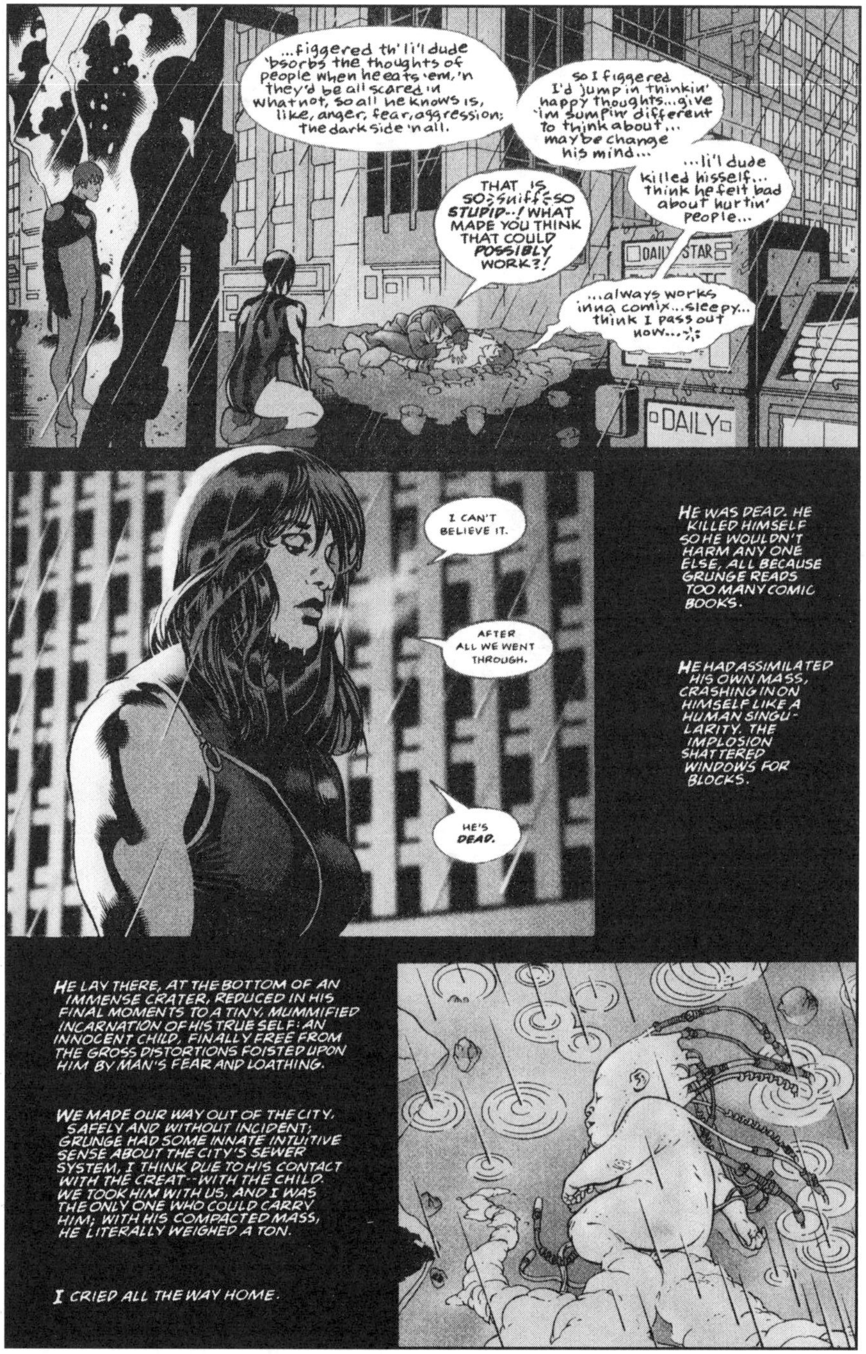
...figgered th' li'l dude 'bsorbs the thoughts of people when he eats 'em, 'n they'd be all scared 'n whatnot, so all he knows is, like, anger, fear, aggression; the dark side 'n all.
so I figgered I'd jump in thinkin' happy thoughts...give 'im sumpin' different to think about... maybe change his mind...
THAT IS SO -SNIFF- SO STUPID--! WHAT MADE YOU THINK THAT COULD POSSIBLY WORK?!
...li'l dude killed hisself... think he felt bad about hurtin' people...
DAILY STAR
...always works inna comix...sleepy... think I pass out now...
DAILY
I CAN'T BELIEVE IT.
AFTER ALL WE WENT THROUGH.
HE'S DEAD.
HE WAS DEAD. HE KILLED HIMSELF SO HE WOULDN'T HARM ANY ONE ELSE, ALL BECAUSE GRUNGE READS TOO MANY COMIC BOOKS.
HE HAD ASSIMILATED HIS OWN MASS, CRASHING IN ON HIMSELF LIKE A HUMAN SINGU-LARITY. THE IMPLOSION SHATTERED WINDOWS FOR BLOCKS.
HE LAY THERE, AT THE BOTTOM OF AN IMMENSE CRATER, REDUCED IN HIS FINAL MOMENTS TO A TINY, MUMMIFIED INCARNATION OF HIS TRUE SELF: AN INNOCENT CHILD, FINALLY FREE FROM THE GROSS DISTORTIONS FOISTED UPON HIM BY MAN'S FEAR AND LOATHING.
WE MADE OUR WAY OUT OF THE CITY, SAFELY AND WITHOUT INCIDENT; GRUNGE HAD SOME INNATE INTUITIVE SENSE ABOUT THE CITY'S SEWER SYSTEM, I THINK DUE TO HIS CONTACT WITH THE CREAT--WITH THE CHILD. WE TOOK HIM WITH US, AND I WAS THE ONLY ONE WHO COULD CARRY HIM; WITH HIS COMPACTED MASS, HE LITERALLY WEIGHED A TON.
I CRIED ALL THE WAY HOME.

THE MERITS OF BEING GROUNDED

Though he had artistic influences growing up, Hughes is, for the most part, self-taught. He found himself attracted to art and trouble-making and both proved formative.

ADAM HUGHES: Art is something I naturally gravitated towards. I wouldn't give anyone the credit and say, "It was this person's responsibility, this is the person that is the reason why I do what I do." I guess what I would say about my family is that they never told me I shouldn't do it. I had the appropriate amount of positive feedback, positive reinforcement. Much like a political prisoner, I was provided with pen and paper. Which is kind of funny, because when I got into high school, I was always getting into trouble. Not *real* trouble, not the kind of stuff the Bureau of Alcohol, Tobacco, and Firearms get called in on, but I was skipping school just because I hated it. And my mother would ground me, my mother would punish me, and she'd say, "Oh, go to your room! You're grounded for two weeks!" I was like, "Well, great, I'll sit and draw for two weeks! Woohoo!"

And it wasn't until she realized that that was not punishment that she started to say, "Okay, no pen and paper for two weeks!" All of a sudden, I was like the *Man in the Iron Mask* or something, I was just like, "Oh my God, this is horrible!" But yeah, yeah, I have a bit of art in my family. My uncle, my mother's only brother, was an artist. He was the family artist, growing up. He went to art school. And to this day, is the only Hughes that went to college. We're a bunch of ignorant oafs. Of course, he had to go to Vietnam to go to college. He didn't go for real, as they say. God bless the G.I. Bill. But he went to art school and was won over by photography. So a career as a cartoonist, he loved drawing Disney stuff, but when he came back from art college, he was a master photographer and had thrown away all his pencils. Actually, he gave me all of his art supplies when I was an infant.

I use a technical pencil, more like a lead holder rather than a regular pencil. I just like the fact that the same object is in my hand every time I draw. And I had that thing since I was five years old, and I lost it late last year. It was like an heirloom, it was my father's light sabre, it was *Excalibur*. And I lost it, and I'm going, "How did I manage to not lose this puppy for a gajillion years and..." That really sucked. So it's not like I came from the Wyeth family or something, it's not like there was art everywhere. But there was enough around to basically make me realize that there was a little bit more than just comics to like.

SELF-AWARENESS

Hughes has a healthy respect for the comics medium and was in the right place at the right time when he broke into the field. He was fully aware of the potential of comics storytelling and found the task of producing art for 24 pages on a monthly schedule daunting. By being self-aware, he knew that he must be better prepared for the workload of a monthly book.

ADAM HUGHES: For anybody who's reading this who's not old enough to remember, there was a hell of a boom [in the comics field] during the mid- to late-1980s, '85, '86, '87, there was a black-and-white boom. Anybody with, like, two thousand dollars could publish a comic book and make a pretty good profit, because, hey kids, they used to sell a lot more than they do now. And I got in on that boom. I got in because everybody was looking for artists. It was real easy, you just go to a comic book convention, show your work around. Somebody was bound to notice your stuff and say, "Hey, kid, you oughta be in pictures!" And that's what happened. It happened to a lot of people, though. The Eighties were good to a lot of us.

Blood of Dracula was my first comics work. I was doing assistant work–backgrounds and breakdowns and layouts–everything but the actual meaty stuff. In sort of an oddly portentous event, my first assignment was a pin-up for a black-and-white comic called *Eagle*, from Crystal Comics, which was one of those little publishers from the Eighties. They were Jersey guys; I knew them locally. And they were like, "Hey, kid, how about a pin-up?" And I was like, "Hey, my first assignment! I'm a pro now!" And that's how I started.

My first big job was probably the *Maze Agency* for Comico, because it was in color. That just felt like the day that our town got cable. Because when you're working in comics, at that point the Holy Grail was color. For me and all the guys I know, we were like, "Oh, man...to work in color comics." That was just like going to Hollywood or something. So when I first saw my stuff printed in color in *Maze Agency*, that was the big, glorious moment when I was like, "Hey, kid, you made it."

The process of doing interiors was like, "Oh my God, I gotta do 24 pages a month plus the cover!" It was like every artist's first exposure to that much work. I was discovering that I didn't really have a sense of discipline. I would take my time for the first three weeks of the month and then realize, "I've got fifteen pages left, crap!" And then it would be seven days of caffeine and Vivarin and not sleeping. And it's one of the things that really soured me on the whole monthly thing. I felt like I was working all the time, and because of the amount of work that I had to put out in that amount of time, I wasn't happy with anything I was producing. People ask me, "Why don't you do a monthly book?" Well, because I kind of like spending

The Maze Agency was a proving ground for Hughes, who found himself overwhelmed with the rigor of producing 24 pages of continuity in a month's time. A page from *The Maze Agency* #2 and the cover to *The Maze Agency* #3. Maze Agency TM & ©2004 Mike W. Barr.

some time happy. And I know that if I have the time, I can do better work. I don't like walking around soul sick all the time. People come up and say, "Oh man, I saw your latest comic, it was really nice!" And I'm sitting there in myself, I'm not enjoying the compliment; I'm not taking that compliment and rolling around on the ground with it and wallowing. I'm sitting there going, "Yeah, but...if you could have seen what I'm capable of..." And I realize everybody wrestles with that. I lose those wrestling matches. Other artists, better than me, they do the Teddy Roosevelt thing, "You do what you can with what you got with the time you have," and they're men about it. I'm sorry, I'm a

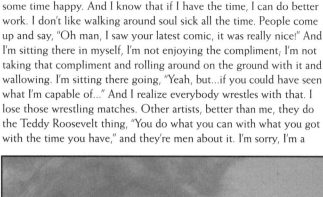

By concentrating on cover art, Hughes is able to devote his energy to producing some of the most stunning covers in comics. He finds the challenge of combining traditional and technological skillsets to produce a single illustration satisfying. Tight pencils to *Tomb Raider* #33 (below) and the final computer painted cover (right). Lara Croft TM & ©2004 Core Design, Ltd.

lightweight, pansy artist. I have to be happy with something that I'm producing, otherwise I feel like I'm wasting my time.

For somebody else, my *Maze Agency* comic, they can read that in twenty minutes. That's a month of my life, a miserable month, so that somebody can spend twenty minutes going, "Oh, nice." Why did I just do that? I love interior stuff, I love telling stories, I just can't do the monthly thing. It's not satisfying.

I'm doing some interiors now. Unfortunately, the industry right now is very niche-oriented. I've talked to so many artists who were like, "No, if you're not doing a page a day, you're not a real comic book artist. And if you're not doing a book a month, you're not a real comic book artist." And I'm like, "Okay, then I'm not a real comic book artist." I put my hands in my pockets like Bugs Bunny and shrug. "Oh well." But because of this niche-oriented industry we have right now, they don't try to fit square pegs into round holes anymore. They go, "All right. You're better at covers than you are at interiors? We're going to give you cover work. Okay, you really can't do a monthly book? Here's a mini-series." So for this time, right now, there's a place that can be found if you're not your prototypical, page-a-day comic book artist.

But you know when it's time to tell certain stories. It's just a matter of feeling. It sort of can't be quantified into, "when the entrails are right, that's when I shall proceed." No, there's a fine line between the concept of "Man, know thyself," and Dirty Harry saying, "A man's got to know his limitations." I think the smartest people in the world are the ones who realize what their limitations are and then work within them. If you can have even a shred of self-awareness, you've got an edge on a lot of the people around you. And I've got that ounce of self-awareness, where I'll sit there and go, "I have aspirations for this, I want to do this, but I know I'm not ready yet."

It's like, imagine an overweight person that wants to run the New York City marathon, and they know, "I'm not in shape, if I try to run that far, I'll pass out, I'll die, my knee will explode, my heart will collapse, I'm not ready yet. I know I can't run that distance yet. I'm going to work out, exercise, diet, train, whatever it takes, and I'll know when I'm ready." And in many ways, it's like that. I'll have ideas for covers or illustrations, and I'll go, "I don't have the chops to do that yet." And I'll put that idea on the shelf for later. And you know what? Ten years from now, I may know enough about color to pull that off. Because one of the reasons why I'm perpetually miserable is I have this phenomenal Adam Hughes gallery in my head of amazing images that I never pull off. People can look at my stuff and go, "Ooh, gosh, that's swell. Oh, gee, you did a nice job. She sure is pretty." Whatever. But I just, in my head I'm going, "Man, that's nothing compared to what I wanted to do." And I realize every artist says that. But it's that self-awareness thing again. I'll hopefully get to those beautiful images the more my skill level increases.

THE BOTTOM LINE

Typically, the cover artist doesn't even read the entire script of the comic being produced. If the cover artist is lucky, an editor may be able to offer a one sentence or one paragraph description. In today's comic books, the role of a cover is less about telling a story and more about simple economics.

ADAM HUGHES: Well, a good comic book cover makes someone buy the comic. The bottom line is, did somebody pick this up off the stands and buy it? That's a successful comic book cover. If it's a book that somebody's already going to buy—like Superman...where 90% of your readers are people who read *Superman* regardless—they could just print a white cover and people would still buy it because they've got to have their *Superman* every month. Well, then, that comic doesn't really need an amazing cover, does it? I feel that my job as a cover artist is to basically stand on the street and go, "Hurry, hurry, hurry, step right up," and get the rubes to shell out a nickel. That's the bottom line. Because the meat of the deal is the story on the inside. My job is advertising. It's on-site advertising, it's point-of-purchase sales. And that's really what it boils down to in the final analysis: did you get somebody to buy this?

It's like your boss saying, "As long as you do your job, I don't care how you dress." You can wear a clown suit to work as long as the grommets and O-rings are assembled correctly. As long as what I produce is an asset in selling the comic, then any pretensions of art or storytelling or anything like that, I'd say it's icing on the cake. And that's all within the purview of the artist. If a particular artist just basically wants to help sell a comic, then he can do whatever commercial, superficial, nutty thing he needs to do to sell a comic. But if you're into art, if you're into sort of like a little bit of substance, if you'd like people to look back years later, after the sale's done, and go, "That guy was an artist. Wow. That guy really knew what he was doing," then you might be inspired to go, "Okay, this is a commercial venture, but there's room for art here. How will I use that freedom? How will I exploit that license?" And right now I have that opportunity, so I'll exploit it.

But things have changed so much. I mean, right now, in this dwindling profit margin of an industry we've got, how can companies get the most bang for their buck? Well, if you can make a comic book cover that you can also reuse as a t-shirt, a mug, a mouse pad, whatever, that's great. It's something that Marvel's really big into right now. It seems like they don't want story-specific covers. They don't want, like, "We really need to have page five, panel ten on the cover just to show everybody whatever's happening." They want iconic images, because iconic images are what people like to walk around with on their t-shirts. Nobody's going to walk around with a t-shirt that's got Clark Kent saying to Lois Lane, "Wow, we're all out of coffee." But Clark Kent ripping his shirt open with the Daily Planet on fire behind him,

people are gonna wear *that* shirt, because it's an iconic, non-specific moment. And comic book covers have gone towards that. It used to be, back in the old days, back in the twentieth century, people would tell me, "In the next issue, this is what happens." And I'm like, "Oh, okay." Sometimes I would talk with the writer. Nowadays, it's like, basically, "Please give us something that'll help sell this comic book in this dwindling market." Fortunately, I'm all about challenging myself and doing different things that I haven't done before, whether it's out of boredom or fear or repetition. So I'm always trying stuff out, and that, I think, hopefully keeps my work from having a very "samey" kind of a quality.

Wonder Woman's bracelets and tiara are iconic. Hughes concentrated on these elements in *Wonder Woman* #152 (left). By not illustrating a plot point for a particular story, and instead producing a timeless piece, the art can then be reused in other ways. The sketch for *Wonder Woman* #152 (bottom). Wonder Woman TM & ©2004 DC Comics.

As a storyteller, the demands for producing a *Tomb Raider* cover are very simple: Lara Croft must look sexy and she must be wielding weapons–the bigger the better (far right). Hughes often adds his own sense of humor to enjoy his assignments. Here, Lara Croft jets to Ireland in *Tomb Raider* #43 (right). The preliminary sketch (top). Lara Croft TM & ©2004 Core Design, Ltd.

LARA CROFT

For some titles, editorial demand is light. For Tomb Raider, Hughes found himself with almost too much freedom to work with. Known for creating stunning "good girl" art, Hughes often wrestles with challenging himself on a given cover.

ADAM HUGHES: Again, nowadays it's not so much about what is this particular *issue* about, it's what is this book about…what is this character about? I'm working on a *Tomb Raider* cover right now, and it's part of a two-part thing where Lara Croft goes to Ireland, something

PACK APPROPRIATELY

about an old castle. I got like a book of one-paragraph descriptions of these two issues. She goes there, there's an old castle ruins, at one point she gets menaced by the spirits of the dead, that's all I was given to go on. And they're not even asking me for cover sketches, which is bizarre. They just basically say, "Please send us a finished cover every month." I could have Lara Croft in a clown suit and they might scratch their head and go, "Hmm, we can't use this." But really, I think they'd go, "The clown suit will be okay, as long as she has enormous breasts." Let's face it…I know that the one *Tomb Raider* cover that I'll never be able to sell will be the one where she's wearing a parka, because she's at the North Pole, because they'll come back and say, "We need to see cleavage!" So I'm left to exercise my own, ahem, air quotes, "judgment" and decide what does this cover need?

I have no idea if the tone is very serious–if these two issues are like the *Dark Knight Returns* meets *Tomb Raider* or whether it's fun and light or whatever. So what I've done for this first cover is Lara Croft standing in front of a beautiful backdrop of Ireland, blue skies, green hills, there's like a Celtic cross from a cemetery behind her, she's just standing in front of it like a tourist. She's holding up, in one hand, a British passport and a British Airplanes plane ticket, so she looks like a tourist. Emblazoned behind her head it says, "Take a trip to scenic Ireland." And she is wearing more guns than the Punisher ever wore on those classic Michael Golden covers. This cover is my tribute to Michael Golden *Punisher* covers. She is literally laden with every type of gun I could draw a human being wearing and you could still believe they could stand up. At the bottom it's going to say, "Pack accordingly." And I have no idea if this is appropriate for the story. People talk about, it's sort of like, it shows that she's taking a trip to Ireland, and wherever she goes, there's trouble, there's danger, so she's gotta take guns with her. It's a funny cover, it's cute. It might be entirely inappropriate. If I'm lucky, it'll make somebody go, "Oh my goodness," and they'll take it off the stands and go, "I gotta see what this is about." So it can be, nowadays, comics can be more about the overall concept of the characters and the theme of the book than the actual specifics.

ROSE AND THORN

Hughes is a storyteller. When he is offered a script, editorial and writer input, the challenge for Hughes is to understand motivation and characterization. When Hughes does his job, he produces results that contain stunning visuals as well as provocative content.

ADAM HUGHES: For the *Rose and Thorn* covers, I read every script. They sent me every script; I talked with Gail Simone, the writer, about each issue, and I asked her about the character. My covers for *Rose and Thorn* are really story-specific except for one, the cover to the third issue. But, according to Gail, I nailed what the book is about. And my covers are very figurative, they're very abstract, they're not concrete blow-up-a-certain-panel, but I read the scripts, I understood exactly what the book was about.

The cover to #4, I hope it creeps people out. There's this sort of like wife beater t-shirt landlord character that is smarmy towards Rose and puts the moves on her–just this completely unlikable character. And at one point, Thorn takes over and just really just rocks this guy's world. And I handed in a sketch with her, she's got the guy, she's behind him, she's got him by the head, she's holding one of her kama blades up to his throat. He's weeping and crying, he looks terrified. She's reaching over, and his head is squashed up against her right breast, and she's licking the sweat off the side of his forehead. And they flipped out at DC when I handed in this sketch. "Oh my God, you can't have it, oh my God!" And I'm like, this book is about a mentally disturbed teenage girl with multiple personalities who's trying to avenge the death of her hero cop father who was murdered by the mob, and her alternate personality likes to cut people. How PG is this book? How mainstream is this? This is a disturbing concept.

People who read the mini-series will see this; Rose isn't the real personality. Thorn is the real personality. Rose is an artificial construct created by her psychologist, psychiatrist, whatever it is, to basically make her a socially adaptable person. Her "normal" personality is a creation. The real personality is this disturbed teenage girl who likes to cut people. It's an amazing concept on the old cliché of the somnambulist character who's a sleepwalker and has a split personality and fights crime at night in their pajamas. And Gail's done an amazing thing with it. And I handed in this cover concept, because I thought, "Okay, this isn't exactly *Peanuts*. This isn't exactly *Family Circus*. There's some high concepts going on here." At it's core, I thought this book should disturb people. This book is all about a teenage girl getting screwed over mentally by some nefarious people. It's about the mob, it's about retribution. And I'm thinking, "Okay, I should do some covers that are disturbing." It should be about disturbing people.

And like I said, they wigged out about this DC comic "superheroine" licking a bad guy. In the book she toys with the guy,

she taunts him, she cuts his hand, takes his gun away, and then plays with him mentally up until the point when she lets him go. She's basically making this guy suffer. And you know there's that old expression, "I can taste your fear," and I thought, "All right, well, my abstract cover will be her literally tasting his fear!" And we worked it out at DC, ended up doing the cover, and it's icky. And people look at it and go, "Ewww, Adam, why'd you do that? That's nasty!" And I'm going, "It's *supposed* to be nasty. My intention was for it to be nasty." Hopefully it'll be so nasty somebody will pick it up and go, "I gotta find out why this girl's licking this pimp! This is terrible!" How many comic books come

Sometimes cover art elicits an emotional response. *Rose and Thorn* sketches (top and right), inks (bottom) and the finished cover (left) for issue 4. Rose & Thorn TM & ©2004 DC Comics

out a week? If somebody wastes ten seconds of breath going, "Did you see that Adam Hughes cover with the girl licking the guy? Eewww!" Then I did my job as a cover artist, because somebody took time out of their day to reflect upon *Rose and Thorn #4*.

The editor was like, "Thorn isn't that kind of character and this isn't that kind of book!" And the writer, Gail, when she saw the sketch, she was like, "Oh my God, that's perfect! That so captures what this book is about!" And I was like, "That's my job." And I was able to do that because they let me interact with the writer. But if you're working with a good writer and you've got a good comic, then you've got an ideal situation.

Possessing great technique, Hughes walks the fine line between flat detail and over-rendering. To make Wonder Woman both athletic and beautiful, Hughes will flatten graphic detail in her skin and hair. By doing this, she appears youthful. However, Hughes will render her costume with detail to add athleticism. Wonder Woman #150 (right) is a perfect example of this balance. The rough sketch (below) used to plan this cover. Wonder Woman TM & ©2004 DC Comics

LEARNING THE ROPES

Producing art is a constant battle. There are many ways to solve the same visual problem, but only experience can dictate the clearest solution. Hughes battles with his art constantly. Color, composition, and movement are all hard fought principles, learned and conquered by the act of producing art. And as beautiful and detailed as Hughes' art is, these are the guiding principles for his covers' success.

ADAM HUGHES: Rendering can be cocaine. It's a whole lot of trial and error. You can basically sit there, "Oh, my brush is workin' today!" or "Ah, man, look at this!" And you can get lost in the details, and when you're done, you're going, "Oh, I really over-rendered this." For me, and it's a terrible thing, no fan wants to hear this, no aspiring artist wants to hear, "Hey, kid, it's all about eyeballing. It's all about just sort of doing it until you think it looks right." But I don't have a whole set of rules. For me it's all a matter of what looks right, what doesn't look right. And when I've got what looks right, can I put it in words? Can I sit down and figure out, "Okay, what was it about this that actually did work?" Because my theory, my personal theory, is if you can put a name on it, if you can figure it out, then you control it. Then the next time, it's not an accident. You can use it the next time. It's all about gaining control over those happy accidents.

So it's a lot of trial and error. That's why I like Photoshop, because you can get rid of all the errors very easily. I'll never let people see what I throw away. But a lot of times I've discovered that it's a sense of balance. When I'm working on a piece, I don't want to render it everywhere. It's all about positive space versus negative space. It's all about rendering versus non-rendering. Let's take Wonder Woman, for example. People will look at my Wonder Woman: I try to draw a very athletic, very fit Wonder Woman. I'm not a big fan of Wonder Woman as a curvy, hippy, vivacious soccer mom. My theory about Wonder Woman was, even before she was given superpowers, she was the greatest athlete from an island of athletes. Paradise Island had, like, two percent body fat, total, y'know? And she kicked everybody else's asses in their Olympics to get to come to Man's World. She's gotta be an amazing athlete. Some covers I failed, some covers I said, "Gee, how to you draw that balance between feminine attractiveness and power? Where do you find that line?" And I found that at a lot of times, it was in the details.

To make a female character look muscular and athletic while still looking female, I discovered that I could draw the crap out of Wonder Woman's costume. Layer upon layer of detail on her bodice, in the gold, her boots, stuff like that, the bands, every reflection. But keep the flesh tones open and simple, then she can still be glamorous and beautiful. That's where I started to find the balance. People don't want to feel cheated by a graphic, abstract image, because only five percent of the population "gets" graphic. Simplicity is over the head of the average layman. Most people look at a comic book cover and they go, "Ah, look at all that detail! Gosh darn it! That sure is sweet, Martha! Shine up your tooth, we're going to the comic shop!"

I discovered that Wonder Woman's hair is supposed to be jet black. I discovered that I could get away with drawing Wonder Woman's hair with two values: black, which I do in the line art stage, and then I would leave highlights open for color. Now, on my earlier covers, I would go into those highlights, and I would try to render several values of color in the highlight area. And I realized, "You know what? That's working at cross-purposes here. So what if I put a really, really, really dark color in those highlight areas..." Wonder Woman's hair is two values, black and nearly black. By simplifying Wonder Woman's hair, I could render, say, the gold on her chest.

And that's where I realized, okay, it's all about where you put the details. "Decide! Where do you put the details?" Sometimes nature will tell you where to put the detail, where not to put the detail. If you over-render women in the face and the body, unless you're Travis Charest or the guy that draws dollar bills, it's going to look like a wrinkled, nasty-looking lady. Good girl art–it's all about putting the detail in the hair or the costume, the accoutrements, leaving the flesh tones open, under-rendered, so they have a soft quality to them.

And like I said, sometimes nature will tell you. Any painter knows that red, in the visible light spectrum, just swallows light. There's no such thing as dark red, there's no such thing as light red; It's brown or it's pink or orange. But with all the other colors, you can go light blue, dark blue, light green, dark green. Red just exists in this part of the visible light spectrum where anything that's truly red goes very flat. So, if I'm doing Superman on a cover, when I do the reds, I know that I'm going to under-render the red values, because I know that's how red works. I know that I can get away with my line art, red, and maybe a shade darker for shadows. That's it, that's all I need to do. Nature has told me how much rendering to do on the red, if I were doing Iron Man or if I were doing Daredevil.

Everybody knows Superman's costume is red, yellow, and blue. But if you were going to do Superman at night, they wouldn't be cyan, process red, and yellow. It all depends on what the overall color theory of the illustration or the page is. With the Superman and Hippolyta cover, because it was supposed to be outer space, I wanted to go cooler. It was my silent tribute to the sour palette of Kevin Nowlan. I wanted it to be very cool, very blue; it's not a happy moment. I didn't want any exciting colors, I didn't want any of the hunger colors, I didn't want any reds or anything like that. So I was like, "All right, I can neutralize the blue of Superman's costume, I'm

going to render most of it in the inks, it's going to be mostly black. I'm going to neutralize his flesh tones, I'm going to take that red of his cape and his ass and his trunks and his boots and push it over towards the violet, and the yellow of Superman's chest, I knocked that down too." It was just kind of skewing that cover to the blue end of the spectrum because it was appropriate for that piece.

Somebody sent me an e-mail, he asked, "What's a good flesh tone?" And I said, "The fact that you're asking me this question means that you don't get it. It doesn't matter. You can make somebody's flesh tone green, you can make it purple. It all depends on

Superman, Wonder Woman TM & ©2004 DC Comics

Color theory is another important key to Hughes' success as an illustrator. Atmosphere dictates how colors are rendered. In *Wonder Woman* #172, Hughes utilizes cooler palettes to narrate the story of Superman and Hippolyta in outer space. Flesh tones are neutralized and Superman's reds read as almost violet (left). Hughes' development roughs searching for the perfect moment (top) and finished inks (right).

what the overall color theory of the illustration or the page is." I remember Mike Mignola, another god along the likes of Kevin Nowlan, he did a *Batman: Legends of the Dark Knight* issue, and there was a monochromatic red sequence. And I took a step back and I realized that Batman's cape and his trunk and his boots and his gloves were colored brown, and the gray of his tunic was colored like a mauve or even a pink. And I said, "Batman is brown and pink! That's insane!" But it was a color theory moment, it was a compositional thing. It wasn't like Batman was walking down the street in Gotham City in broad daylight in a brown and pink costume.

Hughes discovered that Wonder Woman's lasso could be utilized as a graphic device to direct eye movement. Here, in *Wonder Woman* #188, the lasso creates a strong rhythm behind Diana, connecting detail. Wonder Woman TM & ©2004 DC Comics

Guys like Brian Stelfreeze, Kevin Nowlan, they understand it way more than I do. I'm messing around with the tip of the iceberg. Again, most of the times, everything I do is based on what looks good to me. And a lot of times you can put two colors together and go, "They don't look good together, they don't play well together." But good color theory, that's the secret to success in a color endeavor. It's indisputable and irrefutable. And I think there are principles of color theory that work. I don't believe that art has any rules, but I do believe that it has principles. I believe that there are time-honored things that work and things that don't work. And a grasp of sound color theory separates a mediocre illustration or painting from an excellent one. And even with the great illustrations—you can sit there and say, "Hey, Adam, but what about paintings that are all about dis-cord, that are all about wild, contradictory color theory?" Well, if it's successful, that's because the artist understood color theory and knew how to break the rules. Color theory isn't just knowing that this color goes with that color. Good color theory also entails knowing what two different colors, two different hues, two different values that are next to each other do to each other. Individually, they look a certain way, but when they're put next to each other, they affect each other. They're not mixed with each other, but they occupy the same space. They're arriving in the viewer's brain at the same time. Good color theory means you understand how all the colors in your palette and their various values, not only how they look on their own but how they affect each other. Like I said, it's all about control and once or twice I've actually pulled it off. That, again, goes back to knowing something but knowing you're not ready to do it. I know that there are combinations of various colors and various values affect the reader in different ways. I'm just at the beginning of understanding how to implement it. And I know that it'll be ten, twenty, thirty years before I've got a really good grasp of it.

I also don't know the principles of composition the way I probably should. I struggle with composition because I know I'm not pushing myself as far as I could in a lot of instances. I get to the point where I'm going, "Oh, I need to go with what works." I resort to the medium pin-up shot because, "I know I can pull off a cute-looking chick in this circumstance. Whew! Dodged a bullet, there!" But I'll reach a moment where I'll go, "I really need to challenge myself in a design sense, here," and that's when I'll start to do something a little different. But it's tough, because there are some very serious principles of composi-tion that I barely have a grasp of, and I'm trying to get a better hold of it.

Ideally, when I'm working on a composition, my main thoughts are about positive and negative space. It's all about, where is this piece going to be busy with information, where is it not. I think that a lot of times, if you can break a composition down to two values, if you can do a thumbnail of your composition in black-and-white and it still reads, you've got an amazing composition. Because you know that you don't need any more detail, you don't need the contrast between any other values, you don't need the contrast between any disparate hues. If your composition imparts the information that it's supposed to impart with the two values, black-and-white, your composition is solid. At that point, any further contrast you create, whether it's through value or color, is compositional icing on the cake.

Another compositional principle that I think about is…I think it's called "path of interest." And I apologize to any learned people who are reading this. Remember, I've never been to art school, I'm overhearing stuff when other artists talk, or when I read books, and I think, "Oh, okay, I think I know what that means." Path of interest: where does your eye start when you look at this cover? Where does it end? Does it go anywhere? A lot of times I will compose a piece and I'll go, "Okay, the eye is supposed to stay right in this area here, so everything that's outside that path of interest in my composition, I've got to make sure that I don't draw attention to it." Well, how do you do that? Well, contrast draws your eye. If you've got an art board, and it's filled with all sorts of gray dots, light gray/dark gray, light gray/dark gray, but right in the middle, there's a yin and yang sign, black-and-white. Your eye is drawn to that. All the little medium gray values of all the little gray dots all over the place, they just form a melange in your peripheral vision. You're looking at that black and that white. As soon as you walk into that room, you see that black and that white right in the middle. Everything else just turns to gray mush. I think like that when I'm working. I'll go, "Okay, where's the information in this cover? Where do I want them to start? Where's the business on this cover?" And I'll go, "Okay, that right there is where my greatest contrast will be. That's where my greatest color versus color contrast will be."

And the day I sort of realized that I could use Wonder Woman's lasso to move the eye…Normally, Wonder Woman's lasso is a series of ellipses that hang from her hip, and when I realized that I could use them as a design element, it was a very freeing day for me. I was like, "Oh, man, I can use this!" The lasso on my covers is always moving. It's always in the middle of a whoosh! Wonder Woman's lasso, to me, became a design element. My love for art nouveau, which I got while working on *Ghost*, came through. I didn't do a whole lot of art nouveau rendering in *Wonder Woman*, I didn't do a lot of art nouveau elements, but that graceful, cursive shape to her lasso… Her lasso ceased to be a weapon, it ceased to be a lie detector, and it became a graphic device to me, and I'll always use it that way. And the thing is, if I was drawing a character that had a cape, if I drew Superman or Batman regularly, their cape would do the same thing. It wouldn't necessarily flow into art nouveau shapes, but I would use that gigantic swatch of fabric as a compositional element.

"I really, really, really loved the cover where Wonder Woman goes back in time and encounters the Golden Age Wonder Woman. Doing the Golden Age Wonder Woman cover style and to have my Wonder Woman standing on the cover, reacting with this old line-art Wonder Woman with the 65 line-screen colors was an absolute, absolute joy. And that one was fun the whole time. And I've gotta give DC a lot of credit, because they let me use the old logo, they let me use the old DC bullet, they let me use pretty much everything that used to be on old DC comic book covers. The only concession was that we had to have a UPC box. We fought to try to get it put on the back cover, because Marvel does it all the time. As long as the UPC box is somewhere on the comic, it's fine. But apparently that interferes with the sales of advertising on the back cover. It's like the people buying the ads feel gypped, because they're paying for 100% of the back cover, and they might feel that 'why are we paying this much money when we're only getting 99% of the cover?' Because I really wanted people to walk up and look at that comic and go, 'Who left this old Wonder Woman on the stands?' We came pretty close to pulling it off on that one."

"The cover where Wonder Woman fought Clayface and was covered in mud...I can't believe they let me do that. The editor at the time always handed in her descriptions of what was going on in the *Wonder Woman* comics as if they were boxing matches. 'This issue is Wonder Woman vs. blah, next issue is Wonder Woman vs. blah-blah, and then the next issue is Wonder Woman's rematch with blah.' And I'd be like, 'These are all "versus" covers!' And then they [assigned]: 'Two issues, Wonder Woman vs. Clayface.' And I said, 'All right, look. On the second one, I'll give you your "versus" cover, I'll give you your boxing cover' (and I think that second Clayface cover is one of the worst ones I handed in, too), but then I said, 'You gotta let me try something on the first one. Let me experiment. If you don't like it, we'll come up with something else.' And I handed in the sketch, and people were just like, 'I can't believe you did that!' And it was so funny—Wonder Woman doing that three stooges schtick, pulling the pie out of your eye. I was just like, that's funny. If I saw that cover on the stands, if I never read *Wonder Woman*, I would have to sit there and go, 'Oh, I've gotta check this out. I gotta find out how Wonder Woman gets covered in this crap.' Even though she doesn't. Hey, if I fought Clayface, I think it would be a dirty experience." The classic cover to *Wonder Woman* #160 (right) and original sketch (below). Wonder Woman TM & ©2004 DC Comics

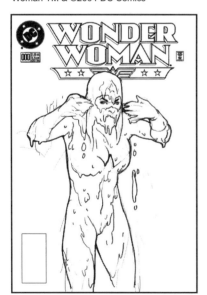

For Hughes, the best working relationship is the one he shared with Mark Chiarello on Wonder Woman. *This collaboration produced numerous awards for the team and its success can be attributed to an understanding of art and being an artist.*

ADAM HUGHES: Working with Mark Chiarello is the best thing in the world. He's the art director over at DC and he's an amazing painter. There's so many times you're working with a person who doesn't know art. You have no idea why they got their job, whether they were uplifted from the Neanderthal state, from the mail room, or whether they're somebody's cousin, or whether they actually have a degree in English and actually know what's going on as far as storytelling, or they have a degree in Marketing, perhaps, and don't know what's going on. You don't know. I've encountered a lot of chowderheads in my time as a cover artist and I've encountered a lot of insightful, brilliant art directors. There's one of every type. Mark, in my experience, is the best example of the good type. He's management who knows about art. And Mark knows how to work with his artists. I would say that whatever kudos, whatever awards we won on that four-year run on the *Wonder Woman* covers, Mark Chiarello gets fully 50% of the credit, because they were collaborations. People think they were all about me because I was the guy doing the artwork, but there's gotta be somebody you bounce ideas off of. There's gotta be somebody who doesn't fire you when things get tough or you get behind on deadlines. Somebody who has a little bit more thought other than "I don't want to get yelled at the next hot meeting." We built an enjoyable run of covers on a book, which is a nice thing. Anytime you can have a positive buzz about a comic, it's a good thing. Mark's got that foresight. So yeah, Mark and I are talking about what our next cover project together will be. I've done my *Rose and Thorn* covers for him. So it's the ideal situation when you can work with another artist.

When I took on *Wonder Woman*, I was very excited. I had a wonderful sense of job security, and I felt that while I was doing them that I could screw up on a particular month, I could do something bad on a particular cover, and it would be okay because I know next month I would be able to try something different. It wasn't like, oh my goodness, I've only got X amount of time to prove myself. It's not like a game show: "We've got 48 hours, oh my God! Do it or we're done." After a few covers, I got to the point where I was like, "Wow, I can actually experiment, I can actually stretch." And I learned more on those four years on *Wonder Woman* covers than I probably have in my whole career. It was a great learning experience.

Hughes was able to experiment with technique and style throughout his run on Wonder Woman. *Some covers were lovingly rendered, paintings on computer.*

Other covers were a bit more cartoony, affording experimentation with emotion. All in all, the experience was just right.

HUGHES: Sometimes it can be as positive as, "Oh, I'm gonna grow, I'm gonna change, every day I'm gonna make myself better." Or it can be complete personal dissatisfaction. You can sit there and look at your work and go, "Christ, I suck. God, I gotta try something new." So you just try anything…throw spaghetti at the wall, see what sticks, just try to find something that works. You need to be allowed the opportunity to try that. If you're pigeonholed and you're being told, "You must produce this grommet and this O-ring every day, ka-chung, ka-chung, ka-chung," then there's no room for experimentation or the serendipity of a happy accident that somehow can unlock something new. These accidents seem to be the bulk of my work. "Whoops, I spilled…hey, that looks pretty good!"

Unfortunately, I would say sixty to seventy percent of everything I pull off on one of my covers is an accident. You know, where I'll accidentally stumble across, like, the cure to cancer or cold fusion or something, and I'll go, "I forgot the ingredients! How did I get here? Dammit!" And the bad thing is, especially when I'm coloring in Photoshop—I work at a really high resolution just in case my stuff gets turned into a poster or some kind of merchandisable thing. It chews up too much memory to keep the history palette set to more than one step. So it's not like I can go back and appreciate my steps and go, "Ahhhh, so *that's* what I did."

I sit there and go, "Crap." One out of every ten things that I stumble across accidentally in an artistic journey, I'll remember how I pulled it off and go, "I can use that later." Keeping track of the accidents is the story of my life. The *Wonder Woman* covers, those covers allowed me to do a lot of different stuff. I think we've paid off. It was an ideal assignment, and I miss it very much.

"This is probably my favorite one out of the whole run. One, I got to draw Wonder Woman smiling. I always seem to be having to draw Wonder Woman as this ass-kicking Amazon, which is not how I see that character. I like drawing her happy. I don't see her as DC Comics' version of Xena, Warrior Princess. Wonder Woman doesn't look exactly the same from cover to cover because I'm trying constantly to find the balance that works, I'm trying to find my Wonder Woman, as you would say. And I thought that cover was the closest that I came. If I could have drawn Wonder Woman that way every cover, I'd have been a happy camper.

"I really felt that the Lois Lane cover had a Rockwell feel because it told a story. Superman, who is a classically stoic, limbs akimbo, fists on hips kind of a guy, I drew him with just his chin in his hand. 'Oh, women talking': the look on his face, that to me was funny. That had a personal Rockwell quality to it. If Rockwell had to do a *Superman* cover, maybe he would show Superman in one of his lighter moments." *A Day In the Life*, cover to *Wonder Woman* #170 (near right), initial sketch (top right) and inks (bottom right). Wonder Woman, Lois Lane, Superman TM & ©2004 DC Comics

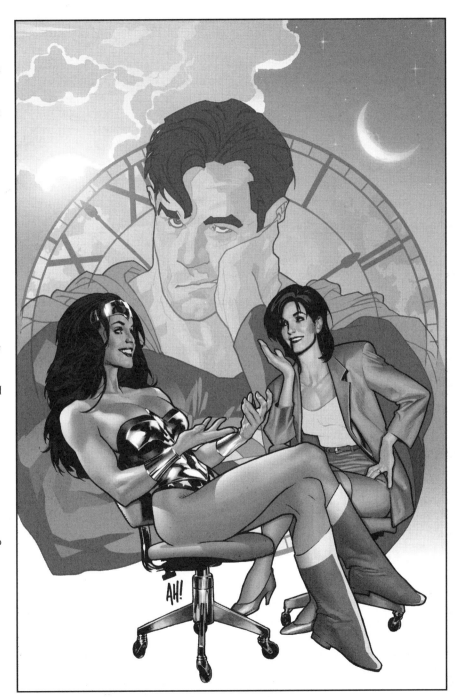

Wonder Woman TM & ©2004 DC Comics

PARTING SHOTS

Art drives Adam Hughes, but a passion for comics keeps him in the field.

ADAM HUGHES: I've always loved comics from an early age. Most of the people that work in comics were into comics when they were younger–I'd say 99%. And it's just when people get older and start to discover other distractions in life that they outgrow comics; they outgrow toys, they outgrow cartoons, they put away the things of childhood. I think the only thing that separates us from them is the fact that when we start shaving and we discover that girls don't have cooties, we still like the comics. We still enjoy that stuff. Maybe, if we're lucky, we appreciate them on a different level. Maybe when you grow up, you can still look at a comic, and rather than go, "Oh, this is so cool! Oh, man!" Then you look at it and go, "Wow, this person really understands storytelling," or you appreciate it as an art form.

I think the lure of comics is that it's a part of your childhood and *most* people probably have good memories of their childhood. When you grow up, you have to put all of that away. When you raise your own families, you have your bills to pay, your home to mortgage. Life is just filled with adult responsibilities and comics are a reminder that it's okay to be child-like. Not childish, but child-like. Even the most serious comics, the graphic novels, the high art, they're still born from the predication that this is all based on something fun. It reminds us of a time when pretty much having fun was the only thing on your action item list. When you're a child, you to-do list is "Have fun. Have fun. Eat lunch. Take a nap. Wake up and have some more fun." And that's what comics are, I think. American comics, anyway.

I really do think there's two types of artists in the world. You've got your happy, successful, content artists that basically are loving life, they're living large, and they're enjoying every minute of it. And then the rest of the art world is populated by Van Goghs: tortured, one-eared artists just basically wringing their hands and dying every day to create, which they feel the need to do. And every day I get more and more scared, "Man, I think I'm in that second category." Hey, man, I have my days when I envy those guys. I just got a bill from the IRS in the mail two days ago, and I was kind of going, "Man, I wish I was one of those happy idiots that just made a lot of money." There's something to be said for that. And if you're happy with what you're doing, then I'm all for you. As long as your happiness doesn't involve knocking down little Girl Scouts and breaking their cookies or something, then more power to you. I envy a lot of those people that are able to function like that. They seem to have a happiness level–even if it's just a purely superficial, "Mwa-ha-ha, I make money!" And they shake their fist, like Doctor Doom, at the sky and like, "I'm a sellout and life is large!" Part of me's going, "Well, that guy's at least having fun. He's not having fun drawing the stuff, but he's enjoying the benefits."

And I'm not trying to play this self-deprecating game. People wonder, "Why aren't you happier?" And I'm like, "I don't know." Dissatisfaction is the water that churns my mill. Not getting it right keeps me going. It probably also keeps me from having an ego problem. I remember when I first started getting into comics, all my friends were like, "Oh, gotta watch it, his head's gonna get big!" Well, it did get big, but I had such a bad opinion of myself when I started that it just inflated enough to the point where I'm like, "Yeah, I'm okay." Whatever sort of accolades or kudos come along, I'm going, "Well, it's nice that other people feel that way, and I'm glad somebody else is getting something from this, but I'm going to keep sweating and struggling and have trouble with it."

I don't care who the artist is, I don't feel that any artist finishes that journey. I think it's like looking for the Holy Grail. You're never going to find it. It's all about who you are and what you discover along the way. I can't even imagine any artist ever finishing a painting and going, "That's it! I have discovered the last principle of art!" It's like that Web page somebody put up that said, "Congratulations! You have reached the end of the Internet. Please shut off your computer and go out and have fun." And it's true, there is no end. If you think about it, people have spent centuries engaged in an endeavor that has no resolution, no hope of climax, no hope of payoff except for the actual journey itself. I'm sure in print that's going to sound incredibly pretentious, but it's true. I know I'm going to go to my grave going, "What did I miss? What did I not get?" And it's going to be that way. It's a sad truth, but it's there. It's tough.

Now breaking into comics…that's tough, because the industry is so different now from when I got in. Vastly, vastly different than when I got in. Ten years ago, I would have had easy advice: like take your stuff to conventions. But it would have been applicable ten years ago. Still, that's the best way to get your work shown around. Brevity helps. No editor wants to be inundated with your life's work, just pick your five best pieces. Very specific tactics. I've talked to people who were like, "How can I be a comic book cover artist?" And I'm going, "I dunno. I didn't set out to be a comic book cover artist." It's this bizarre niche you end up in. The guy down at the zoo who gives rhinos colonics–do you think he wanted to do that when he was a kid? Nooo. "Timmy, it's career day, what do you...?" "Oh, I want to shove my arm up a rhino!" For me, personally, a life plan is a laugh. I'm just going to see where it takes me and adapt.

I ended up where I am because I draw well enough that people still want to hire me. I'm not useful as an in-the-trenches, page-a-day guy, but the industry found a place for me where my particular backwards skills can be useful. If I planned to be here, I don't think I would have made it here. I'm where I am by default, not out of any grand design or scheme. The best advice for any people trying to get into this type of thing is to realize that it is not, for most of us, a lucrative or amazingly tangibly rewarding experience. I mean, you have your Jim Lees and your Bryan Hitches, guys who are buying property on the moon, they're so wealthy. But for most of us, it's a grunty little experience. And if you're lucky, you get a little bit of a living. But you do it because it's better than being rich but in a miserable job. You find some sort of reward. Nobody likes being poor. It's like what Frank Darabont said, sometimes the rewards aren't as tangible as having fun while you're doing it. In other words, it could be not as tangible is having a big paycheck. Anybody who gets into comics for money is probably doomed to failure. But my advice is, if you really, really, really want to do this: just accept it. It's two social steps above being a monk as far as the fame and fortune realm. But if you can find a sense of reward and satisfaction out of that, then give it a shot. At the core, you have to enjoy some aspect of it. There's gotta be some sort of reward in it that's ineffable. And if you're the kind of person who is content with spending your life with only ineffable rewards like satisfaction, challenges overcome... Let's face it, if you become a famous comic book artist, it's a dubious kind of fame. But still, you make do.

Hughes is an incredible draftsman. However, he works hard at his craft in developing each cover. He leaves nothing to chance and will produce a wide array of sketches until he is satisfied with a direction. Like all great illustrators, he uses sketching as a way to get his ideas straight and to plan his compositions. Sketching is the most important part of Hughes' cover process: *Wonder Woman* #144 (opposite top), *Wonder Woman* #151 (opposite bottom), "mini-series proposal" sketch (top far right), and *Wonder Woman* #142 (bottom far right). Once this stage is done, his reward is the challenge of creating art, *Wonder Woman* #153 (right).

Wonder Woman TM & ©2004 DC Comics

Greg Rucka
on Comics & Novels

Though comic books are a visual art form, they are still books. The smell of paper and ink used in comic book production serve as a bridge for older and modern comics readers' sensibilities. Captions, dialogue and thought balloons ground characters to the sometimes fantastic worlds in which they operate. Words are at the heart of a comic book and are gaining importance as visual art forms like sequential art mature.

Greg Rucka is an emotional writer. He is passionate and prolific. Though he has developed an impressive comic books resumé and has earned awards that reflect his stature in the field, Rucka was first a fiction writer, even though comics always held a special place in his heart.

GREG RUCKA: I think I was influenced most by my mother. I was an early reader and I started reading mysteries very early. I started reading mysteries with a series of books by a writer named Stuart Kaminsky. My mother had given me one of these thinking it was a kid's book, and it wasn't. And I loved it. I think that was about fourth or fifth grade. And I started chasing all those down, I went to the library and got the rest of the books in that series and just loved them.

I have an older sister who has Down's Syndrome, and she was just fascinated with the *Incredible Hulk*–the TV show, with Bill Bixby and Lou Ferrigno. Roughly the same time, I seem to remember being out with her at some point and going into a comic book shop and picking up a *Hulk* magazine that used to have these "Moon Knight" backup stories–I think Doug Moench wrote pretty much all of them; I don't remember who drew them. The one I picked up was the Incredible Hulk versus a nuclear reactor. I had gotten it ostensibly for my sister, but she really didn't have

much interest in it because it wasn't the TV show. And I spent a lot of time poring over that magazine and trying to copy illustrations out of it, trying to teach myself how to draw off of that, and just failing abysmally. And that's the first real, cognizant link to comics that I can remember, actually picking up a physical comic.

It wasn't until eighth grade that I started reading comics regularly. I fell in with a group of miscreants and malcontents that were Marvel zombies, and we ended up spending a lot of time with the X-Men. That's what really triggered that field for me, that art form. I wasn't really aware of comics until just before high school. And then it took off, and all throughout high school I was a big fan of the medium.

Now, up until that point, I was a voracious reader. And I was pretty much bored by most of the schoolwork that I did. I would sit at my desk, which was independent of the chair, and rest my head on my arm on the desk and scoot my chair back and put a book in my lap and read for as long as I could possibly get away with it, over and over and over again. And I read a lot of mysteries. I read Sherlock Holmes early. My father read stories to me when I was very young, then I started reading them myself, sort of chasing those down, too. Other writers who were writing pastiches of Holmes; Loren D. Estleman, he'd written two books that I remember reading that were pastiches, and Nicholas Meyer's *Seven Percent Solution*, things like that. So it all sort of conflates.

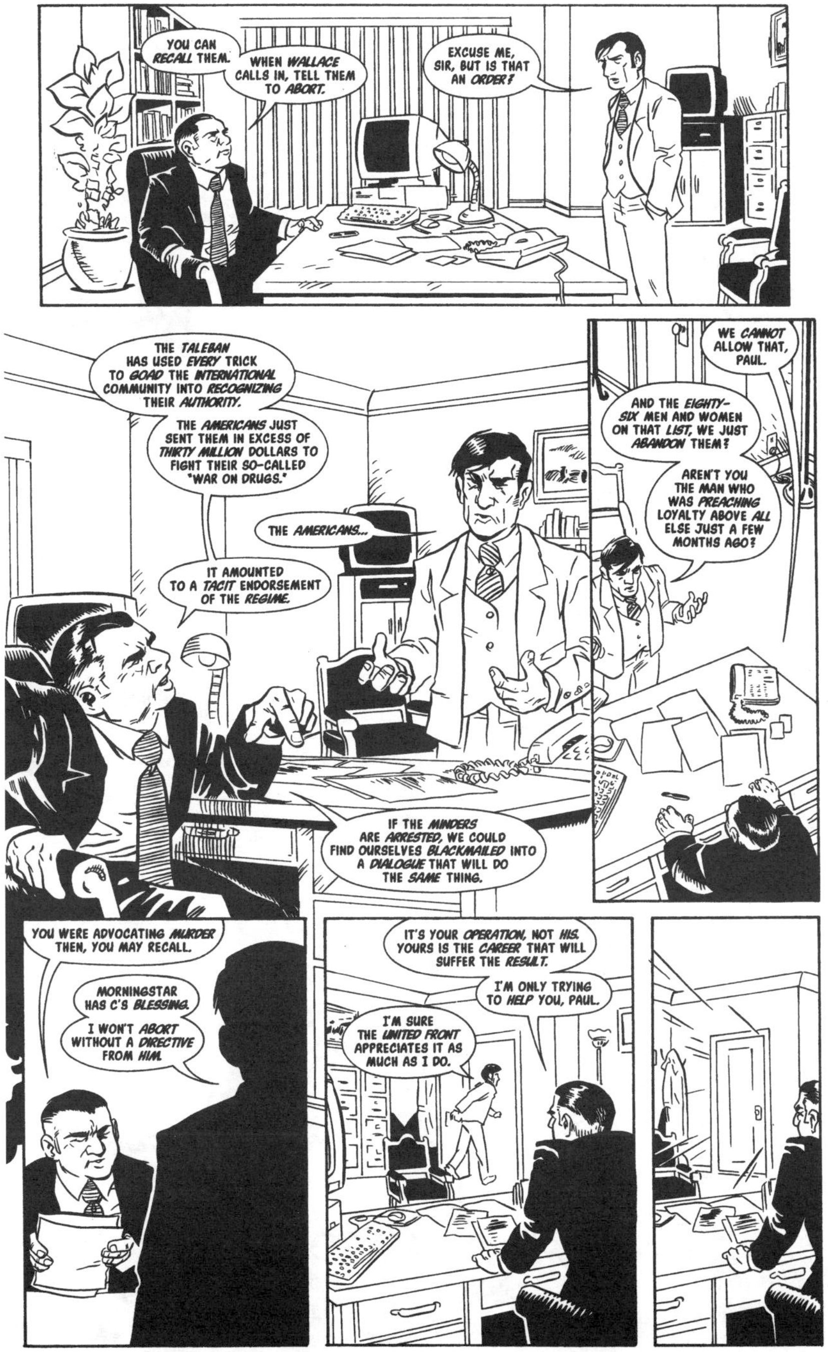

YOU CAN RECALL THEM.
WHEN WALLACE CALLS IN, TELL THEM TO ABORT.
EXCUSE ME, SIR, BUT IS THAT AN ORDER?
THE TALEBAN HAS USED EVERY TRICK TO GOAD THE INTERNATIONAL COMMUNITY INTO RECOGNIZING THEIR AUTHORITY.
THE AMERICANS JUST SENT THEM IN EXCESS OF THIRTY MILLION DOLLARS TO FIGHT THEIR SO-CALLED "WAR ON DRUGS."
THE AMERICANS...
IT AMOUNTED TO A TACIT ENDORSEMENT OF THE REGIME.
IF THE MINDERS ARE ARRESTED, WE COULD FIND OURSELVES BLACKMAILED INTO A DIALOGUE THAT WILL DO THE SAME THING.
WE CANNOT ALLOW THAT, PAUL.
AND THE EIGHTY-SIX MEN AND WOMEN ON THAT LIST, WE JUST ABANDON THEM?
AREN'T YOU THE MAN WHO WAS PREACHING LOYALTY ABOVE ALL ELSE JUST A FEW MONTHS AGO?
YOU WERE ADVOCATING MURDER THEN, YOU MAY RECALL.
MORNINGSTAR HAS C'S BLESSING.
I WON'T ABORT WITHOUT A DIRECTIVE FROM HIM.
IT'S YOUR OPERATION, NOT HIS. YOURS IS THE CAREER THAT WILL SUFFER THE RESULT.
I'M ONLY TRYING TO HELP YOU, PAUL.
I'M SURE THE UNITED FRONT APPRECIATES IT AS MUCH AS I DO.

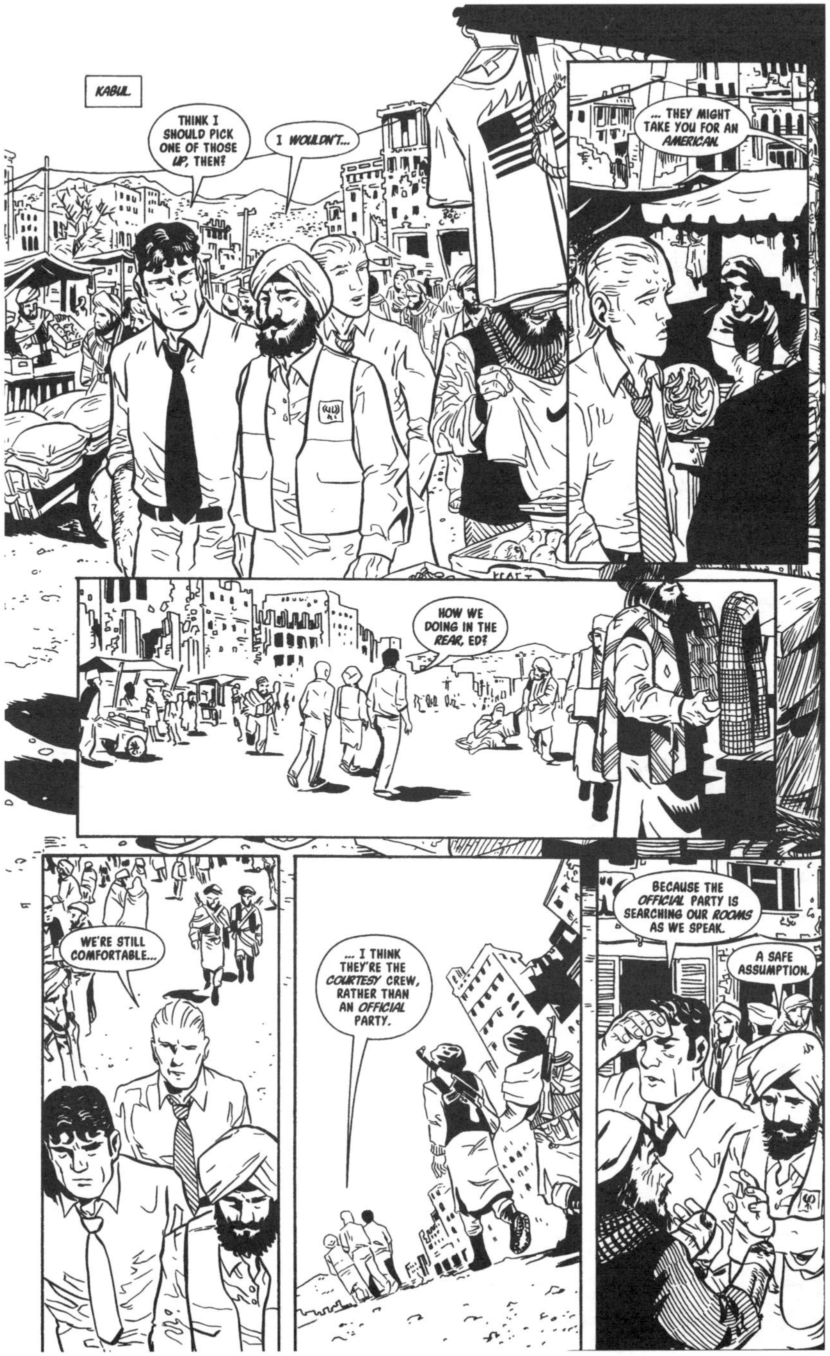

KABUL
THINK I SHOULD PICK ONE OF THOSE UP, THEN?
I WOULDN'T...
... THEY MIGHT TAKE YOU FOR AN AMERICAN.
HOW WE DOING IN THE REAR, ED?
WE'RE STILL COMFORTABLE...
... I THINK THEY'RE THE COURTESY CREW, RATHER THAN AN OFFICIAL PARTY.
BECAUSE THE OFFICIAL PARTY IS SEARCHING OUR ROOMS AS WE SPEAK.
A SAFE ASSUMPTION.

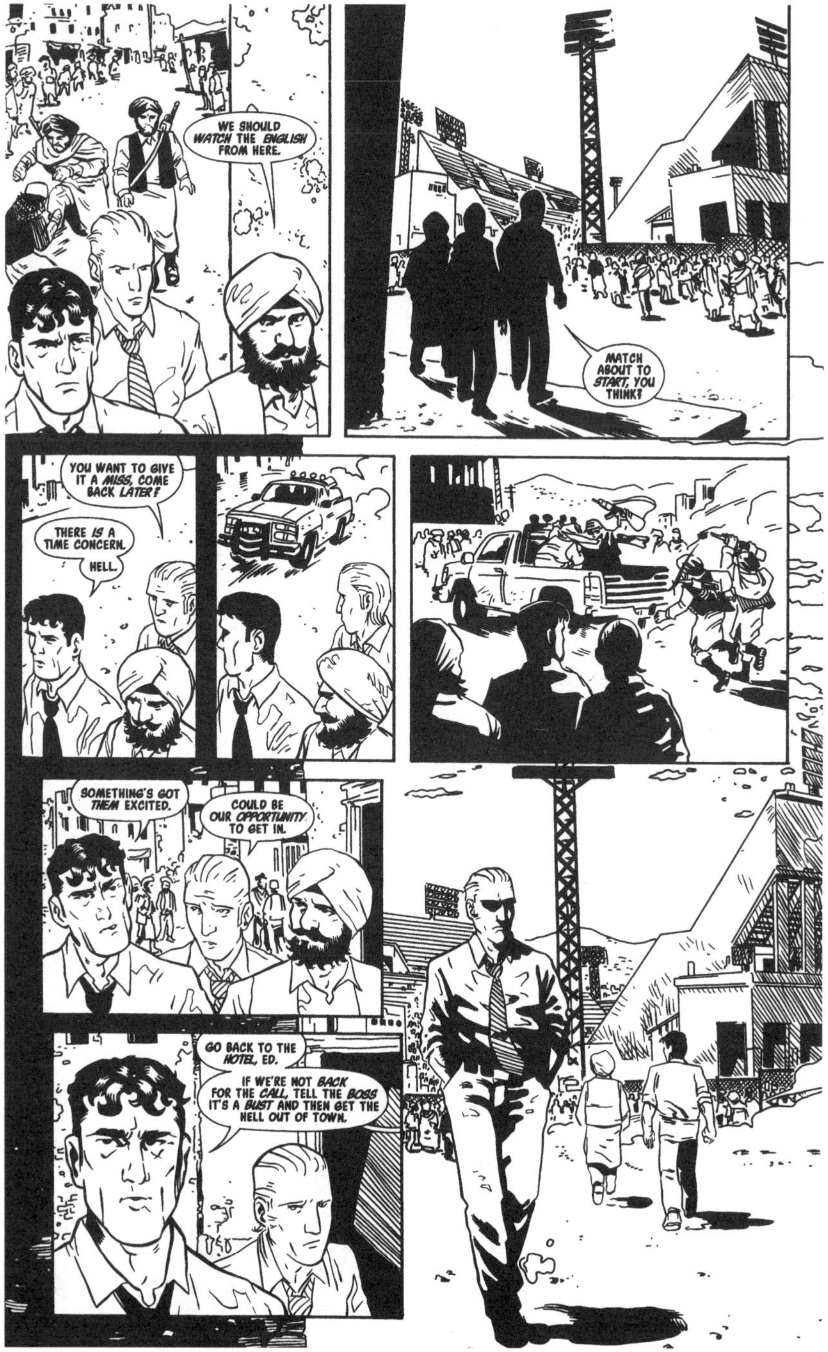
WE SHOULD WATCH THE ENGLISH FROM HERE.
MATCH ABOUT TO START, YOU THINK?
YOU WANT TO GIVE IT A MISS, COME BACK LATER?
THERE IS A TIME CONCERN.
HELL.
SOMETHING'S GOT THEM EXCITED.
COULD BE OUR OPPORTUNITY TO GET IN.
GO BACK TO THE HOTEL, ED.
IF WE'RE NOT BACK FOR THE CALL, TELL THE BOSS IT'S A BUST AND THEN GET THE HELL OUT OF TOWN.

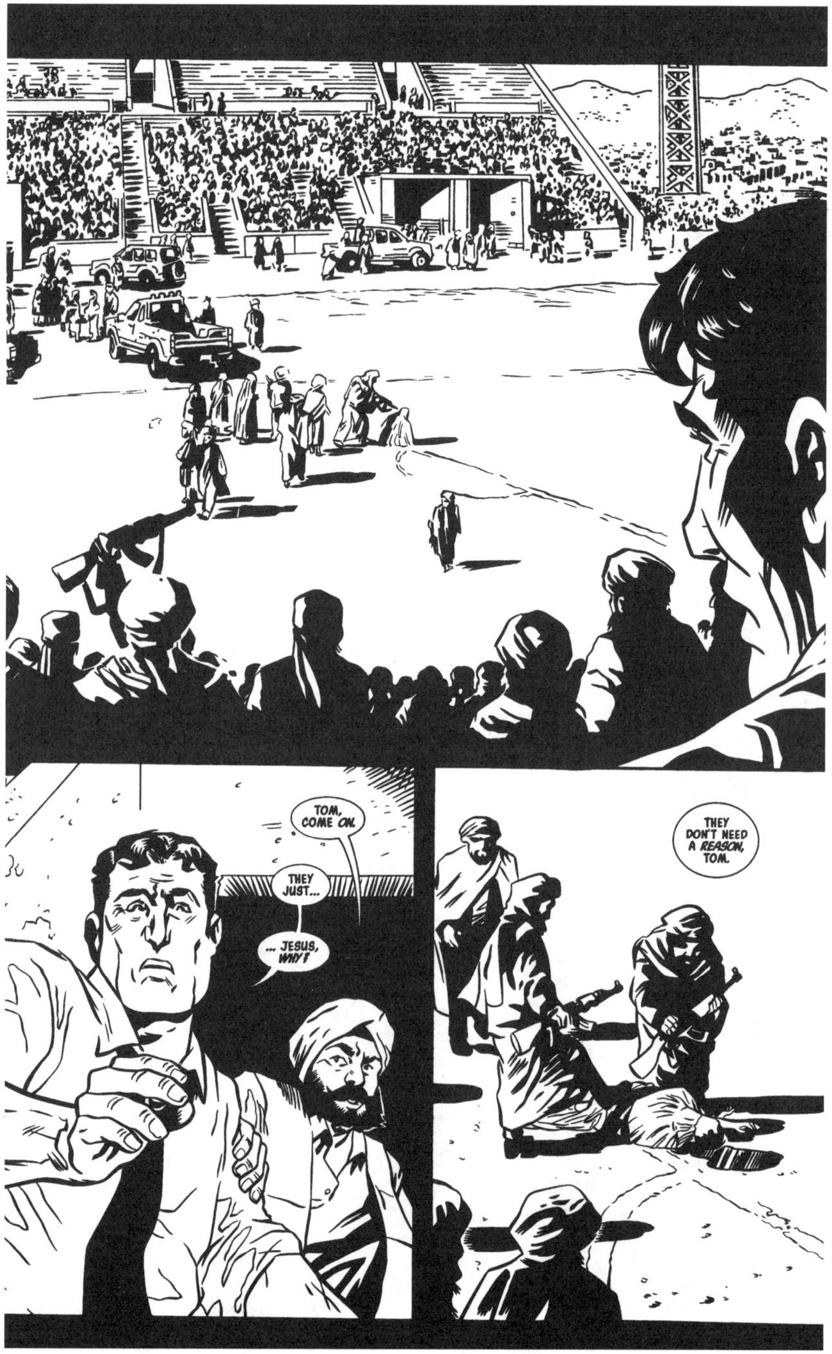
TOM, COME ON.
THEY JUST...
... JESUS, WHY?
THEY DON'T NEED A REASON, TOM.

The value of 250,000 words

Probably the only field tougher to break into than comics is novel writing. You must be passionate enough to write, and dedicated to the craft of writing. And though there are many books on breaking into writing, instead of reading words, Greg suggests writing words to break into writing.

GREG RUCKA: By the time I was a junior in high school, I was spending my English classes sitting in the back of the room writing a novel longhand in a notebook. Again, I think more out of boredom than anything else. But when I got to college, my intent was not to be a writer. My intent was to go into theater. And that lasted for about six months, and then I discovered that most of the theater people I was dealing with were not very pleasant people as human beings. I found them almost universally to be malfunctioning, self-absorbed, thoroughly annoying. So I changed my major. I went into Medieval Renaissance Studies—that lasted about a semester. I did Religion, I did Poly Sci. And sometime during my junior year I kind of realized that I had to declare, and I only had enough credits to be an English major, because that was the only department where I had been consistently taking classes. Every semester I had been taking at least one, if not two, English classes. And all throughout that I had been writing, but somehow the neuron hadn't fired, it hadn't connected, "Well, gosh..."

I remember spending a portion of my early junior year—we got a week off in early October for, I forget what they called it, they didn't call it Autumn Break, but you had a week off—and I remember spending that week in my room on campus typing a novel. And I wrote a quarter-of-a-million word novel, which is insanely long. There's a truism I've heard many times, the aspiring artist who goes to the successful artist and says, "How do I learn to draw?" And the response being, "You draw everything." Or the Dave Sim quote, I believe, is, "You've got a six-foot stack of newsprint, and you draw on every sheet, everywhere, front and back. And when you've finished that stack, you'll be an artist." And I think there's an element of truth in that, in that you have to do the work to discover how not to do the work. And you write a 250,000-word novel, and maybe 3,000 words contiguously are good. They actually did what they were supposed to do—might even be considered literature. You will go through that experience having taught yourself a whole lot of stuff. I don't mean to make it sound like I wrote 250,000 words over the course of a week. I think I wrote something like 100,000 of them over the course of that week, though. But these words were nothing like *War and Peace*, because *War and Peace* was good

and my words were really bad.

But I have felt for a long time that only those artists who can be truly, spectacularly, disastrously bad, only those artists who absolutely, gloriously fail at what they endeavor can ever be really, truly good. I think mediocrity breeds mediocrity and you're sort of condemned to it. I believe that if you can write really wretched stuff, then you can probably write really, really good stuff. But the key word there being "writing" rather than just slapping words down on paper and saying, "See, look! A narrative."

BATMAN: NO MAN'S LAND

Now he had been in Gotham for just over a week, watching and waiting, walking the different neighborhoods, learning the new dynamic of the No Man's Land. The tagging intrigued him; the bat-tag he had seen, in particular, had raised his eyebrow. He had resisted the urge to jump pell-mell into the fray, instead making contact with Alfred, learning what the gentleman's gentleman had to tell.

Finally, the Batman felt ready to face the helplessness head-on.

A dog was barking nearby, and the sound drew Batman's attention back to the present, away from the alley. The sound seemed alien, and he realized that since returning to Gotham he had seen no dogs at all, nowhere on the streets.

The barking grew louder and more desperate, and Batman moved toward the sound, taking the rooftops again, staying silent on the dark and empty street. The noise was deceptive in the stillness of the city, at first seeming merely around the next corner, but Batman had gone six blocks before finally homing in on the source. From the edge of a rooftop he looked down.

It was an adult Airedale, standing in the middle of the street, its tail stiff and its head lowered as it guarded its master, a boy of perhaps fifteen. The two were surrounded by a group of men, all in salvaged and torn winter clothes, all holding makeshift weapons of one kind or another. Across the street from where he had perched, Batman could make out a spray-painted tag on one of the opposite buildings, the crossed spears of the Xhosa.

"Looks like dinner," one of the men below was saying. He held a baseball bat, its end wrapped in barbed wire.

The Airedale's head dipped lower, growling. The boy began backing away, then halted as he realized that he and his pet had been surrounded. His voice drifted up to where Batman had perched, thin with fear.

"Leave my dog alone," the boy said.

"Weren't talking about no dog," the one with the bat said.

Normally, Batman would have waited a second or two longer, timing his entrance to best effect just before any violence could begin. But what he was seeing now made him angry, and he'd had enough. He launched himself off the rooftop with a leap, gathering

· 81 ·

Though Rucka broke into novel writing, he has always had a keen passion for comic books. He has been instrumental in the *No Man's Land* and *Officer Down* story arcs. Writing the *Batman: No Man's Land* novel, Rucka was able to combine both passions. Batman TM & ©2004 DC Comics

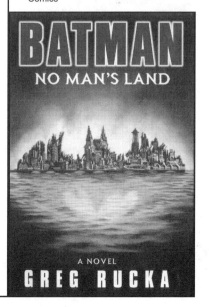

MINDER AND KEEPER

With Minder, *Greg Rucka's college thesis paper, the character of Atticus Kodiak was born. This effort led to* Keeper, *Rucka's first novel with Bantam Books.*

GREG RUCKA: I went to graduate school after Vassar. I went to USC and got what is essentially an MFA. They refer to the program as the "professional writing program," meaning: "You come here and we'll teach you how to write professionally. You can write a play when you leave, you should know how to write a screenplay when you leave, you should know how to do technical writing and novel writing and short story, etc., etc." Which is lofty, and I'm not sure how successful it was, at least in my case. But my Master's thesis was the first Kodiak novel, which was called *Minder*. My thesis advisor, who is an accomplished writer in his own right, Sid Stebel, told me when it was done that he thought the novel was quite good, and that I had certainly earned myself an A, and that I would never, ever sell the book. I asked him why he thought so, and he said, "Because your protagonist is far too fallible." He said, "Atticus makes mistakes. People aren't going to want to read about that, and I think you should go in a different direction with it and do that sort of James Bond/Tom Clancy thing." And I said, "Well, that's really nice, Sid, but that's not what I set out to do."

There's a literary tradition of the American private investigator. It's its own school, and I feel very passionately about the merits of that school. It starts with Edgar Allan Poe, who predates Arthur Conan Doyle, and whose stories are a form of social commentary. If you are writing about crime, Raymond Chandler argues that you have to write about murder, that there really is no other crime worth writing about. You are writing about a dysfunctional society because there's something wrong in any society where murder can occur. And the American private investigator is universally a first-person narrator, universally a character who is liminal in some aspect, and therefore in a unique position to comment on a society. As a result, we have a body of work over the last one hundred-plus years of this commentary. And if you have any questions about that, I steer you to the inimitable Dashiell Hammett. Not the *Maltese Falcon*, but his Continental Op stories, which were all social commentary stories. There's a whole other school of thought behind this about the motion to the West and how the P.I. comes out of the Western. Be that neither here nor there, I was looking at an extension of that, as I saw it, from Raymond Chandler to Hammett to Ross MacDonald, all the way to–at that time–Robert B. Parker, who had sort of taken the P.I. trope and reinvented the character over and over again. And I was like, well, these guys are all great writers, they created great characters and I love them as literature, but they are not relevant to my generation. So my character Atticus was really my attempt to answer that.

He had to be fallible, because in my experience growing up, my experience of the world is that people lie and people make mistakes.

The Challenger explodes. That's a formative event for me. So Sid said, "To prove to you that it cannot be sold, I'm going to give it to a friend of mine, who used to be an editor at a publisher but now is a literary agent. And he's going to tell you why he can't sell it." And I said, "Okay, Sid. Do what you want." And I graduated and I went off to live in a cabin in the Sierra Nevadas with my wife while we were waiting for her to start graduate school, and I got a call one day from this agent, who said, "I would very much like to represent your book." So I said, "Well, that's great!"

He sent *Minder* out everywhere he could and couldn't sell it. We got amazing rejection letters. Normally a rejection letter is a slip of paper that says, "Thank you very much for submitting your fill-in-the-blank, unfortunately it does not fit into our schedule at this time." We were getting letters where the editors who had read it actually bothered to take the time to write up two pages of notes on why they hated my book.

Jen (Van Meter, my wife) had started graduate school. We had moved up to Eugene, Oregon, and I was working on a second novel, what became *Keeper*. I'd work during the day, and at night I'd come home and write 3,000 words, and I just kept hammering and hammering. I could not for the life of me find a steady, good job. I spent six months trying to get work, and the best, most consistent gig I'd gotten was as a house painter. I'd managed to get some work as a technical writer and beta-tester at a software game company and then finally I landed a job teaching four nights a week at a business college, where I taught, get this, job-finding skills. We were very, very poor. We were living at that time a married couple's life where every month you look to your spouse and say, "Whose parents did we call last month to get the rent?" And your spouse says, "Mine, it's your turn this time." So we had scraped and saved and we had planned to take two weeks off to go to San Diego [Comic-Con] before Jen had started her next semester. And I went in to the last day of classes before break to discover that the doors had been chained shut–the school had gone out of business overnight. I was like, "We have no money, we have nothing." And Jen and I decided, "Well, we're going to take this trip anyway." We went down to San Diego and when I got back, I called Peter, my first agent, and I said, "I don't care what you have to do, you gotta sell *Keeper* now." He said, "All right, I'll send it out." I had rewritten the draft something like four or five parts at that point and about two weeks later, he gave me a call and said, "We have offers, and the book may go to auction, but Bantam has come in with a preemptive that basically says they will pay X amount for a two-book deal, or if the book goes to auction, they'll guarantee a minimum bid of this amount." And I said, "What do you think we should do?" The idea of auction is very nice, publishers throwing money at me. And he said, "I'd take the preempt." And I said, "Why?" And he said, "Because if it goes to auction and it gets out of control, this'll be the only book you're ever gonna write. If this book brings you $800,000 and it doesn't sell and clear it, you're dead. They're

Keeper, first published novel in 1996, launched Rucka's writing career.
© Greg Rucka

gonna write you off. But if you take the reasonable, good amount of money that they're offering here, they're guaranteeing you two books. That's a career." I was like, "You know, that's good advice."

So that's what happened. So we sold the book to Bantam, and I had a conversation with my editor—and she still is my editor to this day, a woman named Kate Miciak—and she made it pretty clear that she thought the novel had horrible problems. The thing that had sold her most was Katy, and in particular—and this is a spoiler—when Katy died. She saw something in the writing of that, I think, that gave her hope, made her think, "Hey, maybe this kid can write." So that's how I first got published. I was very lucky. I was 23 when the book was sold and I was 24 or 25 when it came out, because, again, it had to go through a couple other drafts between the time it was purchased and the time it was released. It was released in '96.

Keeper tackles difficult contemporary issues, including abortion. Rucka made sure that that both sides of the issue were discussed in the novel. In this excerpt, Jonathan Crowell explains his view on abortion.

---

128   GREG RUCKA

dered how much it had cost him. "I don't know anything about the letters," Crowell said.

Bridgett opened the folder and set each letter out, chronologically, on the coffee table before Crowell. It took a minute and all the space on the table, and Crowell made a sour face to pass the time. Barry never moved; I'm not certain he even blinked. When Bridgett was finished Crowell looked at them briefly, then out the window. "I've never seen these before."

"Didn't Detective Lozano show them to you?" Bridgett asked.

He considered that, then looked at me again. "Yes, yes he did. And the FBI men, too. I meant, I've never seen the originals."

"So you have seen these before?" Bridgett pressed, the glint of a very sharp edge in her voice.

Crowell stood and walked to the window and stood there, admiring the expensive view. At least, I thought he was admiring the view. He pointed. "The Jewish Museum is over there." He lowered his arm and waited. When he got no response from us he waited some more, then said, "It's all just decay down there. You do know that, don't you? This city is only a small part of this country, but it embodies everything in this nation. Everything here can be found between Maine and Alaska. And it's all falling apart."

"So you have seen these before, Mr. Crowell?" Bridgett repeated. The edge in her voice was clearer now, and the muscles in her jaw tightened after she spoke.

Without turning Crowell said, "And it is falling apart from the heart, from the center. As this city is the center of this nation, this nation is falling apart. As the family is falling apart, so is this city, corrupted, diminished by parasites who refuse God's law. The true values of the American family have been distorted by all those people who now live here, groups with their perverted special interests and their selfish, hedonistic concerns. They are slowly tug-

KEEPER   129

ging the thread that built this city, unraveling it, and thus the country, leaving us a ruin that may never be repaired."

It was as if he spoke to a huge audience beyond the pane of glass and had forgotten we were in the room. Barry was staring at his back, probably expecting Crowell to sprout wings and a halo.

"I'm right, you know that," Crowell continued. "You never hear about a Christian being arrested for dealing crack. Godless is what we have become, forsaking the Word for our own petty delights. And unless we find God again, we shall be destroyed." He turned and his eyes rested on Bridgett. "Unless our women understand their duty, we shall be destroyed." He looked at me. "Unless our men lead the way, we shall be destroyed."

He turned back to the window and raised both his arms so he looked, in silhouette, like Christ on the Cross. He rolled his head back and said, nearly sobbing, "Unless each and every baby killer is stopped, each and every factory of death is dismantled, we shall all be destroyed. Unless we stop the holocaust of the unborn innocents, we shall all be destroyed. There can be no rest, no hope, no salvation for any of us, until we stop this mad butchery of our own children."

It was grand theater. He didn't move, rigid in his own imagined crucifixion. Bridgett shifted on the couch, making the leather sigh, the tension coiled in her, looking for an out.

Considering the scene Crowell was playing, his apartment was remarkably secular. Only one religious artifact, a large stainless-steel cross wrapped in barbed wire, hung on the wall over the television cabinet. He had two shelves loaded with books, a large easy chair for reading beside them. A well-shined brass lamp stood beside the chair. On the floor beside the coffee table, where Bridgett had moved them to lay out the letters, were hardcover copies of his two books, *Abortuaries and the Death of America* and *Innocence Slaughtered*. Neither copy looked to have

BREAKING IN AND WRITING FOR COMICS

Though Rucka maintains that his breaking into comics is a matter of circumstance, many factors keep him in the forefront of the medium. His writing philosophy stays the same and he adjusts his goals from novels to graphic novels.

GREG RUCKA: As I said, we would go to San Diego [Comic-Con] trying to get work. When I was in college, I tried doing a comic. I wrote my first comic script for a friend of mine named Scott Nybakken, who tried to draw it and got through most of the first issue and then decided that this was not something that he could do. Scott then went off and worked at Fantagraphics, and then from Fantagraphics ended up working at DC. He started at DC in Marketing working for Patty Jeres, alongside Ivan Cohen.

When *Keeper* and *Finder* came out, I'd give editors the novels, and they would be, like, "That's very nice. Just go away now." San Diego is actually not the best place to try to meet an editor because there are too many people. And Scott had received copies of all the books, and every time he got one of the novels, he handed them around the office. I guess it was like, "Hey, my friend wrote this." So Patty Jeres had read both *Keeper* and *Finder*. At one point she said, "Okay, you should meet this guy I know." And she walked me over to meet Bob Schreck the first year that Oni had a booth at San Diego.

Patty made the introductions and said, "Greg is a novelist and he wants to do comics, and you guys should talk." And Bob and I went out on that little second-level veranda that overlooks the Bay. We sat down and I gave him copies of the books, and he got this kind of scared, trapped look in his eye, and he said, "You don't want to adapt these, do you?" And I said, "No, hell, no!" And immediately he goes, "Okay, we can talk." I said, "They're two different mediums." And he said, "Well, what's your idea?" And I said, "This is the idea," and I pitched him *Whiteout*. And he said, "All right, let me talk to my partner (Joe Nozemack); I like the sound of that." So that was how I got into comics. That's how *Whiteout* happened. Joe and Bob took the chance on it, and I started writing it.

A novel is a one-man show for me. I'm not a writer/artist, I'm a writer. So at the end of the day, the novel is me, the blank paper and what I put on it. It lives or dies on the basis of that and it suffers and excels as a result of that. The collaboration in a novel is very limited. My editor is outstanding—I would take a bullet for her in a moment. She makes me a better writer, but she doesn't force anything on me. So at the end of the day, the book is mine.

A comic is always a collaboration, and as a result, suffers and excels on the basis of that. In the best possible world, a successful comic is something where I have written the script, given it over to the editor and the editor reads it, approves it, and sends it over to the artist. The artist takes it and creates, from what I've written, something that is greater than the sum of its parts. Because then it goes to the inker and the letterer and the colorist and there's a whole bunch

In *Queen & Country: Operation Morningstar*, the British SIS sends male Minders into Afghanistan to retrieve vital intelligence information. Tara Chace is forced to sit on the sidelines. In the script (right and opposite), Rucka describes Chace's mental state while the telly delivers news of Minder MacMillan's execution.

Greg Rucka

Page 24

ONE:
Exterior of CHACE'S flat in South Kensington, night. It's late. Rain is falling.

All the street is dark but for the few lampposts and a single light coming, faintly, from Chace's home.

1 TELEVISION/elec/inside: …result of continued economic sanctions in the region.

TWO:
Interior, from behind Chace's sofa, to the television, where the BBC World News is playing.

CHACE is visible on the couch, propped on her side. Cigarette smoke swirls in the diffused light, the only illumination coming from the television itself.

2 TELEVISION/elec: In Afghanistan this morning, journalists Nicholas Buck, David Macmillan, and Alain Roux
                            were EXECUTED by the Taleban Government after being found GUILTY of ESPIONAGE.

of people involved in the process. It's not just mine. And it is arrogance for any comic book writer to think that it is all about them. Just as it's arrogance for any artist to think it's all about them. Successful writer/artists out there are few and far between. I cannot imagine anything harder to do in the medium than to do both.

When I write a script for a comic, I write a full script, meaning I write "Page one, panel one," the full description, dialogue, everything like that. I don't break down the page–or I very rarely do. Sometimes I'll say, "I'd like this done in four horizontal panels, Panel One, Panel Two, Panel Three, Panel Four." But normally what I do is I hand it over with the understanding that my visual sense is in the toilet. I'm the writer; I'm not an artist. The artist has a very acute, professionally-honed visual sense. My visual sense is weak.

And if I've done my job in the script, then whoever I give it to, be it Brian Hurtt or Steve Rolston or Michael Lark or Drew Johnson or Darick Robertson or Matthew Clark, they've read the script and they know what I'm trying to accomplish in the story. They understand the emotional movement of the story, they understand what's happening thematically, they understand what's happening with the plot. And as a result, they can throw all my descriptions out the window. As long as they can tell that story, they're going to have a better way to do it. I mean, if I say, "Over-the-shoulder angle" or "six panels on this page," and Michael Lark comes back to me–and he's done this before–and he says, "I need eight. Do you mind if I make it eight panels?" And my response is, "Hell, no!" I'd be mad to say anything else.

Axel Alonso and Eduardo Risso and I got incredible props for the *Tangled Web* #4 story "Severance Package." And I believe very firmly, no offense to those people who love that story, that that is a mediocre script, at best. I don't think it's bad, but I don't think it's brilliant. It is Eduardo and Axel who made it brilliant. They took what I gave them, in particular Eduardo, and brought magic to it. That's an example of a perfect collaboration.

There have been times artists, who shall go nameless, have taken a script and have in some cases completely missed the point, and in other cases decided that I'm wrong and they're the better writer and changed the story. Which I can't stand. And it's unique to the medium and is one of the frustrations of the medium. No writer in the business would go to an artist's pencils and redraw them. Never. It would never happen. Artists somehow feel they have a right to change the writing. It pisses me off like you wouldn't believe. Like I said, there's a difference between telling the story that we're setting out to tell as best as possible, and then changing the story. My job– I've been hired for this; there's an assumption that I'm good at it, they're paying me a fair amount of money for it. That's the biggest frustration I've ever had.

But when a [comic] comes together it's magic. Artistically, that's the most satisfying thing–when an artist takes my words, elevates them and makes them more than the sum of the parts. And at the end of the day, that's got to be the most gratifying thing. Because, as much as it's wonderful when the fans say, "We love it! We love you," you can't go to the bank with that.

The finished page (below), penciled by Brian Hurtt. Queen & Country and all related characters TM & ©2004 Greg Rucka.

3 TELEVISION/elec:	Macmillan, a British national and twenty-two year veteran correspondent, had been charged specifically with spying for S.I.S..

THREE:
On CHACE, on her side on the couch. An overflowing ashtray sits on the end table at her side.

CHACE is half passed out on the couch, blearily watching television.

| 4 TELEVISION/elec/off: | The Foreign Office has denied the allegation. |
| 5 TELEVISION/elec/off/linked: | In related news, a report released by Amnesty International today estimates… |

FOUR:
CU of the an EMPTY BOTTLE OF SCOTCH on the floor, beside CHACE'S limp hand.

| 6 TELEVISION/elec/off/link: | …that TENS of THOUSANDS of Afghani women suffering from various medical conditions face certain death if continued to be denied medical treatment by the Taleban government…. |

CHARACTERS

Many writers have problems fleshing out characters. Often times, especially with comic books, readers are left with skeletal archetypes slogging their way through a story. For Rucka, the imperfections of the characters make the story robust with opportunity.

GREG RUCKA: Stories are character-driven for me. I'm not very interested in plot-driven stories. And I'm always amazed whenever I see a criticism that actually accuses me of putting plot over character. My greatest weakness is that I put character way ahead of plot.

Perfect people are boring as spit. They're not real. I think one of the reasons why people love comics is that they're soap operas. *Superman* is a soap opera. People get more excited not when he wins the fight, but when he loses it. They get more worked up when he and Lois are fighting than when they're happy. That's why we keep going back to *The Days of Our Lives*. And foibles are critical.

Also, I believe very strongly that the artist has a social obligation. The job isn't to write a polemic, but we have the public ear and we have to make a statement. You don't have to agree with what I'm saying, but regardless of whether it's *Batman* or it's *Whiteout* or it's *Queen and Country* or it's *A Fistful of Rain*, I am obligated to at least say something. At least put an idea across. That becomes very hard to do when people are just perfect and idealized. For a hero to be heroic, they have to overcome obstacles. And there are no greater obstacles than the obstacles we've created for ourselves. To me, that's being a hero. When we talk about the novels, specifically the Kodiak novels, there's a very specific reason that Atticus has to be fallible. If you're in the personal protection business and you don't make any mistakes, then you don't have much of a story because nothing ever happens. Something has to slip through. That's where the drama comes from.

I think ideally the artist grows, right? So if I'm writing a female character today, regardless of who that character is, I'm going to bring to it things I've learned during the last twenty years of writing. I was slated to take on the book *Wonder Woman* almost three years ago, and for a variety of reasons, that didn't happen. Now I think that's really for the best because what I can bring to it now serves the character far better than what I could have brought to it then. I know more about the form than I would have three years ago, and I certainly explored with other characters other issues that are going to help arm me for how I'm writing Diana right now. She's such a unique character, and she's pretty much radically different from all the other women I've ever written because she isn't as haunted. She does not have the tragedies in her backstory that are tragedies in continuity, you know what I mean? They aren't things that have been sort of *sui*

generis with the character, that are deep in the backstory. She isn't born out of a tragedy. Well, actually, you can argue that she is, if you look at the George Pérez origin. But she doesn't carry her tragedy with her, she doesn't go around saying, "I am the spirit of the first murdered woman!" or anything like that. And it's interesting, in *A Fistful of Rain*, Mim is horribly damaged. We got a *Publisher's Weekly* review yesterday. My editor sent it. And it's tepid, which is not surprising, because I knew that I was going to get this review eventually. One reviewer loved the book and was going crazy about it. I'm looking at it right now. The reviewer says, "Even the wildly improbable plot has strong moments of real terror and palpable personal tragedy. The real problem is Bracca herself. As a tough female cop shouts at her, 'I have never encountered someone as stupid as you about helping herself.'" Um…yeah! Quite intentional! She's exceptionally dysfunctional as a protagonist. She is horribly flawed. She's alcoholic, she's self-indulgent, she's a liar. And she tells the reader that she's a liar! She tells the reader, "Don't believe anything I tell you." And most readers are going to ignore it and are going to slide right by it.

You know, in *The Great Gatsby*, [F. Scott] Fitzgerald spends a whole chapter to get to the line where Nick can say, and I can't remember the exact quote, "Everybody has some personal flaw or weakness or something, and if I have one, it is this: I am the most honest person I have ever met." Fitzgerald does that so you will read the rest of the novel knowing that Nick is telling you the truth. He's not lying to you. Mim tells you, "I'm lying! I make things up!" For me, that makes her compelling. But it runs the risk of making her compelling in much the same way that a car crash is compelling. You look at Tara in *Queen and Country*, she's got baggage and some of it's clear, some of it's really deeply inside and unseen. A lot of that will come out in the *Queen and Country* novel, actually. Carrie's damage is clear in *Whiteout*. Her husband dies shortly after they're married, and then she kills somebody. You look at Bridgett, for instance, in *Shooting at Midnight*, oh, hey, she was hooked on heroin. I've been accused alternately of being a misogynist because I'm "mean" to my characters, and of being a great feminist because I'll treat my female characters the same way I'll treat my male characters.

There's a difference in how I write them, there's not a difference in how I'm going to treat them in the narrative. If I write a female character the same way I'd write a male character, then she's not female, she's a guy who looks like a girl with a girl's name. The female experience is entirely different. There are things that are very similar. There are things that are almost identical. But all those things being equal, I'm sure that, speaking as a male, my experience walking down a street at three in the morning is totally different than my wife's. Especially if she does that alone. I do not have to worry about my gender making me a target at three in the morning when I'm alone. I really don't. My wife does. Society tells her. Not only that, society says, "Come to grips with it." 'Cause we're not doing anything about it, really. One of the reasons that I love writing female characters is that you can take situations and stories that we have seen hundreds of times, thousands of times before, and if you recast your protagonist as female, it becomes entirely different, because dynamics change. Sex enters into every interaction on some level. We live in a society that is dominated by a male gaze that objectifies women. All

that's incredible grist for the mill. One of the things *A Fistful of Rain* is about is the toll that that objectification can take on you. It's heightened to an incredible extreme. We take a character and we set her up as pretty and famous. She is already very well known. And then we start to exploit that. It is a horrible burden. Mim cannot shoulder it. There is a huge difference. I think anybody who doesn't write with that in mind is making a horrible mistake. A female character is not a guy with tits.

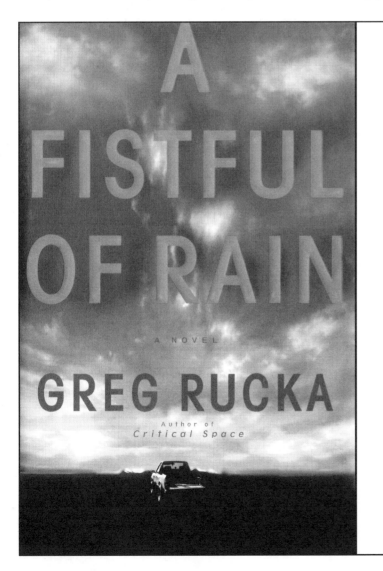

A FISTFUL OF RAIN   5

take it. Celebrity status has perks, but it also means that there's always someone looking to take you down a peg or ten. It's not as if musicians—or more precisely, musicians who play "popular music"—are known for living a Seventh-Day Adventist lifestyle.

The search was thorough, and the agents were, too. They asked if I had any contraband, specifically drugs. They asked it repeatedly, trying to trip me up. They had me turn out my pockets. They shook out my jacket. They patted me down. They even tore open my packet of cigarettes, checking each tube of precious nicotine to make certain it was filled with tobacco, nothing more.

When they'd finished with my bags I started to take off my shirt but the supervising agent stopped me, saying, "What are you doing?"

"Isn't this what you want?" I asked. I impressed myself by not slurring. "I mean, isn't this what, you know, what you want?"

His eyes went to flint. "No."

"Oh," I said, and tucked back in. "Well, then, my mistake. Right? My mistake?"

"I'd say so."

I got my things together and he held the door for me out of the little examination room, letting me pass through. I impressed myself again by not wobbling.

"I've made a few," I told him.

"I'm sorry?"

"Mistakes," I said. "I've made a few."

I had to stop in a ladies' room before switching terminals, and I gave until it hurt. When I emerged, there was a photographer waiting outside—he must have picked me up coming through customs—and he shouted my name when I emerged.

"Mim! Bracca! Hey! Gimme something I can sell!"

I got my hands up before I heard the whirring of the speed-winder, one to shield my face, one to let him know just what I thought of him and his Minolta, and then I was shoving through clumps of fellow

With the reader's first introduction to Mim in *A Fistful of Rain,* Rucka establishes a successful celebrity with more than her fair shares of troubles and regrets.

RESEARCH

There's the writing adage that you should both write what you know about and write from experience. Though the majority of us will never fly, take on the Joker, or run military covert operations, Rucka manages to make us believe that his characters do these things and more. He prides himself on research for his stories, and the payoff is in the details.

GREG RUCKA: For realism in my storytelling, I've had those experiences where if it's practical, I try to experience it. My key resource for the Kodiak novels is a guy who was a personal security expert, and he took me shooting, for instance. I try to get it firsthand, if I can, either through interview or through experiencing it myself. That has scared my parents at times.

Somebody once asked me, "What's the worst thing your parents think you've done? Not that you've actually done, but think that you've done?" My response was, "heroin." I'm pretty sure my parents think I've dabbled in heroin as a result of *Shooting at Midnight*. And I'm sure there are people out there who read *Finder* and are, like, "Oh, Greg goes to bondage clubs all the time."

No, Greg doesn't.

Greg went to bondage clubs with a notepad in his lap for *Finder* and sat at the bar drinking Coca-Cola and taking copious notes and talking to people. But there're some writers who need to get out there and experience it, meaning they have to do it themselves. I find that that occurs only at certain times for me.

Mim is a guitarist in *A Fistful of Rain*. I needed to know enough about how to play guitar that I could write that convincingly. And I couldn't get that solely through interviews, I had to buy a guitar and sit in the basement and try to learn how to play this thing.

When Atticus got a motorcycle, I thought I needed to know how to ride a motorcycle because I didn't know how I was going to use it. I was intrigued. It's important to me to know how to fire a gun and know how to treat those weapons.

Those become the story detail elements that will make or break a story, to an extent, for a lot of readers. But there are some things that I'm just not going to experience. I can't dance ballet to save my life; there's a lot of ballet in *Critical Space*. I don't do yoga. I wish I did, but I don't. But that's a lot of research. I did a lot of research for *Shooting at Midnight*, for instance. I spent a lot of time talking with the D.E.A., talking to different local politicos, visiting crime labs, talking to the F.B.I. at length. Especially when I was doing *Keeper*, trying to understand how the FACES [Freedom of Access at Clinic Entrances] legislation would work, how RICO [Racketeer Influenced and Corrupt Organizations] processing works, things like that. Mostly these days I read. There's a lot of source books here. I just finished a book called *Hatred's Kingdom* by a man named Dore Gold, who's actually been in the news a bit recently. I believe he's a policy advisor for [Ariel] Sharon right now. But the book is a doctorate thesis, I think, that he had started something like twenty years ago, and it's about Wahhabist Islam, and in particular about how Wahhabist Islam and the Kingdom of Saud are intrinsically linked and the results of that. Great book, great history of Wahhabism. A great little history of the kingdom of Saudi Arabia. That's going to work its way into the novel, but it's going to work its way into the novel very subtly. I've got a friend in the State Department, I've been bugging him for the new novel. And I'm lucky with him, because he's a fantastic storyteller, so even if he doesn't realize it half the time, he's giving me gold. When we talk, he'll spit something out and I'll be thinking, "Oh, I've got to use that."

The reason that the *Publisher's Weekly* reviewer got so pissed off and angry at Mim for being stupid is because he cared about her situation and he got to a point where he couldn't take it anymore. I can hear it in the review; he wanted to throw the book across the room. Not necessarily going, "This is horribly written," but because he's like, "Oh, that stupid woman!" See what I mean? That frustration. And I've always believed if I can get readers to invest that much in a character, I'm home free. And it doesn't matter if that character is Wonder Woman or Batman or a sentient pillow from Epsilon 8. If there's a connection made, then you pretty much can drag the reader along for the rest of the story. When they get to the end, they may not appreciate having been dragged along, because it runs a risk. Mim is a very risky character. Some people are not going to respond well to the novel, especially since…she ain't Atticus.

And that's actually another example of the research. Atticus can deal with problems, especially physical threats, in a very specific way. He knows how to punch and kick and jump and shoot and dive and roll and drive and this and that and the other thing. Mim knows how to play guitar. Not really a life-saving skill when somebody is holding a gun to your head. And I didn't want to cheat her in the novel. I didn't want to have her suddenly go, "Oh, I will punch you!" She's tiny. She's described as being very small and very slight. And these are all very calculated things for the narrative.

In *Finder,* Atticus, Natalie, and Erika shoot off some steam at the City Hall Rifle and Gun Club. Rucka's deft use of descriptions reflect the hours of research he spent at gun ranges.

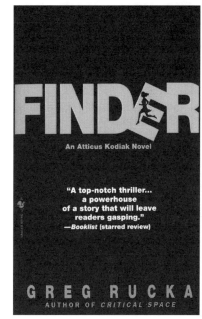

©2004 Greg Rucka

114   GREG RUCKA

back to watch as I put up a clean target and held the button down until it hung roughly seven yards away. The targets could be automatically sent out to the fixed distances of ten, twenty-five, and fifty yards, but since those fixed ranges weren't that relevant to my or Natalie's work, I didn't drill at them, and neither did she.

Most engagements take place at seven yards or closer, and that's what I needed to be prepared for if things ever went so bad on a job I had to start shooting.

But if things ever got that bad, the odds were I wouldn't even get my weapon out.

Natalie and I took turns, and between us we fired off almost two hundred rounds in about an hour, doing our drills. We started with double-taps, firing two shots as fast as possible, then switched to vertical tracking where we would work our way up the target. We'd start with the gun either in its holster or in the hands at what's called the low-ready position. Then we switched to one-hand drills, first the strong hand, then the weak one, firing off shots again and again, five or six from each presentation position in each drill, and changing the targets for the different exercises.

When the papers would come back, we'd hand them over to Erika, asking her to circle where we'd missed the shading with a pen from my bag. The Q targets we were using are the same ones the FBI utilizes for qualifying work, and the shaded portion on them represents the human central nervous system. Shots to different areas net different results. In vertical tracking, for instance, the goal is to draw a line up the body, starting at the abdomen, with the hope of taking out the CNS. If it works, the target goes down and doesn't get up again. End of problem. Shots to the pelvic girdle, on the other hand, are motor shots, used to cripple a target, to keep him or her from moving. Shots to the cardiovascular system are bleed-out shots. They'll put the target down, but it can take up to fifteen minutes, sometimes longer. They're not much use in our line of work.

Natalie and I finished up by sending a target out to

FINDER   115

fifty yards and taking some aimed shots with our good ammunition. When I'd emptied the magazine, I started to pull the target back in, but Erika stopped me.

"Can I try?"

"Sure," I said. I reloaded the magazine, set the gun down, and stepped back.

She made certain her goggles were in place and took the weapon, sighted, and cracked off a shot, looking back my way almost immediately. "What happened?"

"Different ammunition. You were firing some cheap stuff before. Now you're firing the stuff we use at work. It's a faster bullet."

"Kicks more."

"Yeah."

She readjusted, then emptied the gun. I cleared the weapon, reloaded it with the good stuff, then put it back in my holster while Erika called the target back from downrange and took it off its hanger. The three of us spent another ten minutes cleaning up, picking up our spent brass and dropping it in the buckets that were left for collection purposes.

We returned the eyes and ears to Lonny, and Erika thanked him again.

"You had fun?" he asked her.

"It was great."

"You can bring her back anytime," he told us. "She's a good little shooter."

We waited for Dale in the lobby, with Erika going over the targets while Natalie and I kept watch.

"You were right," Erika told us. "I did group better. Why is that? You guys shoot more often than I do."

"You're taking more time and you're using the sights more," Natalie said. "When we shoot, we're just trying to hit the target as best we can. We don't worry about the placement."

"The emphasis is on speed," I said.

"Don't you worry about where you hit, though? I

HAVING A CHIP ON YOUR SHOULDER

When asked to sum up his inspiration, Rucka has a powerful, yet eloquent one-word response.

GREG RUCKA: Anger.

My best writing tends to come out when I'm pissed off. With *Keeper*, I got angry. You don't shoot doctors. If you believe abortion is wrong and should be made illegal, then you do everything you can legally to get the law changed. We live in a country where there's a rule of law. And the rule of law says it's legal for women to get an abortion. You do not, therefore, shoot doctors for providing a legal service!

Regardless of whether or not you're pro-life or pro-choice or however you want to put it, shooting a doctor is wrong. And I just couldn't cotton it, so I had to understand it. And, of course, the explanation for murdering a doctor is, these people say, "It's not murder, it's self-defense. They're saving babies." But it took me writing a novel to really see that. That's sick! That's sick. You don't see PETA members murdering furriers. So what's going on there? It pissed me off like you wouldn't believe.

"Operation: Morningstar," the second arc in *Queen and Country*, was the exact same thing. The Taliban made me spit. I was bright red angry. And I was struggling with that story arc. It was Jen, it was my wife, who sat down and said, "I don't understand why you're not writing about this." She said, "Every time you speak about the Taliban you get that flame in your eyes. I don't understand why you're not writing about it." I said, "Uhhh…that's a good point." Part of the reason I didn't write about it and I was avoiding it is that I get nervous. Because the flipside is that the anger risks it becoming a polemic, because I want to sit there and say, "I'm right! I'm right! I'm right!" Or, more specifically, "They're wrong! They're wrong! They're wrong!" And that gets a little boring.

Keeper only works if both sides–and that implies there are only two sides–of the abortion debate are actually discussed fairly, so that you can see the rational voice that says, "I'm Pro-Life and I believe that abortion is wrong. And worse than wrong, I believe that it is murder." Because you need that. If that's not there, then you cannot then put next to it on one side the extremist that says, "Therefore killing somebody is appropriate," and going the other way, saying, "No, you're wrong, the right to choose and your determination of what is right for me is incorrect, or not your position to make." Bridgett's got a line in *Keeper* that I've always liked. She asks Atticus, "What do you think, where are you on abortion?" And he says, "I support a woman's right to choose." She says, "Oh, you're one of those." He says, "One of what?" She says, "You're a sensitive, New Age guy. 'Whatever you want, honey. Whatever is best for you.' Of course women have the right to choose. Women have always had the right to choose. That's not what this is about. This is about men believing they can give women the right to choose." That's her specific thing and that only works if everything else is out there. I get ticked off and that's what I write about. *Smoker* is another example of being ticked off. I mean, really angry. Spittingly angry.

And I gotta tell you, in writing the *Queen and Country* novel right now…politics are always present. And I mean "politics" here in terms of story rather than politics in terms of the art, if that distinction is any good. Politics is an element of the story in *Queen and Country* that's always a factor, there's always political dealing. One of the other things that's going on in the story is that there is–Tara does something at the order of her government that once she does it the government says, "Oh, God! What did you do?" And essentially her response is, "Well, I killed the man you told me to kill." And essentially the government says, "We didn't mean like that!" And I make it clear, one of the things that happens in the novel is there's a terrorist strike that happens very early. A horrible thing, several hundred people die, and they die horribly. The government turns around and they authorize a covert response. They want, essentially, the Wahhabist cleric who fomented and encouraged this dead.

So Tara does it, but when she does it, she kills the guy in a mosque. While he's praying! So in terms of Islam, and we're not talking Wahhabism, we're talking Islam–can you imagine anything more sacrilegious? There's this woman, she's not Muslim. There's a man, he's on his knees, praying toward Mecca, and she shoots him in the back of the head. That's horrific. That's ghastly. Is it more ghastly than the terrorist action? Is it more ghastly that it was done at her government's request? Those are political questions, and those are the things I get angry about. What's the double standard here? It bugs me.

I'm not a big fan of Bill Maher, but the quote that lit ABC up–"What's more cowardly, firing cruise missiles from a thousand miles away?"–it's a fair question! I never heard anybody answer it! And answer it with thought, rather than with the emotional "How dare you?" And the implication is that in asking the question, you're not patriotic? That you do not honor those who were murdered on 9/11? That's unfair! Americans ask questions, and one of the things that democracy requires is asking hard questions, asking questions that do not have easy answers. One of the reasons I hate this administration, anytime you throw a hard question at them, they say, "No, no, no. Clearly you're not with the program. You're not patriotic." And I resent that. I resent that like hell. I resent that the White House press secretary said, "Maybe now's not the best time to be asking questions like that." Yes! Now is absolutely the best time to be asking questions like that! You don't ask after the people are dead! Because then you can't do anything about it! Unless there's some secret project you guys have that brings people back from the dead, but I doubt it!

In *Smoker,* Rucka shares his views on the dangers of smoking.

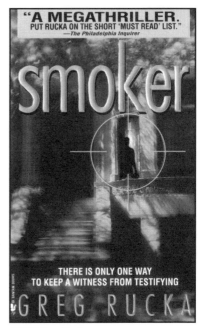

256   GREG RUCKA

ambushed here, we'd have no warning, and almost nowhere to go.

Natalie, Corry, and I kept scanning while Dale drove, and Pugh kept his head down, silent now. When we hit the Taconic, all of us relaxed slightly. The convoy accelerated to a little over sixty, all the cars holding their space.

"We're good," Dale announced.

"You can sit up," I told Pugh.

"Can I take this thing off?" he asked, tugging at his body armor.

"I'd say no," I said. "Ask Natalie, she's more charitable towards automobiles."

"You can take it off," Natalie said. "You'll have to wear it again when we stop, and keep it on until we get you secured at the deposition. But for the ride, you should be okay without it."

Pugh twisted and bent, and with some help, managed to get the body armor off and onto his lap.

There wasn't much talking for the next several miles. Occasionally, Dale would say something to his radio, and the other drivers would respond. Slow down, speed up, watch the car on the right, watch the car on the left, careful of the bend. But that was it; the environment wasn't really conducive to conversation.

North of Yonkers, Pugh asked Natalie, "You smoke, don't you?"

She looked surprised. "No, not really—"

Pugh punched her in the arm. "Don't. It'll kill you. It'll kill you sure as a bullet, and a hell of a lot slower."

"Don't you hit me." Indignation made her voice climb.

"You didn't like that?"

"No."

SMOKER   257

He socked her shoulder again. "That's what a cigarette does to your lungs, hon. That's the tar, that's the ammonia added to the tobacco to increase your nicotine intake, that's the acrolein. I could list a hundred other chemicals, all of them bad for you. Four hundred and twenty-five thousand people a year die from cigarettes, you want to be one of them?"

Natalie said, "I don't—"

"Jesus! Don't lie to me, girl! I was around the stuff for more than twenty years. I can smell a smoker at thirty feet. It's in your hair, it's in your clothes. Eau de Cancer, sweetheart, believe me, it followed you as we tangoed."

"I quit," Natalie protested. "I wasn't even really smoking. I had less than half a pack, for God's sake."

"Well, then, you *just* quit, because you had at least one sometime this morning." His hands were knotting the straps to the body armor now in his lap.

Natalie looked at me, and I didn't have anything to say in her defense, so she looked back at Pugh. "You're right," she said. "I had one this morning, before I drove up."

"Don't do it again," Pugh said, and turned to stare out the front window. We went a couple more miles, before he said, "I'm sorry, I shouldn't have punched you. That's not a way to treat a lady. I just kept smelling it, and I couldn't figure out which of you it was."

"It's okay," Natalie said.

"Hell, I've got no right to cast stones. I smoked off and on for fifteen years myself. Couldn't really work for DTS without sucking on a butt, could I? Billy and I used to sit in his office and sample different brands from different makers. We'd rate them, try to guess what blends they were using, how much fill they'd

WRITING IS ABOUT EMOTION

Greg Rucka has some words of wisdom for those about to write their first novel.

GREG RUCKA: What are the tools of the trade? Well, a working knowledge of grammar. You don't have to know all your rules, you don't have to be a master of it, you can know it well enough. I always say writing is alchemy. You have 26 letters that really mean nothing. They are icons; as Scott McCloud would say in *Understanding Comics*, they're little pictographs. They don't mean anything. They're just a little symbol that we've invested with meaning. We have 26 of them in English, at least, and what you do is you juggle them. And if you put them together in the right sequence, they form a series of symbols that actually mean a concept, a word, that we can phonetically create. And if you do a whole sequence of those, you now have a sentence. And if you do that several thousand times, you have a story.

Writing is about clarity. If you're not clear, you lose the reader. And writing is about emotion. And I believe this is the strongest tool.

There are fundamental tools. You have to be able to read, you have to be able to write. You have to understand grammar well enough to be clear. Having a sense of voice, creating a sense of style. But if your story doesn't have an emotional resonance it's useless to me. I have no time for it. If your story, or actually anything, your movie, your painting, your drawing, whatever, doesn't make me feel something, I could care less. The emotional connection is everything.

Learn the tropes. You have to read. You have to, have to, read. Too many people don't read. And you cannot just read the thing you want to write, you have to read everything. So a lot of people say, "Well, I've read *Watchmen* twenty times." *Watchmen* is actually not a great example of how to write a comic book, just like *War and Peace* is not a great example of how to write a novel. These are accomplished masterworks. What you need to do is you need to understand the fundamentals. You need to know what makes a story a story, how to tell that story. And then you need to start looking at the masters of the form and realize why they're masters. And if you don't like them, realize why you don't like them. For instance, I know a lot of people who hate Ernest Hemingway, hate his writing. I love Hemingway. And I don't care if people hate him, it's just you've got to know why you hate him. And you have to understand why people think he's great. You need to learn to recognize good art and bad art, and then you need to be able to critique it fairly. Which means, yes, I can recognize this as good art that I do not personally like, which is a fair response, rather than just saying, "It's bad." That does nobody any good. Read. Write a lot.

Fear's a great motivator. Hunger is always a great motivator. The feeling that it wasn't good enough and needs to be better is a great motivator. The desire to improve is a great motivator. There's a joy in creation that every creator, I'm sure, has experienced. All of those things factor.

My little brother is in film school at NYU and he was telling me that one of his writing teachers has a cartoon, I guess from *The New Yorker*, on his office door. A writer sits at a cluttered desk, and with his feet up and the pencil in his mouth and his eyes are closed, and it says, "I'm writing." And that's the hardest thing, actually, about being a writer, is that you feel guilty if somebody walks by and you're not actually typing. So much of writing is an internal process. Typing is the easy part. You ask how long does it take me to write a novel, and my answer is four weeks or a year-and-a-half, depending. The year-and-a-half to think about it, four weeks of typing furiously. So I guard and I try to recharge.

Find people you trust. Not people who will tell you what you think you want to hear, and not people who have an agenda in criticizing you–which is one of the biggest problem I think you can run into in courses, in graduate schools, for instance. I hated the fiction workshops at USC where nobody would say anything bad because they were afraid that if they did, when their work came up, they'd be lit up. And that doesn't do anybody any good. You have to develop the ego that says, "My work has merit," the ego that says, "Not only does it have merit, but I believe in it." And at the same time be able to drop the defensive ego enough to hear honest criticism and to take it, which is why you have to find sources that you trust.

Find for yourself a rabbi, find for yourself a teacher who can guide you. I have been blessed throughout my education with a string of teachers who were brilliant, who inflamed and encouraged and did not let me back down. And I can list their names. And they far outnumber the bad ones, whose names I can list as well. Those teachers...Professor Frank Bergon, Sid Stebel, Mrs. Johnson back in fifth grade and sixth grade, Tom Murray during high school...these are the people who put in the spurs and lifted my work and didn't let me slack. My senior year at Vassar I was in a fiction writing seminar; it was the first time I actually got into an official fiction course after trying for three years. And I'd gotten in by surprise. We came back from the summer break, and the professor, who was Frank Bergon, asked, "Let me see what you've got." And I gave him this piece of crap that I'd written over the summer. And three days later he called me into his office, because he was calling everybody in, and he gave me the story back and he gave me a note, a two-page, short, notepad note written on both sides, and just savaged it. And he didn't savage it gleefully. He said, "This, this, this and this. These are the problems. And this, I don't understand it. And this, what are you thinking?" And then he said, "These are the things you must work on." And I went back to my dorm room and I broke down, I was hysterical. I ended

Greg Rucka is acknowledged as one of the finest writers of thriller novels. *Critical Space* furthers the Kodiak series by continuing to utilize edgy and complex characters. ©2004 Greg Rucka

up calling my dad, I said, "Ah, I just got this horrible critique!" And my dad said, "Well, was he right?" "That's not the point!" or something suitably hysterical. "I think it is." And yeah, I'm a better writer because of that note. There are people who would have gotten that note and run away. It would have been over, that's it. But those moments…I understand it's hard. Being criticized is hard. And writing is hard, art is hard. Because to do art, you have to put some of your-self out there. That's why a lot of writers can't be in the same room as somebody who's reading their work. My brother's on break from school and he's brought his films. And I really want to watch them, and I don't want to watch them while he's present. I don't think that's fair to him, and I certainly don't think that's fair to me. They need to be viewed alone for me to be fair to them. So that's my advice. Find for yourself a teacher.

---

138   **GREG RUCKA**

sky. Either the air conditioner in the Passat was broken or I didn't understand the controls, because the atmosphere in the car was thick and dead. I rolled down the window as I came up to Silver Lake Park, trading the security of a closed vehicle for the hope of air.

There was a grotesque monument to modern architecture opposite Silver Lake Park, a block of apartments that looked like it'd been built by the same firm that handled most of the U.S. Army's bunkers in foreign lands. My instructions had me continuing another 1.3 miles before a turn, and as I came over the crest of a small hill, with the Silver Mount Cemetery on my right, I caught a glimpse of the Porsche in my rearview mirror.

"You're still too close. Give me more room."

"There's plenty of room," Bridgett said.

"Give me at least half a mile, more if you can."

Her grunt was sullen in my ear.

I had another left coming up, and as the odometer confirmed the distance, I signaled the turn. "Left onto Clove. Heading roughly south now, maybe southeast."

Bridgett radioed a confirmation. Corry came back on the air, but there was a lot of interference, and I had to ask him to repeat.

"Said it looks like you're actually coming in our direction."

"Hope it stays that way," I said.

The traffic on Clove was busier than it had been on Victory, and I went another half a mile before hitting a light and checking the directions. I was on Step 11 now, and had another left coming up, in less than a tenth of a mile. Ahead of me, past the light, the intersection had been constructed around the Staten Island Expressway, and it looked like I had two choices: I could either make an almost immediate left or I could continue past the highway and make the left there. The odometer wasn't helping much.

The light changed, and I decided to err on the side of caution, making the left onto Narrows Road, then relaying the decision by radio to the others. Everyone acknowledged.

Step 12 said to continue .86 of a mile and then to make a right. Behind me, a black Camaro made its presence known by leaning on its horn. I ignored it, knowing that I was driving like a little old lady, and unwilling to take things any faster. The odometer ticked off eight-tenths of a mile, and I didn't see a right turn onto anything. The Camaro tried to get around me, found that it was blocked by a truck, and gave me more horn. The odometer was about to roll over another mile before I saw a right I could take, a busy intersection onto Richmond Road.

CRITICAL SPACE   **139**

"Right onto Richmond," I radioed. If I had made a mistake, if I had taken the wrong turn when I'd gotten onto Narrows, there wasn't much of a point in sharing that.

Confirmations came back, and once again, Corry and Moore's transmissions were snarled with static.

Step 13 instructed me to continue 2.4 miles before making another turn, a left. The Camaro had gotten around me when I turned onto Richmond, and I drove, trying to monitor the odometer. If it was off, I was screwed, I'd have to double back to Narrows and try again. The road wasn't easy, either; Richmond was just as crowded as Narrows had been, and getting worse as more and more people left their homes to head to work. The Passat had a radio and CD player, and the digital clock informed me that it was now four minutes to eight in the morning.

I'd gone 2 of the 2.4 miles indicated when Richmond did a strange kind of left bank, merging with another road, and try as I might I couldn't get a glimpse of any sign telling me if the names had changed. On my right-hand side I could see a huge and well-tended golf course, but nothing said what I should call that, either.

"I think I'm off Richmond," I radioed. "I've got a golf course on my right, now, but I don't know what it's called."

There was a storm of static, and Corry's voice came through choppy, the words broken. I heard *"Richmond"* and *"club,"* but the rest of it was garbage.

"Corry, you're breaking up, I've got you at five by two, best. Can you hear me?"

More static, and this time I didn't understand anything he said.

She can't be doing this, I thought. She can't be jamming us like this, not unless she's very close.

"Bridgett?"

"Still here."

"Corry and Moore must have hit a dead zone."

"Could be on the bridge, it could be eating the signal. I'm still with you, don't fret."

"I've got another right coming up, Step 14, here . . ." I braked to a stop on the side of the road and stared at where Drama meant me to turn. I double-checked the paper and the odometer to be certain.

"Atticus?"

Once again, despite everything that was happening, I had to admire the skill of it. She'd picked the perfect place, just secluded enough to keep wandering eyes at bay, just public enough that our presence wouldn't raise suspicion.

Clarity in writing is important to Rucka. In *Critical Space*, Atticus travels to a hostage exchange. In this excerpt Rucka is able to establish and describe multiple locations while keeping all of the characters distinct.

Dave Dorman
on Comics & Illustration

As much as comic books rely on the written word to tell a story, the stunning visuals within the panels make the form unique. The art often attracts many life-long readers. There are just as many visual styles as there are kinds of stories that can be told. Most comic book production techniques include a traditional pencil-to-ink process which is colored and separated on computer. However, painters also use the medium for their stories.

Dave Dorman is an acclaimed painter, but it is illustration work that excites him the most. Fine art painting is about self-exploration and reinvention. Though Dorman exhibits these traits through his illustration, he'd much rather be telling stories and refining his technique. Comic books played an early and dominant role in his formative years.

DAVE DORMAN: Well, I was definitely a Marvel junkie when I was growing up. The first books I can recall creating an influence on my psyche were books like *Tales of Suspense* and *Tales to Astonish* with Iron Man and Dr. Strange and Captain America. I definitely read *Fantastic Four*. And I was pretty exclusively into Marvel comics for a very long time. I didn't have any real interest in reading Batman books, or Superman, or JLA, or any of the DC books. The Marvel books are very dear to me because they're the ones that got me into drawing. I can remember copying those comics when I was a kid–sitting down and doing tracings, stuff like that. But comics also got me into reading. And that was a real big thing because I think just to be well-educated overall, you have to be well-read. And having started reading comics and finding there was more to the written word than the boring stuff you read in school, it certainly opened up a lot for me.

I moved on from reading comics to reading adventure books like *Doc Savage* and *Conan the Barbarian*, which were fairly popular in the mid- to late-Sixties. From there I started reading more hardcore science fiction stuff and then I branched off into detective books and mysteries and a little more mainstream fiction. And that leads to where I am today, which is pretty much reading anything that might interest me, no matter the subject matter. So comics probably had a greater influence on me overall than just artwork.

These days what I'm reading in comics is just oddball stuff. I read all of Mike Mignola's *Hellboy* stuff when it comes out. I think he's just a wonderful storyteller and always imaginative. I read *Heavy Metal*. I like the European material, so *Heavy Metal* is something that I keep up on whenever it comes in. I buy a lot of European graphic novels, even though I can't read them, because the storytelling is done very well. You don't necessarily have to read the text to enjoy the stories. So I'm constantly on the lookout for European material and Japanese material, for the artistic sake of what they're producing.

"I've been working on this Wasted Lands project for about six or seven years now, and I don't mean the *Rail* graphic novel I've been working on. I mean just developing Wasted Lands concepts and characters and stories. There are a lot of stories that I want to tell within the world of Wasted Lands."

The Wasted Lands storylines center around Mortal City–a megalopolis of industrial overgrowth and decay caused by the Iron Wars. These wars were orchestrated by the eight Rail Barons, who used the Rail to control transport and lives. Using black line drawings with wash technique, Dorman tells a full comics story in a graphic novel format greatly inspired by European comics. ©2004 Dave Dorman

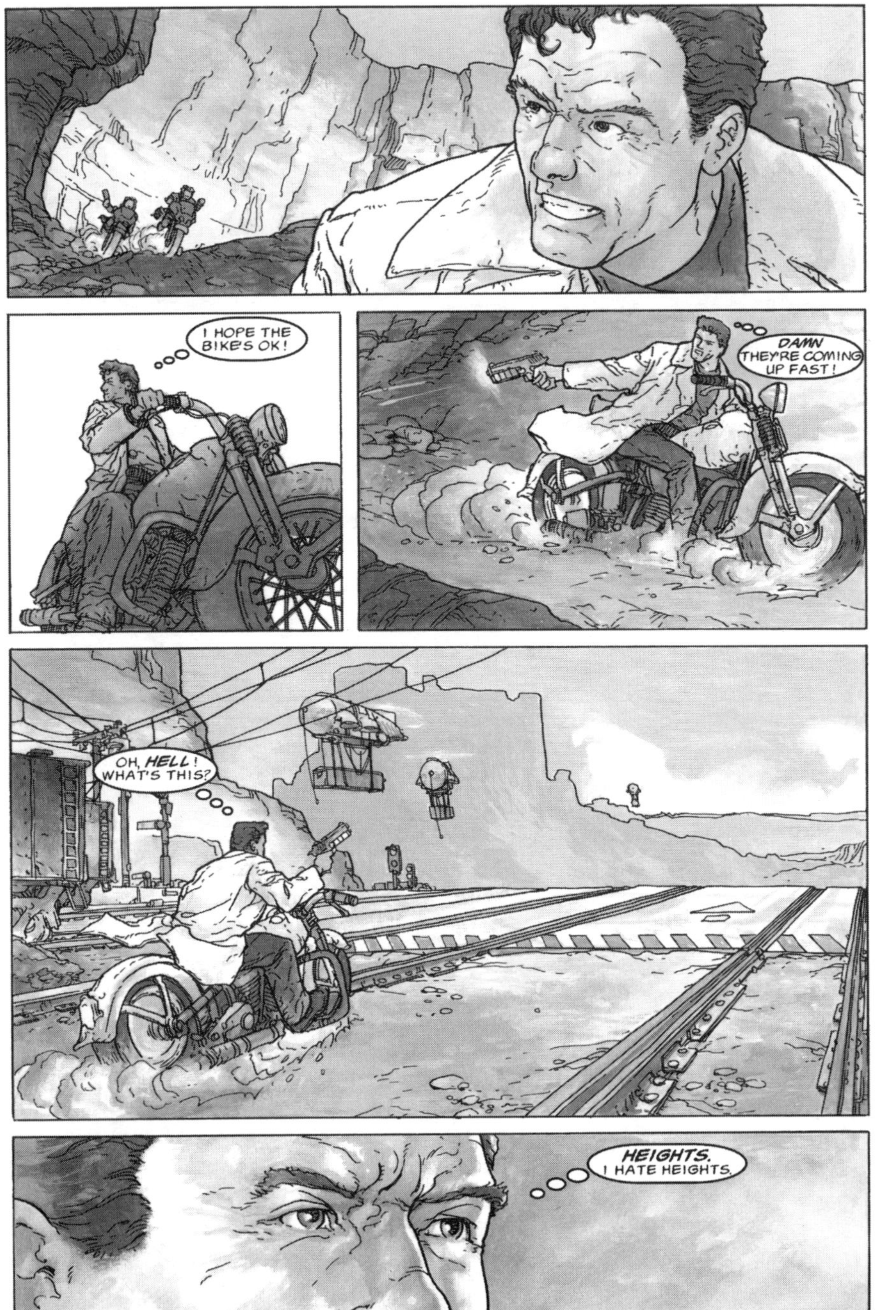
I HOPE THE BIKE'S OK!
DAMN THEY'RE COMING UP FAST!
OH, HELL! WHAT'S THIS?
HEIGHTS. I HATE HEIGHTS.

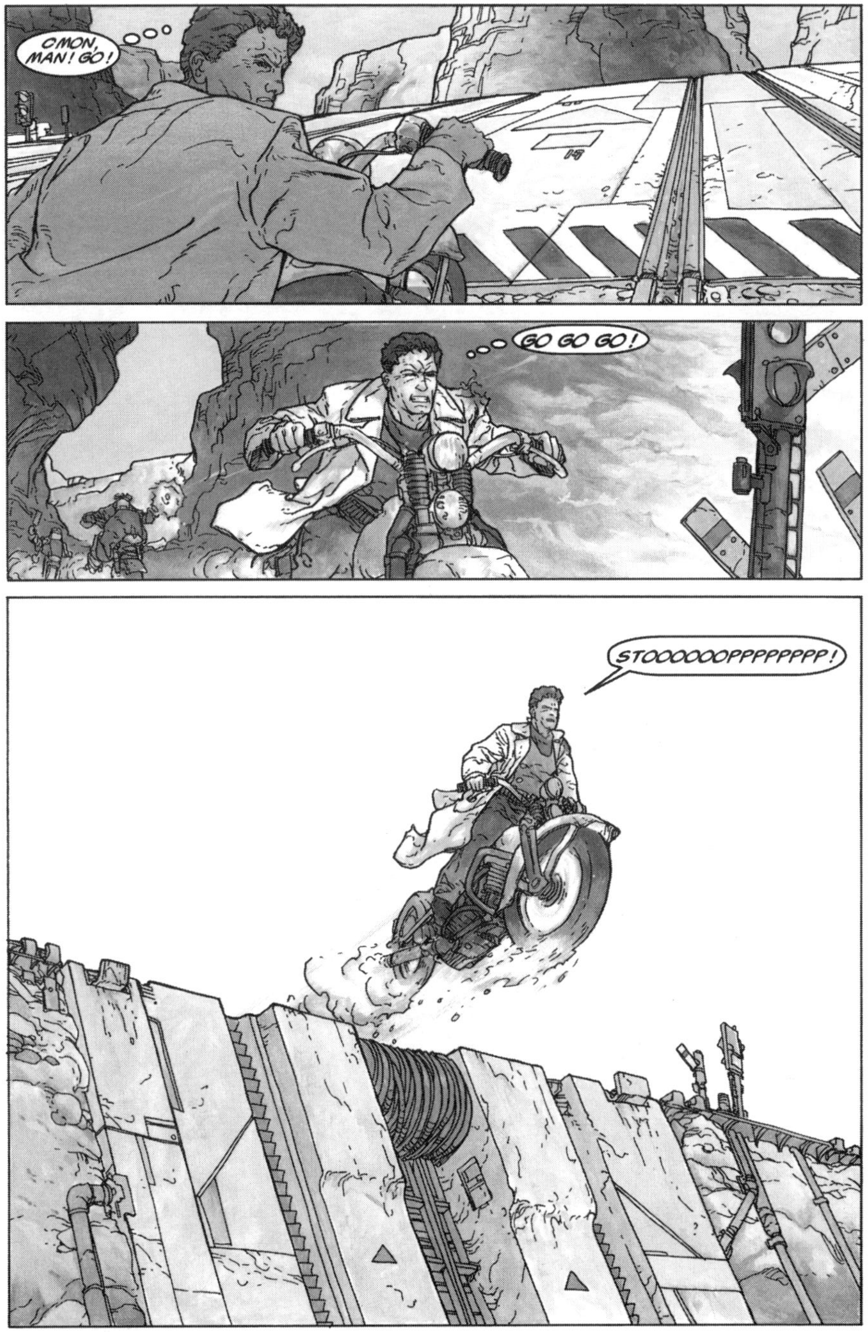
C'MON, MAN! GO!
GO GO GO!
STOOOOOOPPPPPPPP!

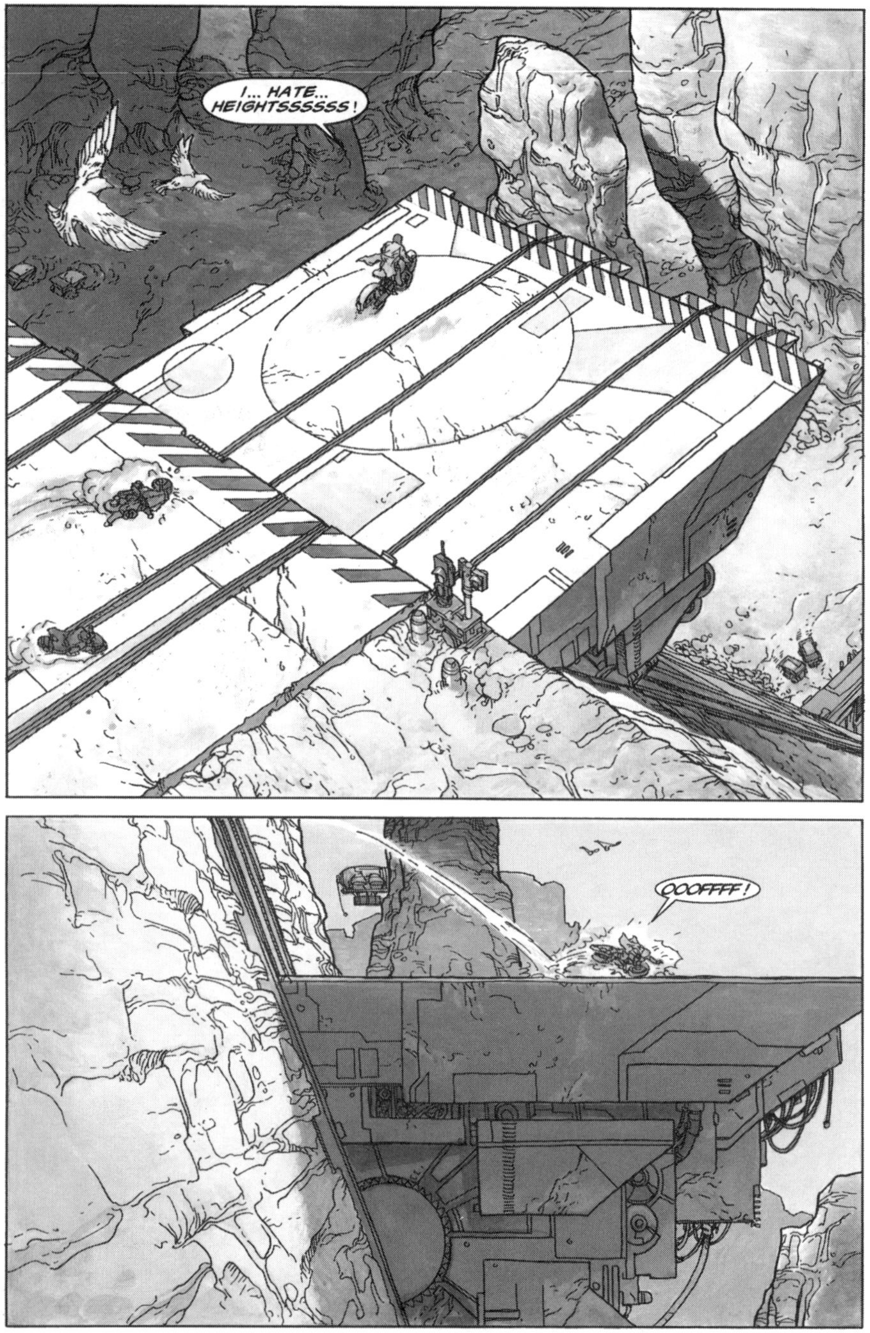
I... HATE... HEIGHTSSSSSS!
OOOFFFF!

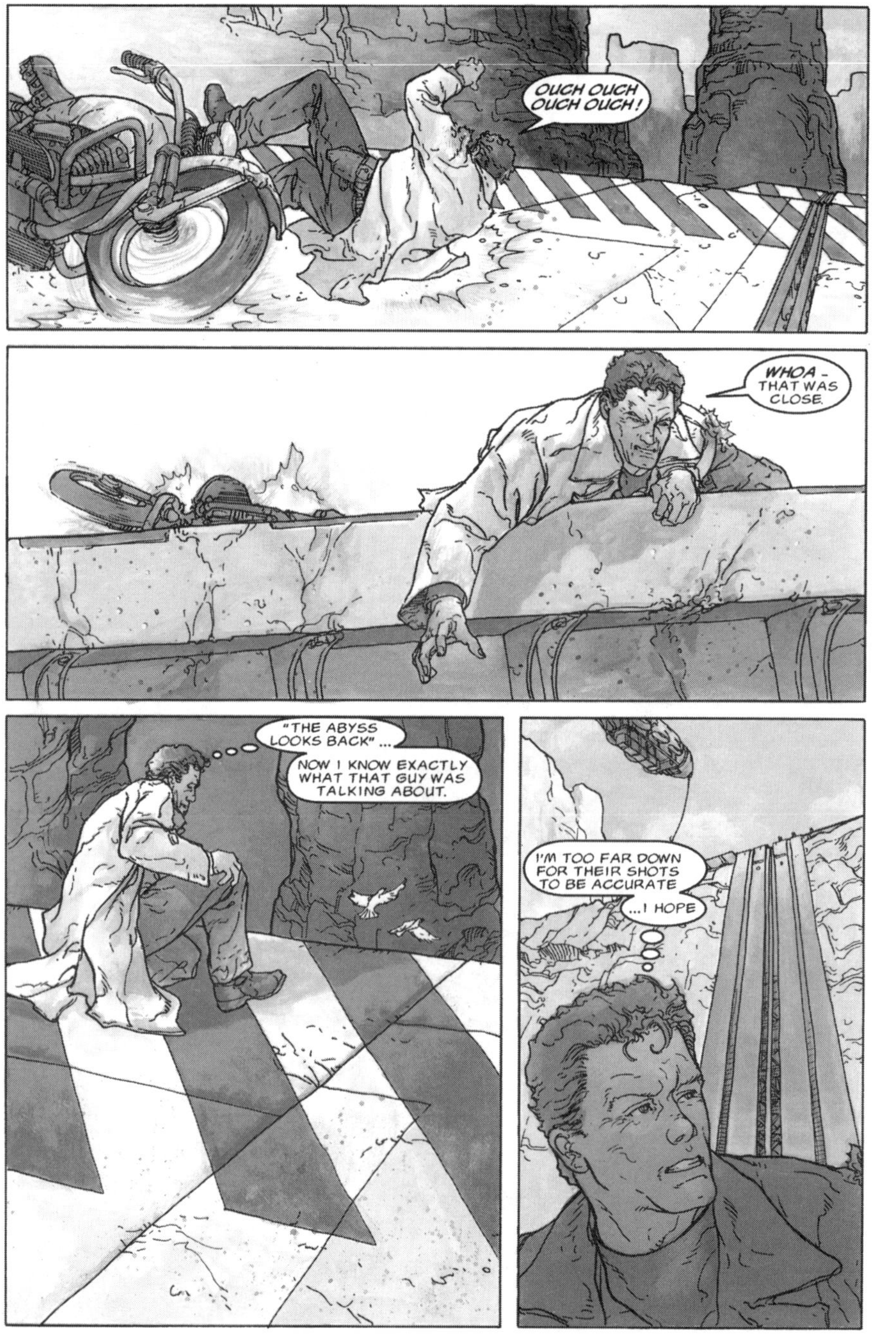
OUCH OUCH OUCH OUCH!
WHOA - THAT WAS CLOSE.
"THE ABYSS LOOKS BACK" ...
NOW I KNOW EXACTLY WHAT THAT GUY WAS TALKING ABOUT.
I'M TOO FAR DOWN FOR THEIR SHOTS TO BE ACCURATE
...I HOPE

KNOWLEDGE IS POWER

In today's society, it's easy to settle into a tried and true profession. It can be a difficult decision to call art your profession, especially when having passion and talent aren't always enough. Being well versed in the craft, understanding the business of art, and constantly receiving new stimuli through reading or other experiences are all important to the artist's lifestyle.

DAVE DORMAN: I think that you need to gain as much knowledge as you can. And the way to gain knowledge is to read, to learn how to read and to educate yourself as best you can. And the more you can educate yourself, the better off you're going to be. For me, reading comics got me started reading, and I look at that as a very big stepping stone. Anything that you can do to get a kid to read is going to be beneficial for that kid. And comics are a very good way to start teaching kids how to read.

You're not seeing that in today's culture, which is a disappointment. You're seeing more and more kids who don't know how to read. But I'm not saying that comics is the only way to teach kids how to read, but it's a very good way to teach kids how to read, and we're missing that.

I try to make a point to kids who come up to me at shows, for autographs and to show their portfolios of their artwork, and want to know how I got started, one of the first things I tell them is, "Work hard, read a lot, and pursue the interests that you enjoy. And nothing is going to come if you don't work hard for it." And the parents need to understand that artwork, art and illustration, is a viable way to make a living. Even in today's society, there's still the stigma that a person who is pursuing art is going to be a starving artists schlubbing around their canvases in New York looking for a dollar. You know, the typical "starving artist" thing. It's not true. There's a million avenues of opportunity out there for a person who knows how to draw well and can illustrate well. They just need the education to know how to pursue those interests.

I think a lot of talent within the comics industry has the respect of other industries. You see a lot of crossover now, more than fifteen or twenty or 25 years ago. A lot of comic artists are doing storyboards and animation and covers for rap music and hip-hop stuff, and you see big corporations hiring illustrators who come out of the comics field for mainstream artwork. So there is respect, more respect now than there used to be for artists in the comics field.

However, technology has changed the way the youth of today is looking at their entertainment. They don't see comics as a viable form of continuous entertainment the way that we did when I was young. And that in the long run is going to hurt the field quite a bit. It's not that the kids don't respect comic artists, because they do.

When you see these artists doing skateboard artwork or, like I say, hip-hop album covers, or advertising—stuff that's being done outside the comics field—the kids do respect that. They're just not reading the comics that the artists are doing to try to make a living.

Dorman's first Batman assignment was his cover for *The Greatest Batman Stories Ever Told* (right, top). Since then, he has done book and comic covers, billboards, and trading cards. Two examples of Dorman's trading cards include *Batman: Saga of the Dark Knight* (right, below), and the *Batman Master Series* (below) which was also used on the cover of the compilation book. Batman TM & ©2004 DC Comics

S T A Y I N G   D I V E R S I F I E D

Art is a difficult field in which to work. Dorman has always been an artist, but he has also worked hard to position himself in front of numerous artistic opportunities. Those life decisions can be as challenging as painting on canvas.

DAVE DORMAN: One of the things that I learned early on was to stay diversified. And that's what I've been doing all through my career. I've never stuck to one particular thing. Comics sort of dictated my interest in learning how to draw originally; that's where I wanted to go first. It wasn't until I started painting when I was a senior in high school that I discovered that my interest in art lay in a much larger field, which was illustration. I didn't just pigeonhole my interest into comics, but broadened it greatly into the world of illustration. And because I didn't pigeonhole myself, I've been able to generate interest in my artwork within many different fields, depending on what I was interested in doing.

Initially, my first sales were in the comics field, doing covers for *Heavy Metal* magazine and Marvel's *Savage Sword of Conan* and some small stuff for AC Comics and Comico, basically whatever I could find that would pay me a few bucks and get my name out a little bit more and show my work into the comic marketplace. But also I would send my samples to paperback book companies and magazine companies and anywhere that would use illustration. So I was never really stuck in comics, because I made the decision to pursue things outside the field, but the comics field has definitely opened doors for me, because there is a lot of crossover in business between comics and books and magazines and films and records and CDs and all types of entertainment media. You find a great crossover that you wouldn't necessarily think would be there, but it is. So my work in the comics industry has gotten me work outside the comics industry

that I didn't necessarily pursue, but certainly welcomed. Other clients would see my comic book work and say, "Well, let's call Dave and see if he's interested in doing some movie designs," or, "Let's call Dave and see if he's interested in doing some G.I. Joe toy designs." So some of it was stumbled upon by the fact that I was able to make a good name for myself in the comics industry by doing covers that attracted buyers and attracted people and generated interest.

What I'm known for primarily, within the comics industry, is doing some nice cover work. However, what really generated a lot of interest for me and sort of took off within the comics industry was when I started doing work with Dark Horse Comics and got involved with LucasFilm and the *Star Wars* and *Indiana Jones* licenses. Those really broke out for Dark Horse and for me, within and outside the comics industry, because of the interest in *Star Wars* and *Indiana Jones* among the general population and not just the comic book industry. So, sort of half-stumbling and half-pursuing the *Star Wars* and *Indiana Jones* projects with Dark Horse really cemented my reputation within the comics industry as a top illustrator of covers. And I certainly wasn't going to argue with the recognition and the fame that that brought. It was a lot of fun work, and I look back on it and it was great.

Still, I didn't really feel that I was an illustrator *per sé* until I started working with Hasbro toys in the mid-Eighties, I'd say '86, when they started having me do some toy designs for them, which was very different from what I was doing for the comics industry. I had done some comic book covers and I had done some paperback covers. I was doing illustration, which is what I wanted to do, so I was satisfied with that. Then I started breaking out of the publishing industry and moving into fields where I created artwork that wasn't necessarily for publication but was still illustration and challenging in a different way than a cover piece would be. And that's when I felt

Dorman has worked on many commercial illustration assignments, including the toy industry. A painting of the Baroness created for the G.I. Joe Figurine Series for Palisades Toys (above) and turnarounds for an Alien Warrior toy (right) for Hasbro Toys. Baroness TM & ©2004 Hasbro. Alien TM & ©2004 20th Century Fox.

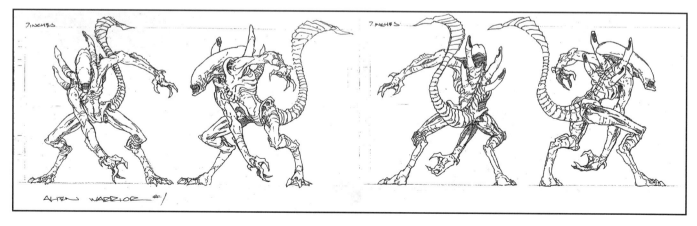

that I was really breaking out of just being, say, a comic or a cover illustrator. My talent was in demand for more than just the ability to sell a product. I was being asked to be more creative, if you want to put it that way, without the context of having to sell anything. So that was definitely an open door to a different path, and it felt good. Something that I've pursued during my career as well is to look for those doors that I could open into different areas to pursue different types of illustration.

I hate trying to define my career, but I can sort of give landmarks to how I ended up where I am. The first *Heavy Metal* cover, my very first sale, was certainly a landmark. That was *Heavy Metal* July of 1983. That was a very big thing for me. Being hired by Hasbro to do the G.I. Joe stuff was a very big thing because that's where I was able to do more than just cover stuff. After that would be the *Indiana Jones* and the *Star Wars* stuff, which was sort of like winning the Oscar. You get a lot of popularity along with that for the work that you do. Winning the Eisner Award for the *Aliens: Tribes* artwork was something that was another landmark for me because that project

gave me the opportunity to do something that I'd wanted to do my whole career, and I still want to do, because I think I'm best suited doing illustrated books rather than continuous panel stories. I think my strong point would be illustrated books, and *Tribes* gave me that opportunity to pursue something that I'd wanted to do up to that point in my career. And having won the Eisner Award, which is the biggest award within the comics field, was very gratifying and very invigorating. To know that something that I'd worked hard to do was accepted and honored by the industry.

Even so, I still want to pursue more illustrated book work. After that, it's just one fun project after another, and there's certainly more to come in the future. But I'm pursuing things both professionally to be a commercial artist, and personally for my own mental health, which is why two years ago I took two years off to work on my Wasted Lands project, of which the graphic novel *Rail* was the first major product. So there I'm sort of coming full circle, in that I learned how to draw with comics, and here I am, finally producing my own continuous panel comic book.

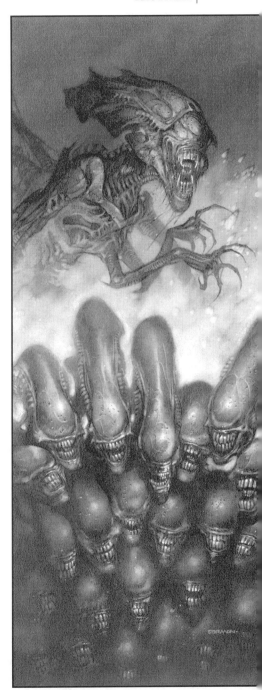

Dorman received his first Eisner for his work on the *Aliens* franchise. Partial front cover for the *Aliens: Tribes* paperback edition (far right). Cover to *Alien: Hive* for Dark Horse Comics (right). Alien TM & ©2004 20th Century Fox.

Dorman's work with the *Star Wars* license began when he first established a business relationship with LucasFilm in the late 1980s. After working on their *Indiana Jones* property, he was invited to try his hand on *Star Wars* projects. A long-time fan, Dorman has gone on to produce *Star Wars* artwork that has been used on a myriad of products all around the world, including comics, magazines, books, trading cards, toys, audio books, compact discs and prints. Examples of Dorman's work: *Leia as Boussh* (below left), *In the Court of Jabba the Hutt* (below right), *Boba Fett: Fall of the Bounty Hunter* (across left), Cover to *Star Wars* #0 for Dark Horse Comics (across, right top) and *Obi-Wan Kenobi* (across, right bottom). Star Wars TM & ©2004 LucasFilm.

THE ARTIST VS. THE STORYTELLER

Just because an artist can draw does not mean they can communicate effectively. In illustration, the artist works to deliver a single image that can freeze a moment or open interpretation. A good illustration relies on the viewer's analysis and demands interaction. Though good sequential art should challenge the reader, the ability to convey information in an effortless way is more important. It takes great effort to render and draw, and incredible effort to make one scene flow smoothly into the next to tell a story.

DAVE DORMAN: One of the most important skills in being a comic book artist is you have to separate "artist" from "storyteller." I think there are a lot of good artists out there that aren't very good storytellers—and I think there are good storytellers that aren't very good artists. There are some that are both, and there are some that are neither. So to be an artist and to tell the story isn't necessarily things that go hand in hand.

Doing a single illustration to convey an idea or to tell a story has to be very textured visually. To tell a story in one illustration requires a lot of elements for the viewer to grasp and to digest within one viewing. In the case of storytelling, you, as the artist, have the convenience of time—you can show action, you can show movement, you can show results of movements and action, you can show drama within movement, you can change atmosphere with lighting

and moving from dark to light or light to dark. You can create a drama similar to what film can do, because you have the convenience of time to work with. With a single illustration, you're stopping a moment in time. And to do that, the visual texture of the piece needs to be much more complicated to tell an interesting story.

Now what I mean by texture are the things within the illustration itself that are visual clues to what the artist might want to say. The artist gives the viewer visual clues so that they may make the decisions on what the piece is saying. The artist can be very distinct in laying out certain elements within an illustration but, on the other hand, the artist may put in elements within the picture to be very vague, so the viewer can make up their own story and not be hampered by any specific idea the artist had in mind. A single illustration can be taken many ways, whereas storytelling tends to be a very direct way of transferring information and entertainment to the viewer.

I don't really consider myself a good storyteller in the continuous panel format because I haven't had a lot of experience doing that. Over my lifetime maybe I've done a hundred pages, maybe 150 pages. But that doesn't compare to other guys in the field who've done hundreds of thousands of pages of storytelling. So I'm definitely still in my infancy in learning how to tell a proper story in the continuous panel format. My strength is in telling a story in a single illustration, and that certainly doesn't translate well when you're hired to do a hundred-page graphic novel. It's definitely a little bit more work

for me to have to structure my way of thinking from producing one illustration that tells a story to 48 pages of six panels a page. Obviously, that's a much longer story to tell, but visually it has to be interesting to the reader to keep the reader moving from panel to panel in conjunction with the text. If the artwork is not fluid enough to tell the story visually, in conjunction with the text, the reader's going to get bored and they're just going to stop reading. Like any badly told tale, if it's not interesting, why read it? So there is a difference for me between being an artist, a comic artist, and being a good storyteller.

In comic book storytelling you have to move beyond just being able to draw well—you have to be able to visualize the story in the way that movies are created, or like real life. People are constantly moving, whether it's one character talking or whether it's an exchange between two characters or more, you don't hold the same visual image the whole time. The artist needs to continually think of a way to keep the viewer visually interested while the course of that conversation is going on. So instead of just having one head-and-shoulders shot and a thousand words of text on a page, you break it down into panels where you move the camera around the room and you emphasize certain things that the speaker may be talking about by having a close-up or reaction shots. Those are all things that the artists needs to think about.

And the artist, to continue the similarity to filmmaking, is the director in this instance. He's setting up where all the characters are in a particular scene. He has to block out the action. He has to decide what shots to make within the course of action that the story dictates, basically photograph it in his head, and then translate that "edit" into a visual medium, which in this case is paper and pencil and pen. And that's not the easiest thing in the world to do. You can be a good artist and be able to render all these things, but to be able to tell that story visually is not simple. You can make it very, very pretty, but if it doesn't flow from panel to panel to panel, or if it's very jarring or very badly laid-out, you're going to force the reader to work to try and read the story, rather than letting the story flow by itself. And that's the worst thing you can do in a book is make the reader *work* to enjoy it.

Star Wars TM & ©2004 LucasFilm.

Indiana Jones has always been a favorite character for Dorman. He had the opportunity to do cover art for the first original comic revival series featuring Indy, which was the start of his working relationship with LucasFilm.

Dorman's first Indiana Jones art was done for Dark Horse Comics in 1991, with *Indiana Jones and The Fate of Atlantis* (above). He has since gone on to complete a wide variety of Indiana Jones work as well as the covers for *Indiana Jones and the Iron Phoenix* (right). Indiana Jones TM & ©2004 LucasFilm.

COVER ILLUSTRATION

Though illustration is utilized in numerous ways, the crowning achievement for most illustrators is to be featured on the cover of a publication. Few illustrators can sustain a living relying on cover work, but to score the cover is quite a coup. With a single illustration, the artist can dictate the look and feel of the content.

DAVE DORMAN: My concept of a cover is the same as an advertisement. That's basically what a cover painting is—an advertisement. It's something that's out there where the viewer is walking by, looking at the book, the comic, or the magazine on the newsstand. You want that piece of artwork to jump out at them and say, "Pick me up and look at me!" And that's what an advertisement does, it attracts your attention. So for me, the approach towards a cover is very much a "grab your eye" type of thing. It's much different from doing an illustration for inside a magazine or a book, where you don't have to rely on certain elements to grab a reader's attention. If you're inside a book already, you don't need to grab the reader's attention; they're already there. But a cover's different. A cover needs to have certain elements that will catch the eye of the viewer. Once they're in, you can be a little bit more subtle within that illustration, but there needs to be some something to grab the viewer almost immediately. Unfortunately, a lot of cover artists don't realize this—even some editors and art directors don't realize it. They think that making a nice painting is everything. Making a nice painting isn't necessarily going to sell a book. It'll be a nice painting, but it's not something that's going to jump off the stands and grab that reader just curiously looking over the stands looking for something interesting.

I always have to look at the bigger picture first, because that's where you get a better grasp of what you're trying to do. If you look at the detail of a piece first when a client hires you to do something, you tend to get lost in the minutia and you lose the bigger picture. And the bigger picture, for most of what I do, is that the client is hiring me to sell a product—whether it's a paperback book, comic book, a magazine, a movie production illustration that a producer needs to sell to a movie company, or box art for packaging for a PlayStation 2 game—they're hiring me to sell their product. That's the big picture. If I am looking at the smaller picture: "Wow, I could do this cool little texture and I could do it in this certain style and make it much more interesting," then I'm losing the big picture. I'm losing the reason for the illustration.

The reason for the illustration will dictate how the illustration is done. You have to set up your dominos in a row. You've got your big dominos first and your little ones last, and everything else will fall into place once the understanding is made between the client who is hiring you to do the cover and your understanding of what they want. And then you can go into what style would best suit the product, what medium will best emphasize what you want to say, what composition will emphasize the drama or the dynamics of what the illustration will be, how much physical texture to put within the piece to accentuate any detail that's going to be put down on the board in the illustration, what color scheme to go with, all those choices are made in the decision to make the project and where it's going to be sold and what it's going to be used for. There's a lot that needs to go on in an artist's head before they take a project, because you don't necessarily just jump and say, "Okay, I'll do it," and then find out two or three weeks down the road that it's not a job you're interested in and it's totally different than what you might be interested in pursuing, either subject-matter-wise, stylistically or compositionally. It just might not even be a product that you would be interested in attaching your name to. So the big picture, the first thing is what is it going to be used for? What is the client hiring me to do? Everything else will fall into place after that.

FULL CIRCLE

As many successes as Dorman has experienced in the field of illustration, comic books were his first love. In 2002, Dorman came home to comics. Rail is a graphic novel that allowed Dorman to develop an efficient storytelling style by using ink and watercolors.

DAVE DORMAN: It was just one of those things where, having been a professional illustrator almost twenty years now, I felt confident enough that I could sort of jump in the water and either sink or swim and do a full comic book story. In the past I've done various smaller stories, eight or ten pages here, five pages there. Nothing extensive. But I've been working on this Wasted Lands project for about six or seven years now, and I don't mean the *Rail* graphic novel I've been working on, I mean just developing Wasted Lands concepts and characters and stories. There are a lot of stories that I want to tell within the world of Wasted Lands. But one of the things that I wanted to do was to do a graphic novel in an European style of storytelling.

I've learned how to draw, how to paint and have worked on my craft, but I have to say that I probably jumped in a little too soon. I should have practiced my storytelling a little bit more. But I felt that I was comfortable artistically to go ahead and do this full-length graphic novel. I felt that now was a good time. I'm getting older, I wanted to pursue some other things. All the pieces of the puzzle fell into place and I just thought it was the right time to do this graphic novel and throw it out to the public and see what they think. I knew that I was going to have problems with it, I knew that I was not the best storyteller in the world. Having grown up reading comics all my life doesn't make me a good storyteller. Being a good artist doesn't make me a good storyteller. But having done it a little bit, and knowing what goes into telling a story visually in comic format, I do know the concepts behind it. And having very good friends within the comics industry being able to help me when I encountered problems within the storytelling was very beneficial for me as well. So it was one of those grit your teeth and jump in with both feet types of things. And I think I pulled it off, for the most part. There are still some weaknesses in it. I still have a long way to go to become a really good continuous-panel storyteller. But I'm going to keep doing it. I've got more stories that I want to tell, and I've broken ground with *Rail*, and I'm going to keep constructing the Wasted Lands universe, both in continuous storytelling and outside continuous storytelling. There are some text novels that will be published with illustrations, some that I will be doing, some that I won't be doing. But the continuous panel stuff I enjoyed doing. It was a lot more work than I thought it was going to be, but I did enjoy it. It's not something that left a bad taste in my mouth.

My generation and generations previous to mine grew up on comics. That was a big part of our childhoods. And for us to retain that enjoyment as we grew older and incorporate that enjoyment of the medium into our adult life means that [sequential art] carries in itself more meaning than if we just discarded it when we were younger and moved on. It's not a fond memory that we have looking back on our youth, it's something that we've carried through on to adulthood. And you hear this with a lot of artists in varied fields. Filmmaking and actors and musicians…people in the entertainment field, they'll talk about how fascinated they were with comics when they were younger. There's something gratifying knowing that something you as an artist were influenced by at the beginning of your life is now something that you're contributing to–adding to so that future generations will be able to see and be influenced by that artwork. It's an amazing thing to think about.

Pages from the *Rail*, showcasing Dorman's European storytelling sensibility as well as his skill wielding the pencil. ©2004 Dave Dorman

Dave Dorman explains his thought process and painting technique for an unpublished *Rail* cover concept:

"The idea for the cover for the *Rail* graphic novel was to introduce the two main characters from the series, Edge and Iguana. I wanted to have an action scene with the emphasis on the figures yet still show a bit of a feel for the texture of the story, what I call a 'motorcycle western'.

"The beginnings of the ideas start with thumbnail sketches of the ideas. No real detail, just blocking out the composition and design. (1) After I decide which thumbnail is the best to represent what I want to show then I do a larger thumbnail (2). This lets me block in more of the figures and compositional elements and I can start working in smaller details as well.

"At this point I know all the elements that will be in the piece and I can arrange for shooting my photo reference. I have friends come over and model for me. In this particular case it was Del Stone, my scripter for the *Rail* book, who posed for both of the characters. I also collected photos of the type of locomotive I wanted for the background and I had a model of a 1938 Harley that I used for the foreground motorcycles.

"After the reference photos are shot, I begin the drawing. From this point on the drawings I do will be the actual size of the painting. I do all my drawing on vellum tracing paper, which allows me to work over previous drawings and make easy changes to make the art more dynamic. The first full pencil is very rough blocking in all the elements to make things work visually within the frame (3).

"Once I am happy with the placement of the elements and look of the final composition, then I lay another piece of tracing paper over the rough and refine the drawing, filling in all the fine details (4). This gives me a finished pencil piece that will be the basis/reference of the final painting." ©2004 Dave Dorman

KNOW YOUR CRAFT

To be a successful artist, Dorman suggests learning the basics of art. The "starving artist" lifestyle of art is easy to fall into. But the craft of art includes the discipline to continually improve your skills, learn new techniques, be a good business person, and to live a responsible life.

DAVE DORMAN: I think that one of the things artists need to understand is that the art field is not limited to any one specific subject matter. You don't need to be a superhero artist to draw comics, and you don't need to be an illustrator to do book covers. One of the things that I try to tell budding artists is the best thing you can do for yourself is to learn to draw and learn to paint anything and everything, if you want to pursue color work. The world is a very big place, and if you know your craft, if you know how to draw something out of your head or even if you use reference, and if you can draw well and if you can paint well, then you can do anything that you want. Though comic book art is a very specific type of work, anybody who knows how to draw can produce a comic. You need to learn the structure of how to tell a story and some of the concepts behind what makes good comic book work. If you're a bad artist, you're not going to succeed in the comics field; if you're a good artist, you will. But if you're a good artist, you'll also succeed in the illustration field and you'll succeed in any field that you want to pursue. And to do that, you need to work hard at it. It's not something you're going to stumble upon and wake up this morning and say, "Oh! I'm a good artist today, I think I'll go out and make a million dollars." You need to have patience; you need to have the guts to go out and show your work; you need to have the ability and the discipline to sit down and draw and paint whenever you have free time and make yourself better. I've been in the industry for twenty years, and I don't think I'm anywhere near the potential artist that I

can be. I am constantly learning from every piece that I do. I do sketches, I do little paintings, I do things to make myself a better artist than I am right now. I don't just sit back and work on commissions. There are some artists in the field who create art only if they're getting paid for it. That is not the way to become a better artist. You have to have the desire and the will and the discipline to work hard to become a better artist.

Becoming a good artist means you have to open the doors to a whole world of work that's out there. But the art is just part of what you need to be to be a successful artist or illustrator. You need to know how to run a business: that is, the business of *you* as the artist. You're running a small business. And as a business person, you need to know some basic things about how to run a business. You need to know how to have more money coming in than is going out; how to make a profit; how to sell yourself; how to go out and present your portfolio to generate work; how to file taxes; how to

put a portfolio together, how to do business cards, and how to present yourself.

The people that think that all you do as an artist is sit at the easel and paint a pretty picture, or sit at the drawing table and draw a page of comic book art, are delusional. That's the fun part of art, but you can't ignore the business part. If you're going to pursue art as a business, you have to look at it as a business. Some artists cannot do that and cannot separate the business side from the enjoyment of the art side, and that's where they're going to constantly fail at being a successful artist. And by successful, I mean earning a consistent living so that you can afford to buy a house and a car and get married and raise a family and continue to do the work that will generate the income to sustain a realistic lifestyle through your career. You could be the greatest artist in the world, but if you don't know the business, and you don't know how to conduct yourself as a business, you will fail. It's as simple as that.

"When I finished the pencil drawing, I looked at it and something just didn't seem quite right. I decided to scan it into the computer and mock-up a cover to see if that might help me figure out what was wrong. Well in looking at it then, it was obvious to me what the problem was: the figures were facing the spine of the book rather than the opening. This may not be a big deal if the painting was a stand-alone piece not intended for publication, but as a cover it needed to draw the reader into the book. So I decided to flip the whole piece and have the action facing right. After making another mock-up of the cover (5) I felt this was a much better composition.

"So I flipped the drawing, and proceed to start the painting. I paint on #100 Crescent illustration board that has a coat of gesso on it. I use the gesso in certain areas on the board to create textures, so that when the paint is applied to the board the texture will show thru and add an extra dimension to the work. After the gesso dries, I make a photocopy of the final pencil drawing and transfer the image, using graphite paper, to my gessoed board. I then sprayfix the pencil and I am ready to paint.

"I first lay down some general tones to get a feel of where I'm going visually, which also helps develop contrasts for the elements in the piece. I let that dry and then come back and work the background a bit more by adding some more details (6).

"When a lot of the background is in, I start working on the main images in the piece, which are the figures. As with the background, I block in the color and contrast and work them into the background. I let this dry and I come back and begin working on the details (7). This is really where the fun starts for me because the painting starts to come alive with the addition of the figures in action.

"As I continue to paint, it becomes a process of just refining the details and playing with the paint and textures to tie everything together visually (8). And as I get closer to finishing, I have to keep myself from putting too much detail in. I want the viewer's eye to travel a certain way within the painting, and if I put too much detail here or there, then I will make the viewer stop in areas that weren't intended."
©2004 Dave Dorman

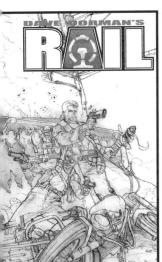
7.

8.
6.

"So here we have, after about 6-7 days of work, a finished painting. I'm very happy with the piece and I feel it captures what I had intended: the action and drama of the story. I decide as an afterthought to do a quick mock-up of the art as the proposed cover. Once again this works very well for me.

"However…after talking with the publisher and finding that they wanted a slightly different look for their marketing of the book, we decided not to use this art as the cover. The final art used was more indicative of a hardback novel style piece, which is what they felt worked better for their marketing (Chapter Introduction, page 38). Now even though this is my creator-owned project and I could put whatever I wanted on the cover, I am still a professional and I know the business that I'm in. I could have insisted on using this art for the cover, but they had very persuasive arguments that I did not disagree with. That other piece, while not as action-oriented, still has a great flavor of what I am trying to put across in the story."
©2004 Dave Dorman

A starving artist is a failed artist. A starving artist means that your artwork is not getting out, people are not paying for it. And that's where we get into semantics of "artist" and "commercial illustrator." I don't consider myself an artist, I consider myself an illustrator, because I don't pursue this craft of art strictly for personal reasons. I don't sit around all day and create totally personal work and just paint canvases and work out my angst and my depression and my joy and sorrow on canvas. That's one definition of artist in my book. There are a number of other definitions. But in contrast, what I consider a commercial illustrator is someone who is being hired to produce artwork for a client and get paid for it, whereas an "artist"—and this is just my opinion—will pursue the artwork first and then try to sell it secondarily. And that's a whole crapshoot there. When you do something like that, your market is one, basically: you're painting for yourself. And when you go to try to sell that artwork, you do not know if there's a market out there for that work or not. And if you do not know the business end, you're going to fail if you don't know where to sell that artwork. As a commercial illustrator, you're being hired to do a specific type of piece, and the craft that a person learns as an artist will enable them to produce that piece of work and get paid for it. So, for me, I would much rather be in the seat of a commercial illustrator, because I know where I'll be making my living. And after I've made my living, then I can pursue the paintings that I want to pursue, my personal piece, and I can be an "artist" on the side and not have to worry that my audience is just one: myself. That's after I've made the rent and paid the bills and I put food on the table, and I support my family. So to me there are two very distinct categories in the art world.

Arguably, Dorman's Rail *project took a lot of planning; he created the graphic novel without putting his professional life on hold.*

Rail *is a personal piece. However, I worked towards making* Rail *happen. I saved up money. I knew that I was going to have to take some time off from my commercial work to pursue it, but I did not give up my commercial work exclusively to pursue* Rail. *Once I got into* Rail, *I worked on it; I finished it; I sent it off to the publisher, and I immediately went back to doing commercial art. I knew that I could not rely on* Rail *to be self-sustaining. There are very few projects for a comic book artist that do that. It's rare that you get a Todd McFarlane* Spawn *to happen, or a Jim Lee Wildstorm thing, or something that will immediately become the sparkle in the eye of the fans who will sustain it with their commercial money and make the creator a millionaire. That doesn't happen every day. That doesn't happen every week, every month, every year, or every ten years. So realistically, as a creator, as an illustrator, as an artist, you can't do your own thing all the* time, because more often than not, you're going to have an audience of one. And that audience of one is not going to sustain a lifestyle.

It was good that I did *Rail*. Right now I'm looking forward to starting the next story, and I'm sure halfway through it I'm going to be pulling my hair out saying, "Why did I do this again?" But when it's done, I'll probably have the same satisfaction I did when I finished *Rail*; a job well done, the best that I could do at the time. And to throw it out into the readers' hands and see what they think about it. I mean,

part of being a commercial artist is knowing that what you're doing is not necessarily for yourself; it's for other people to look at and digest and experience. And this is one of the few fields that a person can work in where you can go to a convention and experience direct feedback from the fans, the people who are putting their money down and buying the material. And they'll tell you what they think of it. That's one of the benefits of working in this field: you can see what the fans want and what they don't like, and either make adjustments or just move on.

The Wasted Lands contains many storylines and characters created by Dorman. He mixes his interest in painting with science fiction, adventure, westerns, and other legendary tales. Anna Lee as a Commander of the Light Angel Brigade (below left) and Anna Lee, a veteran of the war (below right). ©2004 Dave Dorman

GROWING UP AND STAYING YOUNG

Dorman moved around quite a bit growing up. Even as a child, the one constant in his life was the painter's easel in his bedroom. Art dominated his life so he sought education to be the best artist he could be. Very few things have changed in Dorman's life as he still seeks to refine his craft, even if his easel is now housed in a studio.

DAVE DORMAN: I was born in Bay City, Michigan, in 1958. My dad was in the military, the air force, so we moved around a lot when I was younger. Dad got transferred around a couple of bases in the Washington, DC area, so we stayed there for ten years, from 1970 to 1980, which is where I went to junior high and high school. In high school I decided to pursue art as a living, and comics, specifically. And I went to one year of college at St. Mary's of Maryland in southern Maryland with an art major and I learned some stuff there, but I really had my mind set on pursuing comics. And at that time, this would have been 1978, the Joe Kubert school had just opened in New Jersey. I heard about it and I talked to my parents about it. I went up for an interview and they accepted me, so I decided to go to the school. And it was there that I found I was more comfortable doing single illustration as opposed to continuous panel work. I found that as I was getting my assignments to do comic book pages, I'd spend more time on any single panel than I would looking at the whole page. And also during that time period I was pursuing painting a little bit more vigorously; the Kubert school did not have a color curriculum at all, at the time.

So after spending a year at the school and talking with Joe Kubert and some of my teachers, we all decided that the school had basically given me all that it had to offer me in the direction that I had decided to go, which was single illustration. And they weren't teaching any of that. I must say, though, that I learned a lot at the school, and it certainly has helped me when I've pursued continuous panel work. But at the time I was more comfortable doing single illustrations, so I left the Kubert school.

My father got transferred to Florida and retired here. And at the time he came home and said, "Well, we're moving to Florida. You can either stay here in DC or you can come down to Florida with us." And I was still working on my craft at the time, and my folks were very generous in that they were letting me stay at home and work on my artwork. And I was working part-time, generating some income that way. So I decided that I really wanted to continue to develop my craft. And I felt that I was going along a very good path, and my folks had enough confidence in me to let me pursue that. So I came down to Florida. That was 1980. I got some part-time jobs and continued to work on my craft at home. I had a little easel set up in my bedroom, and I'd come home from work and I'd sit down and I'd just draw and paint for as much time as I could during the waking hours, and I developed my craft.

During the next couple of years, I would go to conventions in Atlanta and Chicago and New York, and I'd show my work, get feedback, and then come back home and work on it. Eventually, in late 1982, I made another trip to New York, went to the offices of *Heavy Metal*, got in, and talked to John Workman, who at the time was art director at *Heavy Metal*. He liked one of the paintings that I had and bought it for the cover of *Heavy Metal* magazine. That same trip I went to Marvel Comics and talked to Archie Goodwin, who hired me to do an eight-page text-and-illustration story for *Epic Magazine*. That particular trip turned out to be very bountiful, as far as work goes, and where my first published work came from. And from there, I basically continued to work on my craft, send out samples, and get a little work here, a little work there. Eventually I got more work and got better at what I did and continued the cycle until I was making a living out of it.

So that's where I am now, still living in Florida, still making a living at what I do. I feel like I'm the luckiest guy in the world to be able to paint and to draw and do something I love and have people pay me for it. I get up every day and look forward to coming into the studio and working. Well, sometimes I don't. It's still looked at as an unusual job. People are just amazed. I think there's a little bit of envy, as well, in that being an artist in the comics field in particular, you continue to carry a bit of the child in you into your adulthood. I think that a lot of people who come over to my studio and look at it and see all the toys and all the fun stuff that I have and see that child still in me, I think that there's a little bit of jealousy going because they don't have the opportunity to let that child come out in their lives. I think that more people need to do that. I don't believe—I don't know if this is an exact quote from the *Bible* or if it was just a saying or something, but where it says, "When I was a child, I played with childish things, and as I became an adult, I put away those things from my childhood." I don't believe that. I think that you need to keep something of your childhood with you all the time. And this particular field pretty much guarantees that you'll have some of your childhood all the time. And it makes you feel young. I look at myself in the mirror and I say, "Boy, who's this old fart staring back at you?" But in my heart, I feel very young. And I think that it has to do with my choice of my path in life and continuing to keep these childhood memories and experiences very much in the forefront of what I do every day.

As a commercial illustrator, Dorman has been assigned to produce many kinds of illustrations like calendars, fine-art prints, book jackets, toy designs and role-playing games. Cover for a role-playing game module for Palladium Games (left), and an interior illustration for a role-playing guide published by Wiz Kids (below).

Louise Simonson
on Comics & Children's Books

Though there are differences between children's books and comic books, there are also a surprising number of similarities. In a perfect world, both are mediums for children—old and young. Children's picture books rely on art for visualization and words to tell the story much like comic books. With juvenile books, the narrative still must unfold and excite the reader—it just does so page to page instead of panel to panel.

Louise Simonson understands stories and storytelling. She understands that a good yarn will be a good yarn no matter who reads it or at what age. For Simonson, telling a good story started with reading many good stories.

LOUISE SIMONSON: I read comics in the usual way kids read comics. I wasn't a collector; I wasn't a fanatic reader of comics. I read the usual things kids read back in the Fifties: cowboy comics, *Little Lulu*, Archie comics, *Superman*, all that stuff. But I read many, many more books than I ever read comics. I probably read three hundred books to every comic, partly because I got a small allowance and I could either buy an ice cream cone or a comic book. And every week my mother took us to the library, where my sisters and I could get hundreds of books for free.

Books definitely influenced me more than comics did. That may make my approach and the kind of comics stories I tell a little different from the work of some of the other writers, just because I come at it from a different area of influence. When I was a kid I loved the Louisa May Alcott books. I liked the Jim Kjelgaard Irish Setter books. I loved anything Robert Heinlein wrote. I liked the magic books by Edward Eager. I think those were my favorites. Oh, and Marguerite Henry horse books. I read a huge

gamut, a large spectrum of types of books, of genres of books—historical fiction, science fiction, adventure books, plays, biographies. And anything with a horse in it.

Robert Heinlein and Edward Eager were my two major influences. But in comics, I would say mainly Heinlein…just because his stories were adventure-oriented, with heroes and heroines who were intelligent and extremely resourceful with a strong moral code. Those character traits defined Heinlein's juvenile novel protagonists and influenced the kind of characters that I myself find heroic. Later, Heinlein moved into other kinds of science fiction with less clear-cut characters who exhibited different types of heroism. But smart, resourceful, moral heroes were what I really liked when I was a kid.

I think quite often what children's book authors enjoyed reading when they were kids influences what they end up writing as adults because a lot of writers try to create for other people the kind of wonderful experiences they had as readers. And when I was a kid, I just loved, loved, loved reading. It was—and remains—one of my two or three favorite things to do.

"Of all the comics I've written, I probably had the most fun with *Power Pack*, partly because it was the first comic I wrote. The first thing you do is often the most fun because it's different and it's new and it's kind of scary. Also, probably because I created it. It was a vision that was close to my heart and… was almost a homage to the stuff that I had loved when I was a kid, only done in a comic book hero context." In the following pages, the Pack attempt to thwart their parents' alien kidnappers.
Power Pack TM & ©2004 Marvel Character, Inc.

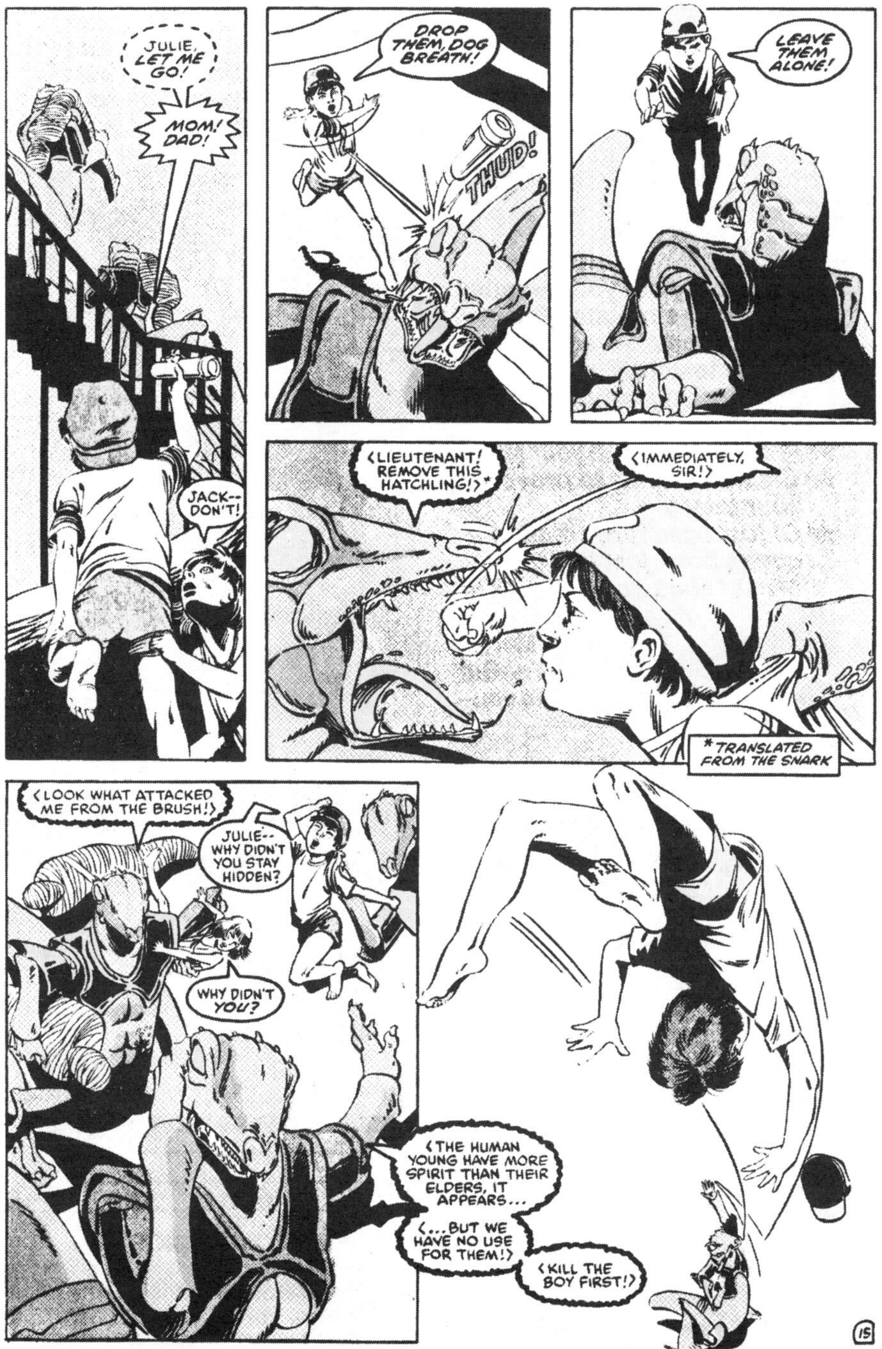
JULIE, LET ME GO!
MOM! DAD!
JACK-- DON'T!
DROP THEM, DOG BREATH!
THUD!
LEAVE THEM ALONE!
<LIEUTENANT! REMOVE THIS HATCHLING!>*
<IMMEDIATELY, SIR!>
*TRANSLATED FROM THE SNARK
<LOOK WHAT ATTACKED ME FROM THE BRUSH!>
JULIE-- WHY DIDN'T YOU STAY HIDDEN?
WHY DIDN'T YOU?
<THE HUMAN YOUNG HAVE MORE SPIRIT THAN THEIR ELDERS, IT APPEARS...
<...BUT WE HAVE NO USE FOR THEM!>
<KILL THE BOY FIRST!>
15

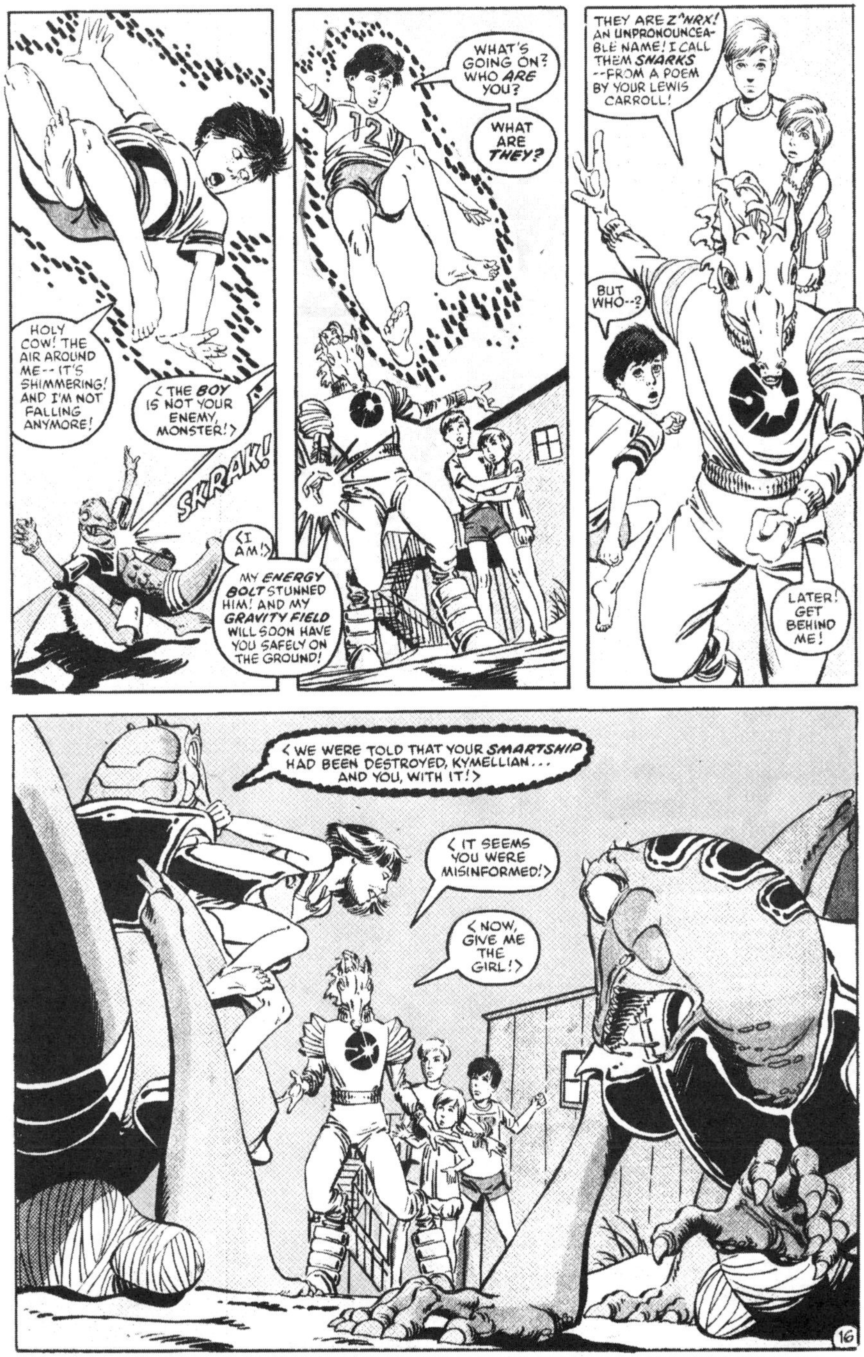
HOLY COW! THE AIR AROUND ME-- IT'S SHIMMERING! AND I'M NOT FALLING ANYMORE!
<THE BOY IS NOT YOUR ENEMY, MONSTER!>
SKRAK!
<I AM!>
MY ENERGY BOLT STUNNED HIM! AND MY GRAVITY FIELD WILL SOON HAVE YOU SAFELY ON THE GROUND!
WHAT'S GOING ON? WHO ARE YOU?
WHAT ARE THEY?
THEY ARE Z^NRX! AN UNPRONOUNCEABLE NAME! I CALL THEM SNARKS --FROM A POEM BY YOUR LEWIS CARROLL!
BUT WHO--?
LATER! GET BEHIND ME!
<WE WERE TOLD THAT YOUR SMARTSHIP HAD BEEN DESTROYED, KYMELLIAN... AND YOU, WITH IT!>
<IT SEEMS YOU WERE MISINFORMED!>
<NOW, GIVE ME THE GIRL!>
16

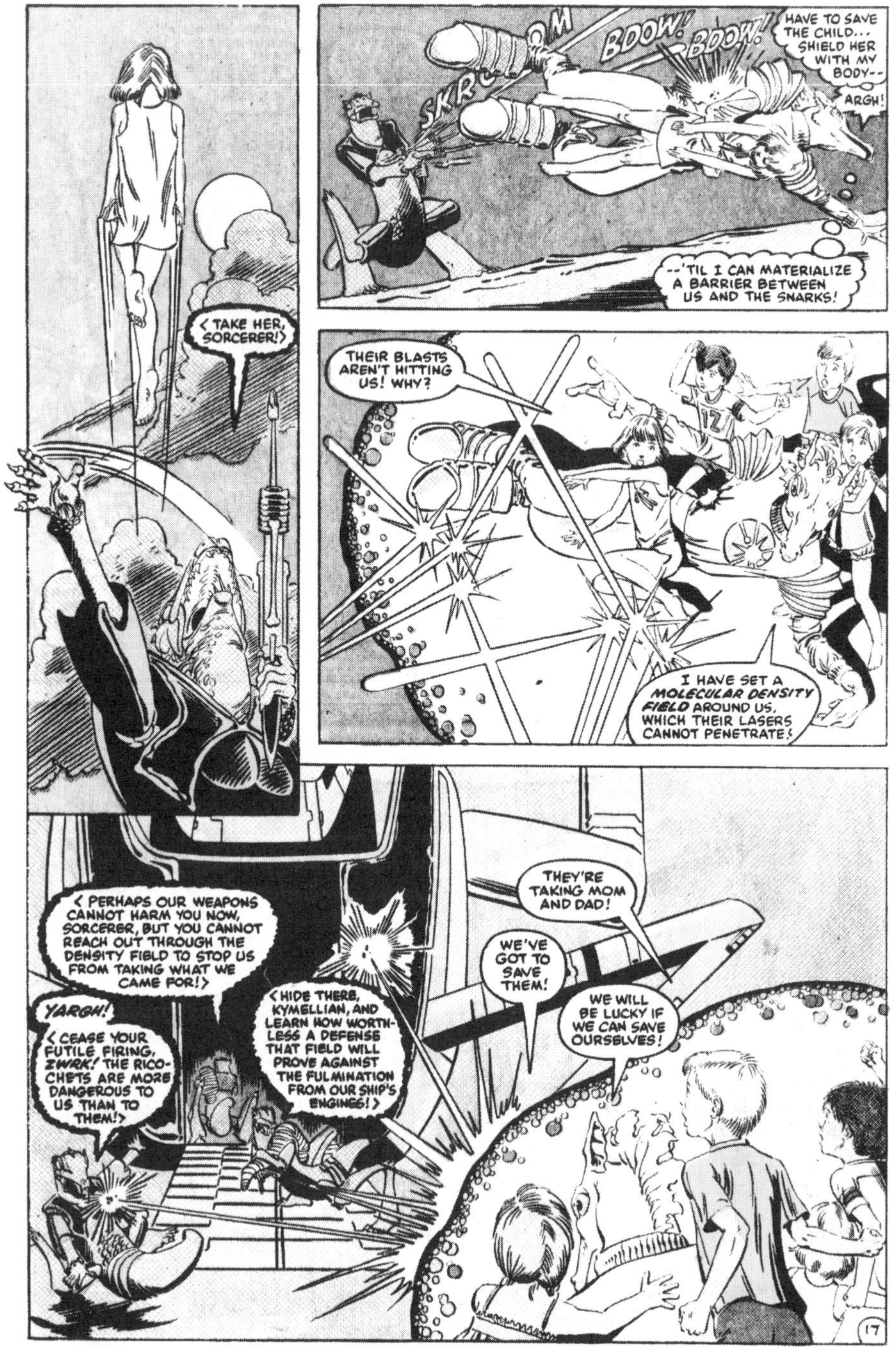
< TAKE HER, SORCERER! >
BDOW! BDOW!
HAVE TO SAVE THE CHILD... SHIELD HER WITH MY BODY--
ARGH!
--'TIL I CAN MATERIALIZE A BARRIER BETWEEN US AND THE SNARKS!
THEIR BLASTS AREN'T HITTING US! WHY?
I HAVE SET A MOLECULAR DENSITY FIELD AROUND US, WHICH THEIR LASERS CANNOT PENETRATE!
< PERHAPS OUR WEAPONS CANNOT HARM YOU NOW, SORCERER, BUT YOU CANNOT REACH OUT THROUGH THE DENSITY FIELD TO STOP US FROM TAKING WHAT WE CAME FOR! >
YARGH!
< CEASE YOUR FUTILE FIRING, ZWIRK! THE RICOCHETS ARE MORE DANGEROUS TO US THAN TO THEM! >
< HIDE THERE, KYMELLIAN, AND LEARN HOW WORTHLESS A DEFENSE THAT FIELD WILL PROVE AGAINST THE FULMINATION FROM OUR SHIP'S ENGINES! >
THEY'RE TAKING MOM AND DAD!
WE'VE GOT TO SAVE THEM!
WE WILL BE LUCKY IF WE CAN SAVE OURSELVES!
17

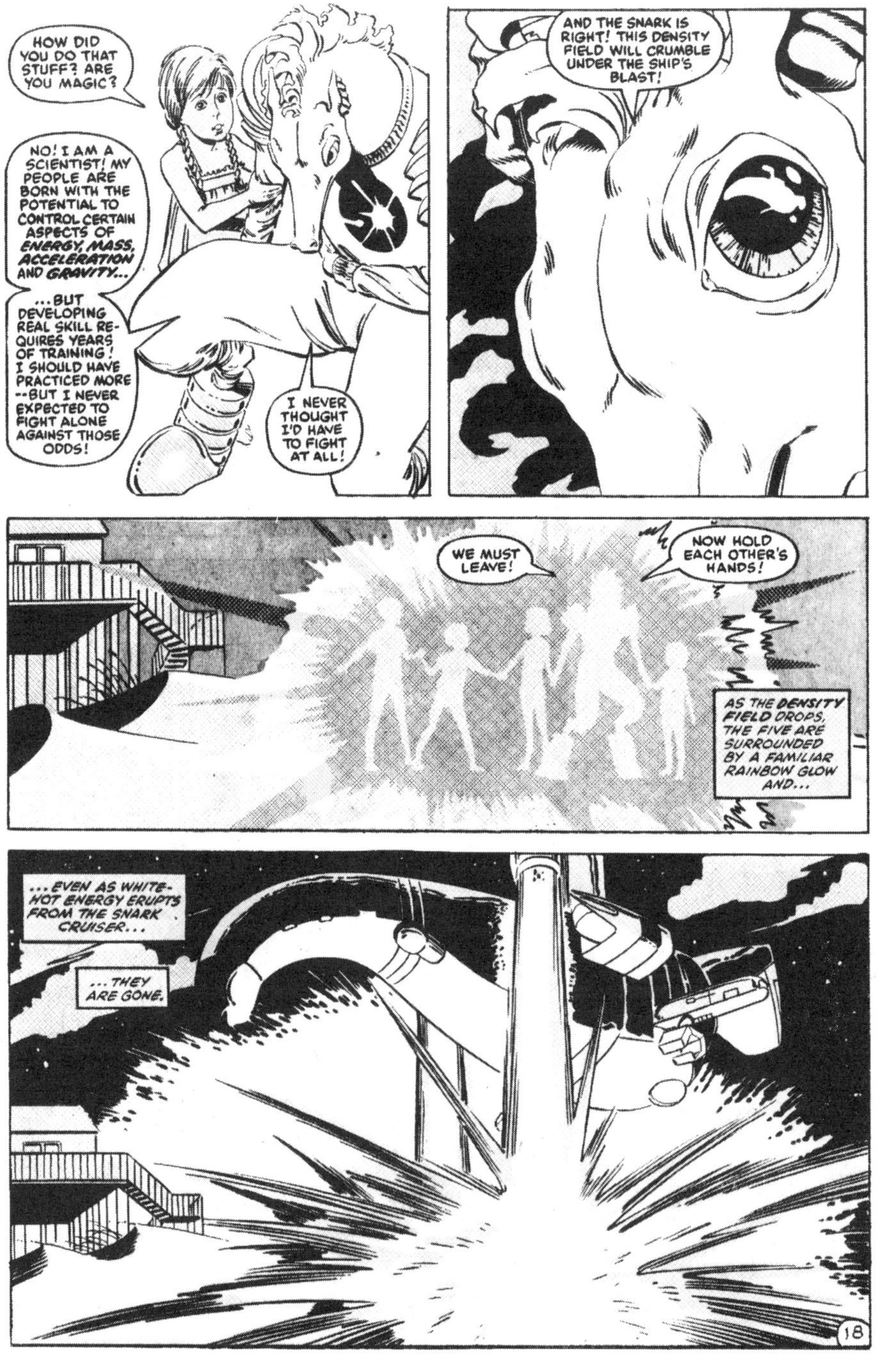
HOW DID YOU DO THAT STUFF? ARE YOU MAGIC?
NO! I AM A SCIENTIST! MY PEOPLE ARE BORN WITH THE POTENTIAL TO CONTROL CERTAIN ASPECTS OF ENERGY, MASS, ACCELERATION AND GRAVITY...
...BUT DEVELOPING REAL SKILL REQUIRES YEARS OF TRAINING! I SHOULD HAVE PRACTICED MORE --BUT I NEVER EXPECTED TO FIGHT ALONE AGAINST THOSE ODDS!
I NEVER THOUGHT I'D HAVE TO FIGHT AT ALL!
AND THE SNARK IS RIGHT! THIS DENSITY FIELD WILL CRUMBLE UNDER THE SHIP'S BLAST!
WE MUST LEAVE!
NOW HOLD EACH OTHER'S HANDS!
AS THE DENSITY FIELD DROPS, THE FIVE ARE SURROUNDED BY A FAMILIAR RAINBOW GLOW AND...
...EVEN AS WHITE-HOT ENERGY ERUPTS FROM THE SNARK CRUISER...
...THEY ARE GONE.
18

POWER PACK AND MARVEL

Louise Simonson has worked in the comic industry for over 30 years. She has worked with popular titles and also created mainstays in comics, including Steel, X-Factor, *and her first favorite children,* Power Pack.

LOUISE SIMONSON: I got into comics through a recommendation by a friend. I had been working in New York publishing in the advertising and promotion department of MacFadden-Bartell, a magazine company. One of my friends who worked at Warren Publishing told me, "There's an opening at Warren and they pay better than your job. Why don't you apply?" I had read the Warren black-and-white horror titles—especially back when Archie Goodwin was the editor and main writer—and had really liked them. So I applied for the job and got it.

I started off in Warren's production department doing art corrections and that kind of stuff, moved into editorial as an assistant editor, where I wrote advertising copy and letters pages and did the usual assistant editor-type stuff. And I eventually became the editor of the Warren line.

Several years later, I went over to Marvel, first as an editor, then as a writer.

Of all the comics I've written, I probably had the most fun with *Power Pack*, partly because it was the first comic I wrote. The first thing you do is often the most fun because it's different and it's new and it's kind of scary. Also, probably because I created it. It was a vision that was close to my heart and was almost a homage to the stuff that I had loved when I was a kid, only done in a comic book hero context. It was science fiction—though the science was actually kind of magical—and it involved kids who were smart and resourceful with, I think, strong moral underpinnings. So in that way, with *Power Pack*, I was able to recreate for the twelve-year-old within the kind of stories I enjoyed reading the most. So probably it really defines me as a writer.

But, y'know, if you had asked me which project was the most fun at any given time [in my career], I would have told you it was the one I was currently working on. I think that's because when you're writing a story or series, you're involved in the problems of your characters and of the stories themselves. And [at the time] that world is fascinating and the most interesting world you could inhabit.

I've never been someone who was working on a series and thought, "Oh, gee, I don't want to be doing this. I wish I was doing that one over there." Usually I can find something in the series I'm working on that I really love and enjoy. And if it didn't start out that way, by the time I'd finished with it, I'd have turned it into something that was really what I loved.

In comics, one of the things that's different than writing novels is that you're working with other creators. You're writing the story, but you have other people who are working on the artwork. And sometimes your enjoyment of a project is mitigated, or enhanced, by the people you're partnered with. I've been very lucky with most of the artists I've worked with.

With *Power Pack*, I initially worked with June Brigman—my own choice. I could not have had a better co-creator for that particular book. Drawing kids is hard if you're used to drawing adult superheroes. For one thing, their proportions are very different. But June had honed her craft doing portraits of kids at a Six Flags amusement park and she brought a realism of proportion and gesture that no one else matched. She made you feel what the Pack—and even the visiting aliens—were feeling. She made you believe kids could fly.

The Pack operated in the very real environment of New York's Upper West Side which June and I carefully photographed, including the schools—PS 87 and IS 44—the same ones my daughter, Juliana, attended. Power Pack even lived in my old apartment—I think that was June's idea—though my office had to be enlarged to become a bedroom for the two boys.

When June left the book, Jon Bogdanove took over, and his work was wonderful, too. He lived in New York's Upper West Side and he knew the area. Jon has an amazing visual memory and his art had warmth, humor and great storytelling. He drew emotion. It made you love those kids and their parents. It made you want to be part of the Power family. I have worked on projects with Jon, off and on, for fifteen years—*Superman: Man of Steel* comes to mind—so obviously I've really enjoyed it.

It was wonderful working with Bret Blevins on the *New Mutants*, a group book featuring teenage heroes. Each of Bret's protagonists was a real being, with his or her own separate thoughts, feelings, and agendas visually defined in every panel by subtleties of expression and gesture. His environments were real three-dimensional places. Move the camera and the characters remained in place in relation to everything else. Not easy, as you may well imagine. And he, too, was really good at action and a great storyteller. (No wonder he's considered a top storyboard artist now for TV animation.)

I loved working with Walter [Simonson] on *X-Factor*—not just because he's my husband. Walter draws beautifully, of course. *X-Factor's* heroes were strong adults and his characters are never wimpy. He is a master of design. He can made even a "talking heads" page seem interesting. He has all the skills. But what he's best at is drawing *power!* He draws *excitement!* His art made *X-Factor* memorable.

Like I said—when I comes to artists, I've been unusually blessed.

Louise Simonson teamed up with some of the best artists in comics. (Above) X-Factor and Wolverine guest-star in *Power Pack #27*, drawn by Jon Bogdanove. (Below) Louise and Walter Simonson collaborate on *X-Factor*. Power Pack, X-Factor, X-Men TM & ©2004 Marvel Characters, Inc.

SKILLS

The art of writing is essential to storytelling. For Simonson, the act of writing still remains instinctual, even though there are many formal processes she employs to solve storytelling problems. She relies on experience and understands how to keep things natural. For Simonson, success is measured in the enjoyment she receives from conceiving and executing a job well done.

LOUISE SIMONSON: Because comics is a very short form–I mean, they are like 22 pages–you've got to understand how to create conflict and resolve it quickly if you want to make each comic a more-or-less complete unit.

The art has to follow not only the action of the conflict and resolution, but also the interior movement of a character from one state to another. And then the story, of course, has to tie those events together and come up with a satisfying conclusion. And you kind of shuffle these events in your mind until you see the pattern sort of leap out. The pattern, the story, must make a pleasing and satisfying whole.

It's like juggling where you've got a number of balls that you know you have to keep in the air, and when you're first starting to do it, you need to think "I move my hand this way, and I move it that way." But after you've done it for a while, it kind of comes naturally. It's a natural movement like dancing. You have to be aware what you're doing on some level so you don't trip over your own feet, but at the same time you don't need to think about it over much. It's planning, but since I've been doing it for so long now, it no longer actually feels like planning.

I know when I first started writing, I was much more aware of different rules and patterns and arcs; I thought things through in a much more formal fashion. And now, in a lot of cases, I just write them and I don't think about what I've done until something goes wrong. And then I'm able to use those particular skills to go back and analyze what I did and straighten out any problem areas. But mostly, the process of writing has become instinctual.

I spent virtually my entire childhood with my nose in a book. And my adulthood, too, now that I think about it. I think you internalize other authors' structures and methods. You sort of learn the way things are done on a subconscious level in the same way that, as an infant, you learn to talk so that it becomes second nature. One of the things that may make my comic book writing different from others is that a number of comics writers have read a lot more comics than I did, and probably the structures they internalized were comic book structures. The structures I internalized were more book structures. I've been told that my comics seemed, at the time at least, a lot more character-driven than usual. I think that character-driven aspect comes from having read so many character-driven books.

And I listen to the way people talk. That's kind of important in storytelling–trying to create natural sounding dialogue. Make the way people say things inherent to the characters they are, so that everybody isn't talking the same way. Superman doesn't talk like Batman, like Lois Lane. To a certain extent, people say the same things in the same way, but in important ways they say things differently; the different ways they say things often says a lot about who they are. And that's something that you want to try to capture.

There is one thing that I found different in children's book writing, particularly in the juvenile novel. In a comic book, you create descriptions so your artist can draw pictures that will help forward the story for your reader. Your reader reads both words and pictures. In a novel, you're putting descriptions onto paper that your readers have to transform into images within their own minds. So your depiction of an environment or an event has to be clear and vivid and atmospheric in a way that it doesn't if you're writing a comic.

In a comic plot, you can write "scary old house" and trust your brilliant artist to give you the ultimate scary house. But a novelist has to bring the scene to life for the audience–involve all their senses–instead of having them receive the pictures fully realized.

But the rest of it isn't that different. In both mediums, the mechanics of plot and the character arcs are very much the same. Now in a comic book, I generally worked in a 22-page format, so each chapter would be 22 comic book pages long. Several comics would form a story arc and several arcs could be compiled to form a larger story–perhaps, if I got lucky, even be compiled in a graphic novel. In juvenile novels, I work in a much longer context, so all the chapters are written before the book is published instead of serially, one chapter a month until the whole, longer story is told.

Point of view is more apparent in novels and more important. So is the need to conjure images by involving all the senses. But, overall, writing comics and books isn't that different. I think it's an easy transition to make, from comics to books.

I really like writing for kids. Most of the time, kids aren't intellectually analytical but they can definitely follow story and character logic. They're honest. They know what they like. And they're smart and not shy about telling you where you went wrong.

As an example, one of my favorite letters ever came from a young *Power Pack* reader. The subject was an introductory sequence where Jack Power–naked except for his underwear–threw his school clothes into the air, used his power to turn into his cloud form, insinuated himself into his clothing and went solid–ta-da! He was instantly dressed. The reader wrote: "When Jack clouded into his clothes, his underwear fell through his cloud body onto the floor. So Jack went to school without wearing any underwear. I'm too smart for you guys!"

6

Bruce Wayne leaned back against the plush leather seat of the limousine and clicked the TV remote.

"Give it up, Bruce. It won't do you any good to keep switching channels," Tim Drake, Bruce Wayne's teenage ward, said from the seat beside him. "The news on every local station is more or less the same."

Not bothering to look up from the comic book he was reading, Tim mimicked a particularly annoying female reporter's breathy voice. "All of Gotham is wondering who the mysterious Batwoman is. . . . Is she Batman's new partner? Batgirl, grown up? Blah, blah, blah."

Ignoring Tim, Bruce clicked the TV remote once again.

This channel showed an irritable-looking Police Commissioner James Gordon, surrounded by shoving, shouting reporters.

"All I can tell you is that this so-called Batwoman is not affiliated with Batman. Otherwise I have no comment," Gordon snapped.

"See," Tim said. "*He* knows nothing. *Nobody* knows anything. Including *us*!"

22

Bruce clicked again moodily.

A black-haired man with a face like a mashed potato appeared on the TV screen. Beneath the image, an identifying line across the bottom of the screen read, *Sgt. Harvey Bullock, G.P.D.*

Bullock—tall, broad, built like a sumo wrestler, and never the picture of sartorial elegance—looked even grumpier and more rumpled than usual.

"I think we got more than enough bat-freaks in Gotham already," he said. "I mean, sheesh, what's next—*Bathound*?"

"Funny he should mention that." Tim looked up from his comic, eyes twinkling. "I've been *thinking* about getting a dog. He could help us sniff out clues!"

Bruce gave him a withering look. Then, when his cell phone rang, Bruce sighed, switched off the TV, and answered, "Bruce Wayne here."

"Bruce, it's Barbara," said a chipper female voice.

Barbara. Commissioner Gordon's teenage daughter. Bruce closed his eyes. He could feel a headache coming on.

"Hey, Barb," he said.

Tim batted his eyelashes at Bruce. "She misses you," he sang in a lilting voice.

Bruce ignored him. "How's college?" he asked.

"Not bad," Barbara said. "But the nightlife here can't compare with kicking butt as Batgirl."

Then her voice turned seductive. "But spring break will be coming up soon and I'll be back in Gotham for two whole weeks. Won't that be nice?"

Bruce shifted uncomfortably. "Yes, we'll *all* be happy to see you," he said.

Tim buried his nose in his comic. "Hey, don't drag *me* into this," he said.

"Anyway, that's not the reason I called," Barbara continued.

23

Ya got me there, kid! Definitely too smart for me!

It isn't hard for me to get into the mind-set of writing stories for kids. I think all of us have an...I dunno...an interior age. In my soul, I'm somewhere between eleven and twelve. It's still one of my favorite ages to be, to interact with, and to write for.

Simonson pays close attention to how people talk in her novel *Batman: Mystery of the Batwoman*. Bruce Wayne, Tim Drake, Barbara Gordon, Commissioner Gordon, and Harvey Bullock all have distinct voices. Batman TM & ©2004 DC Comics

Was that me? *she thought. Was* I *screaming? But . . . why? Where am I?*

In an act of will, she forced her eyes open. Gloomy light seeped through a tiny, barred window and revealed her surroundings—a classic dungeon cell.

What am I doing here? she asked herself.

Memory surfaced slowly, like a goldfish in a murky pond.

The dungeon cell was in the manor belonging to Darkseid's minion Desaad. And the vile Desaad was preparing to study her as if she were a lab specimen—before he destroyed her mind and stole her will.

Wonder Woman fought down her panic, practicing the meditative breathing she had learned on Themyscira. Her mind must be free of fear and focused on her surroundings, on finding a way out.

She struggled to sit upright.

The barred window was set into a sturdy-looking metal door that would be her only hope of escape, once she freed herself from her wrist shackles. Oddly, they were bound to the wall, not by chains, but by a tangle of thick wires.

It figured somehow. Apokolips was, after all, a high-tech world. These were probably power shackles.

Not that it matters. Neither wires nor chains can hold Wonder Woman, she thought. *These, at least, I can break!*

She pulled at the wires. Nothing happened. But that was impossible. She was innately strong, and her magic armor amplified her own power tenfold. It allowed her to hold her own, even against Superman!

Her *armor*!

Wonder Woman looked down and saw, shocked, that she was now dressed in rags. Her glorious red-and-gold armor, her silver bracelets, and her unbreakable golden lasso were gone.

Once more her panic rose and this time she gave it full sway, letting adrenaline surge through her body to fuel her struggles. But without the aid of her armor, she still couldn't break her bonds.

Then, with a metallic clank, the cell door slid open. A hulking guard lurched into the cell, holding a cracked jar and a fist-sized gray cube.

He tossed the cube into her lap. "Energy Block," the man grunted. "Water too. Desaad must want to keep you alive for a while." He put down the jar. "Pullin' at them wires won't do no good. Only old Himon ever escaped this prison in one piece."

In *The Gauntlet,* details are deftly employed to describe Wonder Woman's prison cell on Apokolips. In this excerpt, Simonson delves into Diana's psyche as the Amazon musters her courage to face her captors. Justice League TM & ©2004 DC Comics

THE VALUE OF GOOD WORDS

Adapting stories from one narrative form to another—from comics to novels, for example—can pose challenges to the story at hand. For a younger audience, the rule of thumb is to be more economical with the words chosen. Words must have meaning and clarity.

LOUISE SIMONSON: In the several kinds of writing I've done, I guess there are three stages, three progressions of how much information the words have to carry.

Each comic book is such a short form, you've got to get a lot of information into short snippets of dialogue. There are not that many words in a dialogue balloon. Anything from one to...gee, 25 words would be a really long balloon. I usually run–because I counted it once–75 to a maximum of 150 words on a page. That's not a lot of verbal information, really. The pictures in a comic carry a lot of information and context–where you change from room to room, environment to environment, or initiate action or follow through on an action, a lot of it is visualized in the pictures.

I've done picture books that have twenty words on a page, but included a fair bit of information, because the pictures carried so much of the story. Picture books are very much an interaction of words and pictures. The words present a minimum of (you hope) vividly realized information, but the illustrations expand the information much as a comic does.

I Hate Superman was a comics-related picture book for older children. In it, the words told the readers all they needed to know, while the images fleshed out and expanded the context of story. They enriched the hero's world, presenting a lot of details that a reader wouldn't have gotten just by reading the text.

As an example, as the story opens, the young hero-worshipping protagonist, James, has a red cape–a towel–tied around his neck. It's a "little kid" thing to do. By the end of the story, James, having been through a maturing experience, wears a T-shirt with a Superman shield. His attitudes have shifted. He no longer has to pretend to be Superman, though he still holds his hero in high esteem. Neither cape nor T-shirt are mentioned in the text but the image subtly underlines the story theme.

But, in a novel, you can't fall back on pictures. The story is conveyed by words alone. Words alone create text and context, create mental pictures and sensory images, convey message and theme.

Any theme you can explore in a book or comic for adults, you can do in a book for kids. The details of the stories will be different because you are speaking to a different audience, but the themes of right and wrong, honor, courage, responsibility, love, hate, death and betrayal have been done brilliantly in all these mediums.

You'd want to stay away from scenes of sexuality or graphic violence in stories for younger children. For example, in *I Hate Superman*, there was a scene where James witnesses a robbery and the robbers have guns–important props in the story. The editor was concerned about the guns' appropriateness in a book for kids. Finally, it was agreed that there could be one gun, mentioned once, I think, in the text, but no gun images would be allowed. A gun couldn't be pictured, even in silhouette.

Of course, a writer would have more leeway in novels for older children. And young adult novels, as a genre, don't restrict subject matter, though there might be some concern about how certain subjects are approached.

One of the things I found interesting about doing *I Hate Superman* and other comics-related picture books, is that my editors asked that I not only write the book text, but also provide descriptions for the illustrators. The artists interpreted these descriptions in wonderful ways, but I was able to select what essential visual information needed to be conveyed.

I've been told that picture book manuscripts generally contain just the text of a story. An editor gives the manuscript to an artist who provides whatever images he or she thinks are appropriate. The writer generally doesn't get much input in what the pictures show. But, my comics-related picture books have been a sort of hybrid, created in a somewhat unorthodox manner, and one I think was very effective.

So far, in writing kids' books, I haven't been asked to simplify vocabulary or sentence structure. In comics? Yeah, once. Not by my editor but by a woman from some pro-reading organization–I wish I could remember which one. She spoke to me to complain that my comics were written on too advanced a reading level. Both vocabulary and sentence structure were too complex–I'm remembering fifth or sixth grade level –and she wanted me to dumb it down. Her heart was in the right place. She wanted to make the stories more accessible to younger readers.

I told her I knew a lot of people who had learned to read by reading comics, and assured her that my comics writing was no more complex than most and I suspected the pictures would give kids lots of clues that would help them decode complex words, access the vocabulary, and follow the story. In my opinion, kids who read comics learn to read more easily and develop impressive vocabularies without even trying. I think comics make super beginning readers.

Of course, if I ever write an early-reader book–one created specifically to teach kids how to read–I'll have to give a simplified vocabulary a try. It takes a special skill to make kids want to decode written words, to make learning to read both fun and interesting. But Dr. Seuss did it. And Arnold Lobel does it with his gentle, funny *Frog and Toad* books. And then there's the enormously popular *Magic Treehouse* adventure series by Mary Pope Osborne.

Words. Pictures. Fun. Adventure. Sounds like comics, doesn't it?

WORDS AND PICTURES

Sequential art is a powerful medium because it bridges the visual and the conceptual by pulling together words and pictures. Though it is an incredibly complicated feat to pull off, if successful, even a child can enjoy a comic. So how are comic books and children's books unique?

Children's picture books rely on text to carry the narrative transition while the illustrations show a moment within the story. *Superman: Robot Riot*, (above and below) written by Louise Simonson and illustrated by Bo Hampton and Tim Harkins. Superman TM & ©2004 DC Comics

LOUISE SIMONSON: In comics, the art carries the story, the movement, the action, panel to panel to panel. Whereas in the more traditional illustration-oriented children's books, the actual text carries the transitions, and the illustrations show moments within the story rather than the entire movement of the story.

But then there's the whole spectrum in the middle.

Spread children's books out on the floor, pick a variety of well-respected picture books. You'd see some just have pictures. A lot of those are images held together by a theme like, "What does baby play with," that kind of thing. They are written for very small kids. But not all of them are, by any means.

David Weisser wrote and illustrated a lovely, lovely book called *Sector 7*. It's about a little boy who takes a school trip to the Empire State Building, meets a cloud, and is spirited off to the factory in the sky where clouds are made. The boy ends up being a better cloud-designer than the people who work in the factory and designs spectacular cloud shapes for very happy clouds. Weisser's story is told sequentially, panel to panel like a comic book, but the story itself has no words. The pictures carry the tale brilliantly.

Another Weisser book, *Tuesday*, has eight words–four at the beginning, four at the end. The entire middle, again, is a silent, sequentially told story of a night filled with flying frogs. It is another non-pulp comic book.

Most of the books though, from the deceptively simple *Goodnight Moon* by Margaret Wise Brown to Chris Van Allsburg's slightly disturbing fantasy *Jumanji*, have words and pictures. Like these, most picture books employ sequential art, though some are more sequential than others. In Maurice Sendak's *Where the Wild Things Are*, the jumps are carried by the text so that you get a story with pictures illustrating and amplifying what the text is describing. Neither words nor pictures alone carry the story.

A few others, like Sendak's *In the Night Kitchen*, use a comic book panel format complete with word balloons.

And from there, you can transition to "real" comic books, where you've got the words and pictures together carrying a story. Comics aren't that different from other book mediums–they're part of a continuum.

A while back, I was talking to Bret Blevins about doing kids' books. He'd gone to a children's book convention in California and had shown some of his work there. Several editors were ready to hire him on the spot. They loved what he was able to do because, as a comic book artist, he knew how to make it an illustration that forwarded the story. He understood content, context and story logic.

I thought Bret's insights were interesting, in part because I would never have guessed that the storytelling part of illustration was hard. I had assumed making those beautiful pictures was the hard part,

that illustration-type storytelling was something people did instinctively. But visual narrative is a complicated form and, apparently, a number of very fine illustrators find it difficult skill to master. It seems a good illustrator is hard to find.

LIFE AFTER SUPERMAN

The opportunity to realize a dream can be rare, and Simonson has taken advantage of several opportunities, even if that meant walking away from a proven success. Simonson loves to write, and she loves to write for children. Working on Superman provided her with many options.

LOUISE SIMONSON: I've always wanted to write children's books, but from the beginning, I had a lot of comic book work. During the Eighties and Nineties, comic books could be pretty lucrative, so I kind of stuck with what I was doing.

But the older I got, the more I wanted to write books specifically for kids. So, when I was working on *Superman: Man of Steel* for DC comics, I mentioned to several higher-ups at DC–Mike Carlin, among them–that I'd really love to do kids' books. One of the very cool things about the nice people at DC is that, if you express those kinds of quirky desires, some of them might look at you funny, but if they can, they'll try to make your wish come true.

The Superman team had done a story about the death and return of Superman, which was hugely popular. Because of this, DC wanted to do both an adult novelization and a children's novelization

of the story and release the story in text form. And they asked me to write the kids' novelization because they knew I wanted to write kids' books. So the first children's novel that I wrote was *Superman: Doomsday and Beyond*.

And after that, the editors at DC asked me to write several children's picture books and even a couple of sound books, which I thought was a riot. You know, the books with sound-chips lined up along the side of the page–you punch the Ferris wheel button and you hear a carnival sound, or you punch the Superman button and it plays the Superman theme.

Then, when they made a movie of a character I co-created, Steel, they asked me to write the juvenile novelization for that movie.

By that time, DC knew I like to do "weird stuff," so they asked me to work on a computer-animated choose-your-own-adventure Superman series. That was a lot of fun.

Then later, I wrote several books in the Justice League juvenile novel series. And I just finished a novelization of *Batman: Mystery of the Batwoman*, a direct-to-video animated Batman movie. At present, I'm working on a couple of similar projects. I enjoy writing them and I guess DC likes what I'm doing since they keep asking me to do more.

I really relish writing books right now–although, if I thought I had a story that could best be told in comics-format, I'd gladly do so.

Several years ago, I talked to some of the powers-that-be at DC about creating a line of adventure comics about kids, for kids. I had several concepts that would have made great comics series (at least in my humble opinion) but, at the time, there was no interest because,

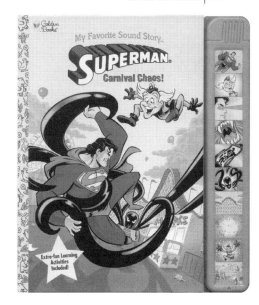

Superman: Carnival Chaos! is an interactive children's book, published by Golden Books in 1996. Relying on various sound chips running down the right side of the book (above), children read the story and press the corresponding sounds when instructed (below). Illustrated by John Delaney and Dave Cooper. Superman TM & ©2004 DC Comics

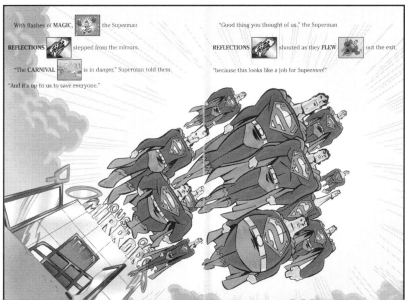

in the marketplace at that time, no one had any idea how to sell a line of comics to kids.

At the time I thought maybe the publishers were right. Comic books seemed to have abandoned the kids' market. Comics had evolved into a grown-up market, catering mainly to adult fans. I realized if I wanted to do stories with kid protagonists, I was going to have a hard time getting a commercial comics publisher interest in that kind of material.

So I decided to try writing one of the ideas as a sci-fi/fantasy juvenile novel. It's out there being shopped around to publishers now. Wish me luck!

I have ideas for a couple of books of historical fiction—one of which could be expanded into a series, a science fiction book and a time travel series. In time, all will become kids' books. The advantage there is I'll own them. In mainstream comics, though you now get royalties if your concepts catch on big and, say, become movies or TV shows, mostly you just give the property away.

I'm hoping the bookstore marketing strategy will be the salvation of comic books, since bookstores reach the ordinary "civilian" reader.

Comic book shops seem to attract the teen-to-middle-aged male crowd: almost no kids and very few women. And most of the comics feature superheroes. I think if comics are going to survive as a genre, they're going to have to expand their audience and their subject matter.

It's great that comics—both superhero and independent, non-superhero books—are being compiled into graphic novel formats and sold, not just through comic specialty shops, but through bookstores. Our local Barnes & Noble displays graphic novels and manga toward the front in a special section, but it also has a special graphic novel section in the kids' department. I've been told that graphic novels are one of the few growth segments in publishing, and I find that very heartening.

This might, in turn, encourage more diverse kinds of comics—in fact, from what I've heard and seen recently, that may already be happening.

Publishing—of books and of comics—has changed in recent years. Back in the "olden days," publishing houses were mostly small family-owned businesses. Now most of the old publishers have been brought up by corporate interests and have been merged into huge publishing conglomerates. These conglomerates make books like they make shoes and frying pans. Everything is a unit for sale, and they have stockholders with expectations and a keen eye on the bottom line. So, these days, it's very difficult for publishers to take chances. I think it's very difficult for the people working in the publishing industry, simply because most of them are there, not to get rich, but because they love the printed page.

The large publishers have deep pockets but they also have a corporate structure and require guaranteed profits. It's difficult for them to justify publishing something quirky or something they can't pigeonhole—something without a huge, instant built-in market. They want bestsellers so they often gravitate toward celebrity authors. Who can blame them?

But, in a lot of cases, the publishing conglomerates can be slow-moving dinosaurs. More and more, I'm noticing small publishers beginning to emerge, like little proto-mammals. They have smaller staffs and thus fewer people in the decision chain. They can react quickly. They require smaller profits. And they're better positioned to take chances.

In comics, the independent publishers are producing some interesting material. Part of it, I think, is because they're willing to publish other genres than superheroes. They're more flexible. They don't have to worry so much about precedent. Like other smaller publishers, they can do with a reduced bottom line, though I'm sure they wouldn't mind having a bestseller or two in their lineup.

That said, DC—one of comics' Big Two—does have the Vertigo imprint. Vertigo take a lot of chances and does a lot of unusual material. They don't focus on a hugely wide variety of genres—a lot of what they publish is horror or fantasy—but some of their properties have a gutsy realism. I think it's very cool that DC is willing to take those chances. The payoff is that some of the work they've taken chances on has become very popular.

Recently, Marvel, too, has begun to broaden their focus. It'd be interesting to see what happens in the next few years.

These days, it's hard for a for a creator to have nerve to take chances, to do something different, to write outside the box. It may be even more difficult for an editor (whose job is on the line) to buy such a project or a publisher (whose profits are on the line) to take a chance on publishing it. Plainly, corporate culture makes it a lot easier to say "No!" than to say "Yes!"

But occasionally, you get that felicitous combination of people-creative creators, editors with brains and good instincts, and publishers with nerves of steel—people who fall in love with a project, take a chance, and have it pay off.

Speaking of which...you've probably heard the famous story that when J.R.R. Tolkien offered *Lord of the Rings* to the publisher, George Allen and Unwin, Ltd. in England, Raynor Unwin, the editor who read it reported to the publisher (who was also his father) that *Lord of the Rings* was a work of genius but that, if they published it, they would lose money. The publisher wrote back that, if it was a work of genius, they had a responsibility to publish it. And Raynor has his permission to lose a thousands pounds.

In fact, what George Allen and Unwin published was the best-selling novel of the twentieth century. Which just goes to show, if you take a chance on a work of genius, sometimes it pays off.

But you know what? Sometimes it doesn't. Sometimes a work of genius sinks like a stone. Publishers need luck and timing as much as anyone else.

CHAPTER 6

As Superman and Lobo left Earth's solar system, Superman adjusted a collapsible transparent breathing mask over his nose. He always carried one with him for just such an emergency.

Speaking into the mask's built-in communicator, Superman said, "Mind telling me exactly where we're going?"

"Remember when you beat Mongul back on War World?" Lobo asked. "Yellow bastich wants a rematch. Hired me to bring you to him!"

Mongul! Superman thought, disgusted. *That maniac ex-despot is responsible for this? Maybe I should've let Draaga imprison Mongul after all.*

The world knew Superman only as the Man of Steel, but he also had a life as Clark Kent, intrepid reporter.

He had several ongoing investigations for the *Daily Planet*, but they could wait. He hoped.

At least Lois is out of the country on assignment, he thought. *So she won't get suspicious because Superman and I are both missing at the same time.*

But next week was his mother's birthday. He was flying both his parents to Metropolis for a visit. And he was going to introduce them to Lois.

He almost grinned, wondering what they would make of her. This was a meeting he definitely didn't plan to miss.

"How long is this little expedition going to take?" Superman asked.

Lobo shrugged. "You fight Mongul four days from now."

Superman sighed in relief. He had given his word he'd go with Lobo. He hadn't promised to do anything at all once he reached their destination. He certainly had no intention of wasting his time fighting Mongul yet again.

He would have to give the situation some thought.

As a juvenile fiction novelist, Simonson revisited the character of Superman in *Wild at Heart,* in addition to Lobo and the JLA. Justice League TM & ©2004 DC Comics

I Hate Superman, written by Simonson and illustrated by Kevin and Kathy Altieri. Superman TM & ©2004 DC Comics

I   H A T E   S U P E R M A N

The challenges of writing for children are the same as in any kind of writing: good characterization, a plot that moves, details, etc. When the story is told and printed, the author receives reactions to it in a number of ways. Traditionally, a well-told story can earn good reviews, a steady paycheck, and kudos from your peers. But when your story earns "best story—ever" recognition, you know you have made more than a positive contribution.

LOUISE SIMONSON: Mike Carlin suggested the title *I Hate Superman*, to Charlie Kochman, DC's book editor (and a really cool individual). Mike didn't have a story in mind, he just thought it was a provocative title since he'd once heard a kid say, "I hate Superman because he's such a goody-goody." Charlie suggested it to me and I loved it. Then I asked myself, "What would make a kid hate Superman?"

When I'm working on a story, I begin with character, specifically, character motivation and conflict. I think I'm happiest in writing a book [at] that instant where I understand what motivates a character and am able to craft scenes that expresses perfectly what the character is feeling and why.

I Hate Superman is the story of a little boy, James, who's raised by a single mother. He has two heroes—his big brother and Superman. James ties a towel around his neck and pretends to be Superman, while his big brother joins a gang and begins spray-painting anti-Superman and other graffiti around the neighborhood. James knows his brother is wrong but he loves his brother, too. Conflict!

Then James' mom sends him out to a local bodega, to get milk. Looking in the window, James sees shadowy figures robbing the store owner. He runs to a pay phone on the corner to call the cops but it's broken. So he shouts for Superman. Superman hears James with his super-hearing and stops the burglary. But it turns out that James' brother and his new gang are the robbers. Supes arrests James' brother and his gang. To his horror, James realizes he inadvertently betrayed his brother to Superman. James now has a larger conflict of loyalties between the two guys he admires most in the world.

I loved poor little James for having to face such a difficult problem. (You know, the more you torture your characters, the more you love them. Especially if they're brave, smart, and resilient enough to face up to their difficulties and emerge stronger.) And, of course, I felt sorry for James, too. How in the world is he going to get out of this, I asked myself. What is he going to do now? How can James reconcile his opposing feelings?

So James goes into the room he shares with his brother, feeling like a rotten traitor. He tried to do something good—stop a robbery—and ended up feeling like a bad guy. Then he spots his brother's can of spray paint. So James takes the paint and begins to

write "I hate Superman," and other anti-Superman graffiti all over the neighborhood, just like his brother did. He uses his brother's tools to attack his former hero. He quits "being" Superman and "becomes" his brother instead.

For me, that really crystallized the conflict for James. He felt like he had betrayed his brother, and the only way he could make things right was to take up his brother's mantle and continue in his brother's footsteps, even if it was against his own moral code.

Superman catches James at the graffiti-painting and they talk about why James is doing this and whether it's a good idea. Superman tells James, "You shouldn't try to be me or your brother. You should just try to be your own best self!" James visits to his brother who's in jail for a short time. The brother says, "Listen to Superman. What I did landed me in jail. Not you. Not Superman." When his brother says, "It wasn't your fault or Superman's fault. It was my fault," James' brother grows up. In accepting that the world isn't black-and-white, and that we all have to take responsibility for our actions, James grows up a little too.

I really like the way that story came out. And I was quite pleased with the art as well.

After the book came out, one of our young friends—a boy eight or nine—was at our house visiting and the *I Hate Superman* book was sitting on the coffee table. Our young friend read it. Then he looked at me and said, "That's the best book I've ever read in my entire life!" Which I thought was so sweet—and exactly what a storyteller wants to hear. That's my final, real reward for having written that book.

But there are other rewards along the way.

Working on a manuscript provides its own pleasure. Sure, sometimes writing can be a pain. But there's also a thrill when you realized you've nailed some aspect of a story…when you've gotten it just right. And it doesn't hurt to get paid for doing what you love either. You want people to like your stories for any number of reasons. One of which is, if they don't like it, they won't hire you to write the next one. You write in part to amuse yourself, but you really hope you're making a positive contribution. It's always a pleasure when a reader tells you that you have.

Later that day James crouched on the blacktop beneath the basketball hoop. The can of spray paint hissed out a Day-Glo "A," the second-to-last letter in Superman's name. *Superman flies over the city all the time! James thought. When he looks down, he'll see this! I can't wait! I want him to see it!*

James thought about his fight with Richard, and for the first time he hesitated. *Maybe Richard's right,* he thought. *Maybe I am crazy.*

-22-

Just then James heard a thump on the blacktop behind him. He looked up, then turned away and kept on spraying. Even when the familiar shadow that fell over him moved closer, James refused to turn around again.

"It looks as if you're pretty mad at me!" Superman said.

"So you noticed!" James replied. When he finished, he read his words aloud. "I hate Superman!"

"It was hard not to notice," Superman said. "Your graffiti is all over the neighborhood."

-24-

"You think you know everything!" James shouted. He turned and threw the paint can at the Man of Steel. It hit him and bounced off his chest.

James plowed into Superman, pounding him as hard as he could with both fists.

"You pretend to be this big hero!" James cried. "And I believed you! But you tricked me! Now Mr. Masire thinks I'm a big hero, too! But I'm not! I'm a snitch! I don't want to be like you anymore!"

Superman let James hit him until the boy was just too tired to move. Then Superman gathered him into his arms and held him until James's sobs quieted.

"I didn't arrest your brother because you betrayed him. I arrested him because what he was doing was wrong. There was a gun. People could have been seriously hurt," Superman said. "It's good to love your brother, but you don't have to act like him. Or me," Superman added.

The two stood in silence for a moment. Then Superman walked James home.

-26-

I Hate Superman is a picture book for older children. The story tackles the mature concept of right and wrong. Even though pictures dominate the book, the text sets the context and drives the narrative. Simonson does not speak down to her audience, instead allowing the narrative be as complex as necessary to tell James' story.
Superman TM & ©2004 DC Comics

RICH'LL COME EVENTUALLY

A successful career comes from enjoying what you do. The more successful you are in comics and children's books, the larger your audience grows. And though many artists rarely think about it, they can make a difference through their work. Simonson's advice is simple: the work is the reward.

LOUISE SIMONSON: I really enjoy writing both comics and children's books. Honestly, I don't think they're all that different.

Power Pack was really a kids' book in comic book form. I wrote it thinking I would get a kid audience. At the time, from the mail I was receiving, I was a little disappointed. I thought only adults were reading *Power Pack* because I got comparatively few letters from kids. Now, twenty years later, I'm getting e-mails from people who read *Power Pack* as kids and had really enjoyed it.

Several times a year, someone will e-mail me and say, "I read it as a kid, I loved it." So kids were finding it. I've even gotten a couple of notes from folks who, years after the book was no longer being published, found an issue at a yard sale or 25-cent bin at a convention, and went on to collect the series. And occasionally I'll get an e-mail telling me "…not only did I read it, but it made a huge difference in my life." Then they'll go on to tell me how. Those e-mails always leave me–and artists June Brigman and Jon Bogdanove with whom I exchange these kinds of notes–misty eyed.

It's really humbling to think your stories made a difference in somebody's life. One of the things that seemed to have made an impression on many readers was the Pack's strong family ties. Some readers didn't have strong, loving families and seeing it depicted in those stories made a big difference to them. What they may not realize is that their stories make a big difference to me.

One of my favorite readers was a kid I met at a comic book convention–I think it was somewhere in the Midwest–a little guy, probably nine years old who was a huge, huge *Power Pack* fan. His parents brought him to a panel I was on and, when he stood up in front of the whole the audience to ask *Power Pack* questions, he kind of stammered. It was a little hard for him, he was such a young guy and public speaking wasn't his thing, but, in the end, he got his questions out. I thought he was very brave. Some of the questions he was asking were ones that I couldn't answer in front of the whole audience because it would give things away they might not want to know yet. So I told the kid to come up to me afterward and I'd tell him privately all the secret stuff he wanted to know.

When I talked to him later, he told me he attended a school for autistic children. And because he was doing so well in school–he said rather proudly that he was the best kid in his class–his parents had been allowed to bring him to the convention.

His dad seemed uncomfortable with the whole experience, but his mom enjoyed it. And he loved it. I was even able to give him a *Power Pack* advertising poster that he told me he planned to hang over his bed. He was a really nice little kid, and his mom said the Pack made a real difference in his life.

I can't stress too strongly that people who want to be writers–or artists or anyone interested any creative endeavor–should read everything and pay attention to what goes on around them. Some of my best story ideas came from watching people and wondering why…or expanding on things that happened in my own life.

For example, I was in Central Park watching a five-year-old try to learn to ride a bike and I realized that having superpowers wouldn't necessarily make developing a life-skill, like bike-riding, easier. That was the beginning of a story.

Another time, one of my young friends lost her first tooth and couldn't wait to put in under her pillow for the Tooth Fairy. So Katie Power lost her tooth in an early *Power Pack* issue and received a most unusual coin in return. The list goes on and on.

One of the things I tell people who are choosing their career paths is, if you can possibly manage it, work at something you love. Don't worry about getting rich. If you work at something you love, rich may come eventually. And even if it doesn't come, at least you'll be happy with what you're doing.

Clark was not an ordinary child. He could run faster than his friends and hear sounds from miles away. Nothing hurt him. He could even see through walls. His strange powers scared him.

One day the strangest thing of all happened. Clark jumped over the farmyard gate to do his after-school chores. Suddenly he was soaring in the air. "Ma! Pa!" he cried. "Look! I'm flying."

Having written for the character of Superman for over a decade, Simonson was the perfect choice to interpret his origin story for children. *The True Story of Superman* chronicles the story of Clark Kent growing up to become the Man of Steel. Illustrations by Mike Parobeck, Rick Burchett and Don Desclos. Superman TM & ©2004 DC Comics

His parents had the perfect solution. Clark's mother made him a special costume to wear. Then no one would recognize him when he used his superpowers.

Clark was thrilled. Now he looked like what Lois Lane had called him. He looked like Superman!

David Guertin
on Comics & Video Games

It's difficult to tell a cohesive story with a video game. Even though it's a visual art, there are so many other elements involved in producing a video game that can detract from or add to the overall experience, including programming, level design, animation, testing, sound, marketing, and player skill. For the best video games, a unifying story keeps all of these elements in line. This is especially important because the medium is at the mercy of continuously emerging technologies.

Dave Guertin has served as character director for the popular video game franchise Ratchet and Clank. A talented artist, he understands the value of storytelling which pervades his character designs. He developed his love of storytelling from numerous trips to the neighborhood drugstore.

DAVID GUERTIN: The first comic I ever had was bought by my father from a CVS pharmacy when I was about six years old. The issue was from the first run of *Iron Man* and featured a bizarre yet interesting combination between himself and Spider-Man. As a kid, seeing those team-ups between two different storylines really meant something special, so I knew I was in for a treat. From that moment on, I found myself immersed into many of the Marvel and DC universes. It was almost as if a new world had been opened not only for comics, but for all forms of sequential art. As a kid I looked at everything from comics to newspaper strips just to follow the adventures of these imaginary characters. I remember waiting days on end for the Sunday newspaper to arrive. The Sunday strips were filled with longer stories, larger panels, and color! What more could a kid really ask for? It was during that time I was introduced to one of my greatest influences, Bill Waterson. Watching

Calvin and Hobbes interact had a huge connection with me and, in many ways, waiting all week for a new strip was torturous. So between the comics and the comic strips, I would draw my own characters—sometimes tracing them so I could give them to my mom for the refrigerator. That's really were everything started for me and continued throughout my entire childhood. When I was thirteen, comics solidified their presence at the sight of a Mike Zeck air-brushed illustration of the Punisher. The book was a special edition hardcover of *Punisher: Return to Big Nothing* wrapped in cellophane. I had never seen a comic character rendered in such detail and at the time it was the most amazing piece of art I had ever witnessed. I still have the book, and it's still in the cellophane. I think in some ways I want to retain that perfect view of it. It was just a great influence for me.

IT'S BEEN THREE HOURS SINCE THE CRASH.

ONCE THE FANS WENT, I KNEW THERE WASN'T MUCH OF A CHOICE.

IT WAS THIS ROCK OR NOTHING.

THE SHIP'S IN PRETTY BAD SHAPE.

AND WITH NO WORD FROM THE REST OF THE TEAM, IT SEEMS I'VE GOT ONLY ONE OPTION.

EXPLORE.

WITH A LITTLE LUCK I SHOULD HAVE ENOUGH FUEL FOR TH--

WHA-?

CLIK-

MAN, LOOKS LIKE THEY GROW 'EM *BIG* AROUND HERE.

I SURE HOPE THE CRASH DIDN'T *THROW OFF* THE VISOR CALIBRATION!

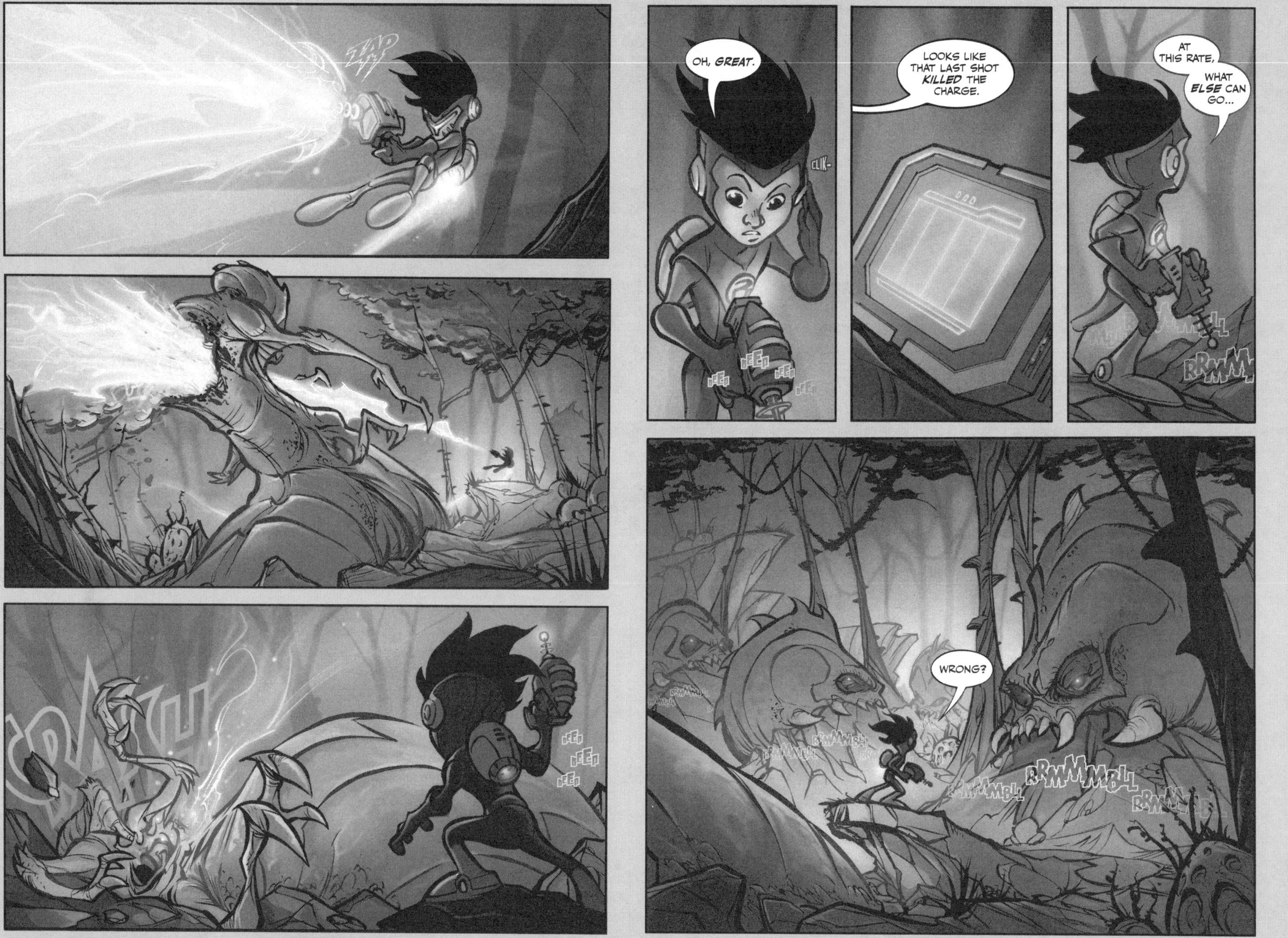
ZAP
OH, GREAT.
CLIK-
LOOKS LIKE THAT LAST SHOT KILLED THE CHARGE.
AT THIS RATE, WHAT ELSE CAN GO...
WRONG?
RRMMMBLL

AN EVEN BLEND

As much as Guertin enjoyed reading and drawing comics, he also found himself drawn to video games and arcades. As long as the medium allowed him to immerse himself into a good story and grand characters, Guertin was hooked. As he found his imagination and artistic skills mature, Guertin looked for a college that would allow him to develop these storytelling skills further.

DAVID GUERTIN: For me, growing up was really an even blend between the comics and video games. So as I moved into games later on in life, it was a pretty natural progression in its own right. About the same time I was staring at comics and newspapers, one Christmas morning brought me an Atari 2600. It was an amazing experience to see so much story-telling with so few pixels bouncing around on screen. I could imagine this entire universe and, for the first time, was able to interact with it. The fascination continued throughout the release of all the major game systems from Nintendo and Sega. I remember playing *Bionic Commando* as a kid; a great side-scroller where you could swing from one building to the next taking out villains along the way. I would sit at my desk for hours creating new maps and obstacles along with new bosses to fight. Around the same time, I found myself heading over to the arcades to check out the larger-than-life characters those graphically superior systems would allow. I spent lots of time examining the sides of the arcade cases for illustrations of the characters to see how they translated. It was very inspiring and I remember running home to create even more characters for video games. The work became an exciting mix for me between the interactivity of games and the different styles of the comic artists.

　　The growth and evolution of these characters quickly became a major focus for me. Whether you were fighting an evil dragon or a fleet of sleek ninjas, in the end you were following the story of a particular hero, watching them grow and change. I was always interested in a character's progression–how they would adapt, confront challenges, acquire new abilities, visually and emotionally mature. That character growth served as the strongest thread for me between both games and comic art.

　　Around the age of thirteen, my family moved from the small city of Woonsocket, Rhode Island to the small town of Inverness in central Florida. The population was quite small and there wasn't too much going on in terms of entertainment. Fortunately I found myself thrown deeper into drawing, continuing the focus into high school. Throughout that time, comics and black-and-white photography took center stage in my life. I began looking at comics as a series of still photographs inter-acting with time through composition, positioning, and detail. There was something really interesting to me about communicating that experience to the reader–almost subconsciously controlling how quickly panels should be read. I think that's the core of what comics were really about for me, just that constant communication of time.

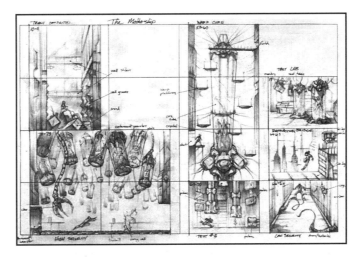

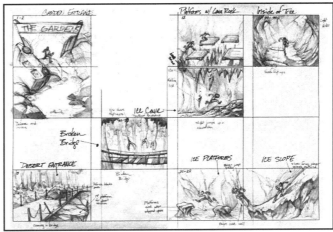

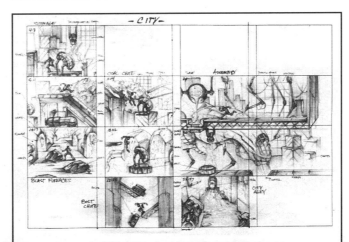

Game maps for platformers are part story-boards and part game navigational tool for the development team. Each rectangle represents what a player would see on the screen at one time and all scenes are connected through horizontal or vertical movements. As a child, Guertin created maps to video games for fun. As a professional, game maps (left) were created for Singletrac Studio for the game *Animorphs: Shattered Reality*. Animorphs TM & ©2004 Singletrac Studio

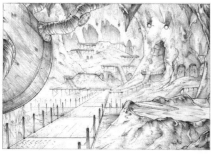

Environmental (above) and creature design (below) created for the PlayStation game *Animorphs: Shattered Reality* while Guertin served as the conceptual artist for Singletrac Studio. Animorphs TM & ©2004 Singletrac Studio

I continued pursuing those concepts through high school until my father brought me to a night class taught by Bruce Miller, a local comic artist. Bruce was penciling and inking independent comics on the side, and one night a week he would gather a bunch of kids to draw and talk about comics. I vividly remember bringing in comic pages or comic characters for the weekly critique. Bruce would then use tracing paper over the drawings to explain correct anatomy, storytelling, penciling and inking–all the important facets of comics that as a kid you don't really hear about. The classes were a huge jumpstart for me and continued to fuel my passion for the medium. I found these sessions really worked hand-in-hand with a lot of my traditional art classes throughout the rest of high school. Suddenly, college was quickly approaching.

Since we were in Florida, I was close enough to Georgia to start looking into SCAD [Savannah College of Art and Design]. My best friend Chris Purdin and I were juniors when a recruiter from the college showed up in art class to talk about what the school offered. Throughout the presentation we were shown all the buildings, galleries, and dorms along with how the classes were set up. What really caught my attention though was the Sequential Art program–the only curriculum in the country built around storytelling and comic art. So I knew right then and there, before even visiting the school, that I was pretty much sold. Just to be sure, Chris and I took a trip to SCAD for one of their orientation weekends. I took part in a comics workshop with Bob Pendarvis and was completely blown away to think that I could go to school for something like that. We sent in our submissions, and surprisingly Chris and I were accepted before the end of our junior year. So we did everything we could to focus on graduating before making the big move to Savannah.

SINGLETRAC STUDIO

In Guertin's senior year of college, he started the methodical search for employment. As a storyteller, he found that he had skills for numerous markets and job descriptions. He accepted a video game conceptual artist position with Singletrac Studio, a small video game company specializing in racing games. It was here that Guertin learned the ins and outs of the video game industry.

DAVID GUERTIN: My senior year [in college] was a pretty stressful time. I think it is for anyone getting ready to graduate when they realize they need a job. But at that time, I'd say about the last four months of school, I wanted to make sure my portfolio was ready to go. The spring was always a great time for students since many companies would visit the college for portfolio reviews and recruitment opportunities. At that time I remember interviewing with Marvel, Dark Horse, American Greetings, Disney, ILM [Industrial Light and Magic], web companies...you name it. Throughout those few weeks, there was a buzz of possibility at ILM with the beginning of new projects. Yet, one thing that I realized quickly is timing is everything in this industry. In the end, budgets, style, availability, experience, and politics all play an integral role to filling positions. Eventually, what was to be a computer-rendered version of *Frankenstein*, fell through. I continued the job search by mailing out about thirty binders of material to various companies around the country from movie houses to web design firms. In the end, I had one binder and about four possible companies to send it to. Singletrac Studio was one of them. The company was a game development house in Salt

Lake City known for popular PlayStation games like *Twisted Metal* and *Jet Moto*. Remembering how much I loved games growing up I figured I'd give it a shot. So I sent the last binder out and Singletrac responded—they asked me to take a test.

The test, which included two varied personality descriptions, was interesting and straightforward. One was what they called a "female race character," for a futuristic racing game, in addition to an alien insect-like creature. Each character had their own detailed design spec from which I was to create two illustrations. Frightened out of my mind, I finished the test and sent it in. The week I waited turned into the longest week of my life. Fortunately the timing worked out and after the interview I came on board with the company as a conceptual artist for a racing game they had in development. I found myself creating very comic book-like art, except for game development instead. I remembered those days as a kid staring at the sides of arcade machines reading volumes of storytelling in one character design. At that point I knew game development is where I wanted to be.

I made a pact with myself that if I got in anywhere I would learn as much as I could technically and artistically about the industry: what software was used, what techniques to refine, what rules to follow. So when I came in, I started doing some touch-up paintings in Photoshop for cinematic graphics for *Streak*, a hoverboard racing game. We were in the final month of production known as "Beta" where many of the game assets are adjusted and refined. I learned volumes about game creation along with the various workflows from the senior artists. It became a great opportunity

to get my feet wet with the various facets of the game—learning both the strengths and weaknesses of the hardware. With the small team size, the concept work eventually lead to storyboards and game design. Since the new project was a side-scroller, the work was strangely similar to those childhood *Bionic Commando* maps. I actually had to call my parents to assure them all the game playing as a kid was paying off! Around the same time, Matt Copeland, a good friend at the company, took me under his wing to teach the ins and outs of 3-D modeling with Maya. The vast program was tremendously complex yet equally powerful. For the first time I found myself really thinking about how character design reacted with an environment in 3-D space. Much like that first comic, it felt as if a new world had opened. Everything from proportion, scale, and efficient use of detail jumped to the foreground as I learned the software. In the coming months, the job quickly turned into a jack-of-all-trades position—I learned a lot of different positions from many talented people, which in turn helped a great deal in understanding how all the pieces fit together

Back then, we had a smaller team of fifteen to twenty people dealing with the game including programmers, artists, sound technicians, and producers. The environment pushed each artist to explore outside of their job description which, even amidst the large team sizes of today, I feel is still important for solid game development. Much like comic artists, a good penciler understands how an inker will approach the page and vise versa. With games, imagining how a character will be modeled in 3-D, including the limitations of poly count and resolution, will drastically affect the 2-D design.

Final creature visualizations for *Animorphs: Shattered Reality*. Singletrac Studios places value on artists who can develop different types of characters for their games. Animorphs TM & ©2004 Singletrac Studio

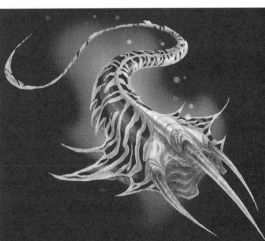

VIDEO GAME STORYTELLING

Video game storytelling is an emerging discipline. Instead of being a linear form of storytelling, relying on the director, editor, or creative team, it relies on the player to define the video game experience. Compound this problem with the competitive need to master ever-changing technology; it is often a miracle when the story is told.

DAVID GUERTIN: First and foremost, I think a good story is a good story; whether it's told with stick men or highly advanced 3-D rendering. Far too often I've seen movies, games, and other tech-heavy media with no soul. The reality is a cool water effect or perfect motion capture doesn't capture the emotion of the viewer. All the polish in the world won't amount to anything if the viewer has no interest in the message. At Insomniac we've attempted to reach the best of both worlds: engaging stories told upon cutting edge technology. One of the constant challenges, however, is the continuous change in hardware and software. Every day, I can honestly say that we go into work and deal with a new obstacle. We continually find ourselves searching for new and more efficient ways to use the hardware to allow more polygons on screen or have better resolution for the characters and environments. It's a pretty breakneck pace, but fortunately we've found with solid understanding of the core concepts or form, design, and color theory the transitions of software can be eased. Even the most advanced computer program in the world won't create great art on its own.

The most valuable tool however in dealing with the technological rollercoaster is communication. With the ever increasing team sizes we've seen a greater need to specialize with specific disciplines. By keeping the lines of communication open, each member of the team can learn more quickly and gain much more ground as a group. This remains one of the most exciting aspects of my job—working together to reach a common goal while learning along the way.

There's been an amazing change in games over the last fifteen years. When you compare the Atari system in the early '80s displaying just a few pixels to the PlayStation 2 with millions of polygons, the jump speaks for itself. Gone are the days where a player needs to imagine, as many did growing up, what the character would look like. Now we're showing them in vivid detail complete with seamless animations, facial expressions, and cinematics. This constant progression over the last few years has also finally allowed the home system to surpass the arcade in every way. The story, characters, environments, and overall experience has become infinitely more immersive. This has provided some great opportunities for developers to create large consistent universes for players to explore. Many, if not all, arcades were designed to eat quarters quickly. These days, games can define a much broader and meaningful message as players watch larger plots unfold.

Personal interaction I think will always be the consistent goal of games. More than art, more than technology, the interactive experience driven by gameplay will continue to be the primary focus. That being said, the constant challenge for every developer lies in removing as many barriers as possible between the game and the player. Confusing stories, awkward controls, and vague goals all lead to a loss of interest. Yet when these elements are brought together correctly, players will find themselves immersed for hours.

Screenshots (below and opposite) from the original *Ratchet and Clank* video game for PlayStation 2. The game featured many worlds and many more weapons, but it was the story of an alien and his robot that captured the imaginations of loyal fans, including executives at Sony. In Japan, *Ratchet and Clank* was packaged with PS2 consoles, the first American game to ever have that honor. Ratchet & Clank TM & ©2004 Sony Entertainment

Furthering the connection possibilities, games are now offering various methods to customize the experience. Personalization such as choosing character classes, adjusting body proportions, and changing texture details all work together to bring the player deeper within the fictional world. In addition to the single player experience, we've also seen great evolution from online play. Ranking systems which track online competition in many of the FPS [first person shooter] titles have allowed players to create a recognizable identity not only through texture and model changes but through playing ability as well. In regards to massive multiplayer adventure games, players are given the opportunity to build reputations and relationships with other players. The experience matures as the added responsibilities of team work and loyalty are introduced and players are held accountable for their actions.

This global freedom of choice has certainly posed new challenges in how stories are told. A common technique found in non-linear gameplay usually involves "pinch-points" where a new scene cannot take place until a set of previous tasks are completed. This allows players to complete smaller groups of tasks in any order without disrupting the overall flow of the adventure. In the future, as processors get faster and AI [artificial intelligence] becomes more complex, many aspects of the story may evolve and change with the player. In the not too distant future, players may find themselves writing large chapters in their own video game adventure merely by the choices they make and the relationships they forge.

A video game story undergoes many stages of production, and every stage relies on a clear game concept or story. In order to create a successful game, this singular vision must be shared by the entire team: from director to modeler, to programmer, to sound engineer.

GUERTIN: Insomniac governs many production decisions by one hardened rule: the deadline is the king. At the beginning of any project, various ideas are passed around and as a group we really shoot for the stars. The best ideas are usually found this way, yet at the end of the day, we stay as realistic as we can about what can get done. The deadline in many ways becomes a promise not only to publishers, but to the consumer as well.

Ideally in game creation, the entire design would be down on paper before all the artists, programmers, and sound designers are brought into production. In reality, that just doesn't happen. Many times production begins with a series of brainstorming meetings to define what the basic framework of the game could be. This structure can include ideas on gameplay, overall story goals, major motivations, and how the character can interact with the environment. In addition, the structure provides valuable information on limitations such as the speed and jump height of the character, game length, and the variety of gameplay styles. In many ways, the framework creates a set of boundaries and gameplay definitions upon which exciting and consistent challenges for the player can be built. With the framework in place, the design, character, environment, and programming departments begin work simultaneously on their respective challenges. With a consistent goal in mind, each department can

Ratchet & Clank TM & ©2004 Sony Entertainment

flesh out in greater detail the games overall style and feel. As with overcoming technological hurdles, communication is crucial in creating a fictional universe across different departments. While the visual style is defined, the game design department can continue to elaborate on core gameplay concepts including character descriptions and level maps. Ideally, design remains several paces ahead of the rest of the team to prevent any department from stalling.

With the first phase of production in full swing, many core gameplay concepts can be tested. In many cases, simple primitive shapes are used as placeholders for characters and environments to track down the elusive feeling of fun. In other words, we'll actually play the game. The prototyping saves months of time allowing the quick adjustment of numerous variables ranging from character scale to attack speed. Once a firm foundation of gameplay is in place, the team then begins work on the final level of polish players expect to see, including millions of polygons, thousands of animations, and numerous effects. Methodically the process continues level by level from anywhere between six and eighteen months until the game nears completion.

Throughout the entire course of production, focus testing provides incredibly valuable information for every department. What may seem like the most amazing idea ever may fail miserably at the hands of a nine-year-old playing the game for the first time. The groups of testers are organized into various age ranges which allow us to organize feedback from different demographics. Through this organization, we can begin to decipher the types of challenges younger and older players enjoy. With feedback in hand, we then begin sweeps of tweaking across the project to adjust any

facet of the game which didn't quite work during the testing. In some cases, pieces are removed while in other instances positive aspects of the game are added in greater number.

Ask any developer and they'll probably tell you the largest challenges rear their heads during the last couple months of production. With game development there's a continuous urge to just "add one more feature, level or character." This in many ways can quickly get out of control threatening both the stability of the game and the deadline. To ensure deadlines are kept, production ends with two major cycles: Alpha and Beta. Alpha is usually defined as "content complete" which essentially means every level, gameplay challenge, and character is included allowing a player to completely finish the adventure. With the full feature set in place, various bugs in the code and art can be fixed without the threat of new features creating more bugs. Throughout this time, various aspects of the game are polished providing the final touches such as breakable lamps, snow footprints, and light bugs. For the first time, during the final couple weeks of Alpha, the true representation of the game can be seen. At that moment, all the late nights, stale pizza, and fried nerves become worth it. Production then ends with Beta. With the game complete and polished, the remaining glitches such as collision holes, missing textures, and text edits can be corrected before final testing. When the team feels the game is ready for the big time, a "Gold Master" is created and sent to the publisher's testing group. Once the disc is free of bugs and approved, the final master is sent to manufacturing and, about a month later, the game can magically be found on store shelves.

With the original Ratchet and Clank video game already a proven success, Insomniac reloaded with *Ratchet and Clank: Going Commando* (below and opposite), creating a franchise. Building upon their existing engine, every element in the second iteration became bigger: bigger guns, bigger levels, and bigger bad guys. Ratchet & Clank TM & ©2004 Sony Entertainment

One of the more interesting challenges faced in team environments is reconciling individual vision over team vision. The reality is when you gather over eighty people together for a project, many will have their own opinion of what something should be like. Yet one of the unique aspects of Insomniac Games is every employee has the opportunity to contribute to the conceptualization of the project at a core level. This openness creates an exciting flow of ideas between the various departments and allows a greater sense of ownership for the company as a whole. In the end, the final decisions are made by the heads of each department, yet usually those decisions include the opinions of many team members. I think every director tries to create an atmosphere conducive to creative output. In many cases this requires allowing enough freedom for innovative ideas to reach the surface. Through open environments, each artist is given the opportunity to not only instill themselves into the world but to accept responsibility for the assets they create as well.

To aid in direction, usually style guides are created to visually define numerous stylistic traits of the universe. Within the Ratchet and Clank universe for example, we tend to treat the bolts on robotic characters in a specific way. This allows us to create characters of all shapes and sizes yet create a connection through a consistent use of detail. Regular use of iconic shapes, representation of technology, and overall level of detail all help contribute to a cohesive appearance of the world.

Even with all the talent in the world, a solid game simply cannot be created without team chemistry. Nothing can be more powerful than collaboration and nothing more destructive than clashing personalities. Throughout the course of multiple projects, a distinct synergy can be forged between team members. This high degree of understanding creates both an enormous amount of creativity and speed. In many ways, decisions become almost instinctive as new character types and gameplay concepts are implemented. Eventually solid instincts can collectively save months of wasted time allowing more involved stories, larger levels, new gameplay, and longer adventures overall.

The industry acknowledges *Going Commando* as one of the most successful platformers ever created. Ratchet & Clank TM & ©2004 Sony Entertainment

Ratchet's final look (below) evolved over time. Guertin experimented with different silhouettes before deciding on an hourglass shape (right). Ratchet & Clank TM & ©2004 Sony Entertainment

RATCHET AND CLANK

Ratchet and Clank is an excellent blend of story, thinking, and playability. Borrowing from animation techniques, Guertin concentrates on shapes and silhouettes to support the game's story.

DAVID GUERTIN: *Ratchet and Clank* was definitely a challenge. With Ratchet, the basic difficulty was this large blank sheet of paper staring us right in the face. What is possible? We must have asked ourselves that question a thousand times during those first couple of weeks. At the same time, the prospect was tremendously exciting for the entire company. To define a new fictional universe is the dream of many developers and for the first time since *Spyro the Dragon*, we were heading down the path. We knew early on the project would be set in a sci-fi universe, yet the struggle involved creating a style unique to the gaming community. After weeks of research we began on merging various traits found in old retro science fiction with some of the grit found in current day space adventures. With many of the broad strokes in place, the team then began to examine the finer details of scale, color theory, and contrast of shape. In addition to the art challenges, the PlayStation 2 console presented many hurdles as well. New toolsets were developed and every member of the team sought to use the hardware to its fullest potential. Witnessing the culmination of both the art and technology in our first Ratchet test level remains the most exciting moment of my career.

Throughout the first couple of weeks, the team tossed around many possible game ideas. The open company environment really fostered some creative input, yet *Ratchet and Clank* began with one simple sentence. We talked about an alien utilizing weapons and gadgets to journey from planet to planet. Amongst the numerous proposals filling the walls in the hallway, it was the one statement that captured the collective attention of the company. We knew we would be introducing something that really hadn't been done in a platformer before–providing the player with a vast array of weaponry allowing a greater sense of freedom to the adventure. It seemed simple at the time but we quickly realized how endless the possibilities could be. Hundreds of ideas filled the conference rooms around the office–we had something.

At that time, I was trying to imagine how we could make gadgets really interesting. We've all seen the James Bond movies with his series of transforming items, yet I wanted to try and find a way to add a bit more personality to these devices. So on the drive home for the weekend, I wondered about the possibility of utilizing small robots for the gadgets. Originally the idea involved a series of these small bots clinging to Ratchet's body completing different functions. One could cling to his head for helmet functions while the second held on to his back as a backpack. The third robot would then grasp onto his arm for wrist mounted weaponry. After a bit more thought, I pitched the idea to the game design staff and Ted Price, the president of the company. We discussed various possibilities and problems with the idea and searched for solutions. With some initial interest, we decided to move forward on conceptualizing the idea. Yet soon after early concept art was created, we quickly realized three robots were overly complicated and created a large

amount of confusion over Ratchet's body. We then began to strip the concept down to its roots and a single robot remained on Ratchet's back. Clank was born.

Clank soon served as many of Ratchet's traversal gadgets including the heli-pack, hydro-pack, and rocket-pack. This provided an interesting symbiotic relationship between the characters aiding us in defining their respective personalities. For clarity on screen, the remaining weapons and gadgets were created to transform from Ratchet's wrench allowing quick intuitive item switching. With the major building blocks in place, we were then able to begin analyzing the overall silhouette of each character.

We knew from the beginning Ratchet was going to be an "alien" species. The idea just seemed to fit with a science fiction universe and allowed the most freedom in creating a pleasing form. That being said, we began research on various terrestrial creatures including dogs, cats, lizards, rats–just about every major form you can imagine. The feline aspects quickly jumped forward and provided the sense of agility we were looking for. With some basic ideas in mind, the animation director Oliver Wade and I began to collaborate on some sketches. Initially I had imagined Ratchet as a small, scrappy creature with a good deal of energy. Oliver's depiction was much taller and a bit laid back. In the end, neither direction captured exactly the feeling we were shooting for. I then began to take the two major ideas and merge them into a cohesive whole trying to retain the most positive aspects of each form. We then began to see some potential and spent several days experimenting with various proportion studies until we found a balance that worked both on paper and

on screen. Once we had a design the company liked, we pitched that character to Sony. After review, they provided some valuable feedback including adding eyebrows and stripes which in turn helped a great deal in defining his visual style. In the end, Ratchet's design, as with many of the characters, was a tremendous collaborative effort.

Clear silhouettes, for Insomniac at least, are the driving force of all character design. If you're not dealing with a very clear and concise shape, you're always going to have confusion due to the shear amount of visual information on screen. Confusion can simply destroy a game, so we continue to strive for as much clarity as possible allowing the gameplay to step forward. We've been teased at times for the large size of Ratchet's hands. From a silhouette perspective however, the hands continue to be our greatest tool in keeping clarity between Ratchet's body and the vast weapons he carries. Our central goal was to allow a large degree of freedom in the gun designs including size, shape, and function–how could he really carry a rocket launcher three times his size if he had small fingers?

In terms of Ratchet's connection with Clank, we purposely combined Clank's box body with the hourglass form of Ratchet's torso. This allowed us the physically layer the characters overtop of each other yet still retain some visual separation. Since the player tends to see the characters from behind, it became a huge motivation for us to keep Ratchet's ears out and Clank facing backwards. We found Clank looking directly at the player for most of the adventure created an immediate connection. By the end of the game we found this connection helped push both his personality and the illusion of life just a bit further.

Clank's shape counterpointed Ratchet by including boxy and round shapes (below). Even when the characters exist in the same space (above), visual separation is achieved. Clank's personality is evident even when he morphs into various gadgets (left). Ratchet & Clank TM & ©2004 Sony Entertainment

THE ADVENTURES OF
RATCHET & CLANK v. 1.0

CLANK   CLANK-PACK   HELI-PACK   THRUSTER-PACK   HYDRO-PACK

Various enemies designed by Guertin (below). Ratchet & Clank TM & ©2004 Sony Entertainment

Technically, my position on *Ratchet* was the lead character designer. What that really involved was defining the overall look and feel of the various character types within the universe. One of the major responsibilities was to work very closely with the design director at the time and examine the character descriptions to make sure whatever shapes we came up worked for the gameplay. I felt my role on the project was to incorporate as many ideas from the team as I could and put them into a visual form. With all the talent in the studio, it was important to include many of the fresh ideas bouncing around the office. To create a truly unique adventure, input is always so important, not only in character design, but in every facet of that game.

Towards the end of the project, as we moved closer to release, the major focus of the character department shifted to marketing materials. Many of the items included covers, point-of-purchase materials, posters, and any other assets Sony would need to market the game. As with any new property, there's a degree of uncertainty in how the public will react. It was a nerve-racking time for the team as we wondered how the game would fare amongst the crowded holiday season. Fortunately, a groundswell of support formed and people really began to enjoy the fast paced gunplay Ratchet brought to the market. As the initial advertising campaign came to a close, word-of-mouth continued to propel the title forward. That's the unpredictable aspect of this industry; if someone really enjoys an experience, they'll talk about it. You never really know until months later what the response will be so all any team can do is put everything they have into the project. The rest lies completely in the hands of the public.

While the movement was steady throughout the country, one of the largest boosts we received came from Asia. *Ratchet and Clank* became the only North American game to be bundled with the PS2 system in Japan. It was certainly an honor for the entire team to be part of such a rare opportunity. Since each country has unique sensibilities in design, humor, and subject matter, breaking into other cultures can be tremendously difficult. The bundle provided an unprecedented chance to reach new markets and players. Stacks of game boxes quickly filled many of the game stores throughout Japan creating literal walls of Ratchet merchandise. Posters lined many of the subway tunnels as shops created custom displays and playable kiosks for the game. It was truly inspiring to see and, as a result, we're fortunate to have a great fan-following throughout the country.

Thankfully, a few months after the release, we realized *Ratchet* had struck a chord with the gaming community. Many saw the game as breathing new life into the platforming genre and we found players enjoyed how the dynamic gunplay created a greater sense of freedom in conquering challenges. Yet, at the same time, we looked very closely at the aspects of the game people didn't enjoy. Issues such as Ratchet's personality and the game's relatively low difficulty topped the list. With the "goods" and "bads" in hand, the team prepared to embark on the sequel.

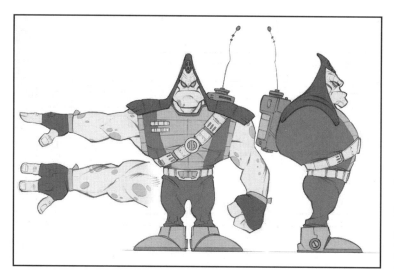

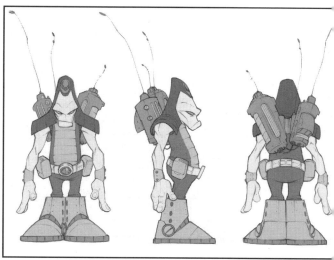

GOING COMMANDO

Unlike movies, the sequel to a video game tends to be highly anticipated. Since most of the core designing has been done in the previous incarnation, it allows the developers to expand on an already rich world of assets.

DAVID GUERTIN: Working on *Ratchet and Clank: Going Commando* was a great experience largely because we had most of the building blocks in place. It was a lot like creating your own playground and finally being able to play in it. With the creation of a firm foundation of art and technology, we were given the opportunity to really examine every facet of the game. In many ways we stripped the game down to its core so see what needed improving as well as which new ideas could be brought to the table.

We found ourselves moving forward on the sequel very quickly. Early on, we decided to attempt another November release providing only about ten months of true production time. In that respect, even with a majority of the art style established, *Ratchet 2* became much more of a challenge that its predecessor. To combat the sheer volume of work, the company almost doubled in size as we sought to create an even larger and more immersive game.

Organization became a primary goal to ensure the workflow could remain consistent. At that time, I was appointed to Character Director which involved designing characters as well as directing the overall process of character creation, including modeling and texturing.

Through consumer feedback, we began the project by addressing many of the criticisms of *Ratchet 1*. First on the list was the overall lack of difficulty. This time around, we wanted to be sure the players needed every weapon in their arsenal to survive. Since the majority of the game revolved around combat, enemy setups included more characters with greater intelligence. Villains could now hide, hunt in packs, and defend each other providing a new dynamic to the universe. Seeking a greater feeling of character growth, Ratchet 2 implemented a new experience points system based on those found in RPGs [role-playing games]. For the first time in a platformer, as Ratchet defeated enemies, he would gain experience which would eventually increase his hit points. The game gained a new layer of depth as players were given incentive to defeat *every* villain in the level. Progressing one step further, we expanded the experience system to include the weapons themselves. With repeated use, each weapon could transform into larger, more powerful versions, wrecking increased havoc across the level. In addition to creating a variety of action, players were encouraged to use every weapon to ensure their entire arsenal was upgraded.

Fortunately we found people really responded well to the changes. It was a charge for the team to get great feedback on the experience system and to see how excited players became over the weapon transformations. Overall the growth added a new depth to the characters and provided a continuous goal for the players.

Everything about the creation of *Ratchet 2* began with passion. I have never seen so many people pull together as they did to finish that project. There were times I wondered to myself, mostly around 3:00 am at the office, if it was even feasible to get everything done that we set out to do. With all the levels, characters, effects,

Conceptual designs for some of the villains in *Going Commando* (below). Ratchet & Clank TM & ©2004 Sony Entertainment

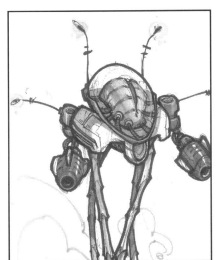

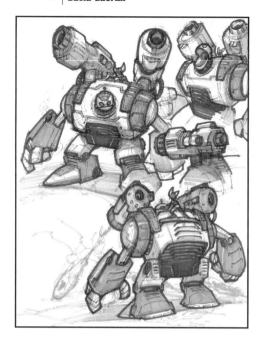

To create a more challenging game, the scope of the enemies became larger. These "bosses" became storytelling elements marking a player's progression: as the bosses become more powerful, the player must muster more fire power and gain more experience to continue the story. Ratchet & Clank TM & ©2004 Sony Entertainment

and movies it seemed we took on the impossible. Uncertainty quickly became the roughest part of the project. Yet with each focus test, the team could see how well everything was coming along. The late nights and stress were paying off and provided the surge of energy we all needed to pull everything together. In the end I think it came down to dedication and the need to create the best experience we could.

Whenever I tell someone that I make video games for a living, I tend to get the same look. Usually it's accompanied by "Wow, so you really get to play games all day, huh?" Sure the work is extremely gratifying, but in reality, it's also tremendously challenging. Making games is a business like many others. Millions of dollars are at stake with every project and there's a constant pressure to create the best experience you can amongst an exceedingly crowded market. Coupled with a constant race for innovation and implementation of new technology, game creation, much like cinema, continues to push the limits of entertainment. We do play games at work, though they tend to be our own as we search for corrupt textures, inefficient collision, slow framerates, broken occlusion, and elusive crash bugs.

As a developer, you don't pull your head above water too often and in some ways it's strange to think someone is buying the game. A couple months ago I was blown away by the gameshow *Jeopardy*. The show was hosting junior week and a young contestant was asked what he hoped to be someday. He responded excitedly with "I want to be the president of a video game company!" He told Trebeck his favorite game was *Ratchet and Clank* and began to ramble about the story and how the game worked. I can honestly say it was the first time it actually sank in that people buy what we make. And I think that's what it comes down to for most developers–sharing an interactive experience with as many people as possible.

TALENT, DRIVE AND PASSION

To Guertin, these are the ingredients to tell a video game story.

DAVID GUERTIN: Video games to me have always been a joint effort between the developer and the player. The game is simply not finished until it's played. I really see the medium as a tool in which you can tell a story while allowing the player to contribute to the overall outcome. Ideally, you allow the player to put their own feelings into the adventure–how aggressive or controlled they play, how quickly they react, how they focus their attention, the overall pacing–it's completely up to them. So you're still telling the same story, but the way they're experiencing the message is left to an individual's play style. That's probably one of the most interesting aspects that I find with games. With improved technology, interaction will only continue to increase and allow the player to become an integral factor in what that story is going to be.

One of the first lessons I learned in this industry is you cannot please everyone. No matter how perfect you imagine a design or gameplay concept to be, someone in the world will disagree. And that's OK. The best anyone can ever do is stand behind what they believe to be right. Far too often in the entertainment industry concepts are watered down in an effort to please as many people as possible. In many ways, when hundreds of people are involved and millions are at stake, an overall fear of failure will drive the project. Unfortunately, what's left is a homogenous mess lacking any real backbone, personality, or purpose. If you ever seek to have a viewer believe in a story, you have to first believe in the story yourself.

The key to creating an immersive adventure or believable design begins with knowing which questions to ask. What's the character's motivation? What's the overall goal? What are the results of succeeding and failing? Who carries the responsibility? What's the balance of good and evil? Is the environment cold, hot, aggressive, calm, undersized, vast, crowded, or open? By answering many of these core ideas, a designer can quickly develop a framework to push against. With defined boundaries, each character can be given a reliable rule set which can then be carried consistently across the imaginary universe. Even the most outlandish concepts can be given a strong foundation to be built upon creating the overall depth interactive stories require.

In regards to an artist building a portfolio for work, the first goal lies in knowing what exactly it is you would like to do within the industry. Each position, including design, animation, modeling, texturing, and programming require specific sets of skills. A motivated artist could be involved in many different disciplines, yet to break in, many times focus on one aspect becomes very important. Most companies, due to larger team sizes, are specializing positions. This is not to say if you begin as a character modeler you can't eventually move to design or animation. However, it's important to display a solid and refined skill to get through the door. In regards to character design specifically, I've found the best tool is being able to draw in as many styles as possible. You never know when a company will require something different visually. Some companies have ten simultaneous productions that often range from hyper-realism to complete cartoons, so you need to be able to handle that change and move with it. Also, speed and efficiency with quick sketches and full illustrations become vital within the production environment. You can never go wrong with a strong foundation in drawing, painting, and color theory.

Regardless of which position you're searching for, incorporating solid art theory is vital. For me, the concepts of contrast and rhythm dominate most the design decisions I make. Through contrasting shapes and color, variance can be created which will retain the viewer's interest. Many times, humor or surprises are born by contrasting against what the player expects. Over the last few years, I've found music theory to be a valuable tool to infuse rhythm throughout visual designs. Collaboration of shape can be closely related to the movements of song. Sharp notes or progressions compare well with aggressive, straight lines while smooth melodies represent soft curves. In many ways, while watching great movies, the organization of the score plays on of the most influential roles throughout the character design.

When everything is said and done, telling a great story or creating compelling designs comes down to passion. The best adventures will always have a strong heart which can only be brought by a creator who enjoys what they're doing. Many times, games can be a frustrating, tiresome, and competitive industry. Yet while reading fanmail or speaking with players around the world who have been immersed in the adventure, you realize, it's all worth it.

Ratchet & Clank: Up Your Arsenal for Playstation 2 is currently in development. Not only is *Ratchet 3* going to be bigger and more polished than its predecessors, but In this new iteration, Clank will have the chance to step out from Ratchet's shadow to star.
Ratchet & Clank TM & ©2004 Sony Entertainment

Jeph Loeb
on Comics & Hollywood

If you can make here, you can make it anywhere. The old saying was written about New York, but it's Hollywood that dominates our current culture. The budgets are in the millions, the casts can have hundreds and the production can involve thousands, but at its heart, the art of movie making is simply the act of storytelling.

Jeph Loeb was influenced by both comics and movies growing up, and does not feel that they are mutually exclusive. He attributes his career in Hollywood (he currently serves as Consulting Producer for Smallville, inset) and in comics to fundamental storytelling.

JEPH LOEB: My broadest influence would have to be my father, who by day wore the mild-mannered disguise of a stockbroker, which he was for 35 years on the New York Stock Exchange. As you can imagine, that may be the most boring job in the world to a child, but my dad had this way of talking about what he had done during the day, and making it sound like an adventure. "I was pulling into the station and I hopped aboard and there were only two seats left, and I sat next to a man who had very deep-set eyes, and wondered the entire time what was on his mind, what was he plotting?"

That was the kind of thing he did, without thinking about it. I don't think he lived in a fantasy world, he just saw life as an adventure. You could go to a boring old post office, or you could imagine it as inside a massive tomb where the walls are covered with pictures of criminals waiting to be captured, with bounties put on their head. It's how you see the world. So I first and foremost think of myself as a storyteller. But it never occurred to me that you could make a living out of it until two things happened in high school. One, my parents got divorced, which meant that my family was uprooted and I left Connecticut and moved up to Boston. And it also meant that I was without my father. So my pipeline for adventures was effectively shut off. But more importantly, what happened was that I realized that the world as a child was not necessarily something that you can count on. It wasn't such a bad idea to escape into your own little rabbit hole. Or at least this is the

way I've chosen to reinvent the history of my life.

So I don't think that it's any coincidence that the summer that my parents got divorced, my mother decided to take us up to Cape Cod and I found a small general store with a spinner rack. I had read comics when I was much younger, *Superman* and *Batman*. But I knew there was something different about Marvel Comics even when I was a kid. There was something much more grown up about them. I think a lot of it had to do with the fact that the stories were continued, whereas many other stories were self-contained. And there was a very large cast of people, particularly in *Spider-Man*, that you had to get to know. Superman and Batman were really pretty simple and had television shows that that filled in any gaps. So I found a copy of *Sub-Mariner #29* with Captain Marvel in the water, daring Namor to jump in, and Namor was sort of turned away, looking girlish, saying, "I can't go into the water, and I can't tell him why!" And I bought it, and I was intrigued because somewhere there was a footnote that said, "If you want to see more, be sure to check out *Iron Man #35*." So now I was on the hunt for *Iron Man #35*. Iron Man had just gotten back from a meeting with the Avengers; I didn't even know who the Avengers were. I found the Avengers, and there was Captain America and Thor, and pretty soon I was collecting everything Marvel put out. And pretty much I never stopped buying comics.

I soon found out that they were collectible things, and started bagging and boxing this enormous collection. My wife would very much like her garage back! So if anything comes out of this interview, if someone would like to trade the entire collection and give me some really, really nice Golden Age comics that would balance everything out, that would be fine. I love the idea of taking a hundred thousand or so comics and trading them for a half a dozen keepers from the beginning of Superman or Batman or Captain America. The good stuff.

Loeb generally feels that his current project is always his favorite work, but when pressed to discuss a comics project that stands out, he turns to Superman. "Certainly in terms of the impact that the work had, I favor *Superman for all Seasons*. By the time [the first issue] came to California, I had gotten over 500 e-mails, mostly from fans who called me, thanked me, or had written to me to say that this was the Superman that they remember from their childhood. I can't tell you how many told me that when they read it, they cried. Most of that was simply drawn from the narration from Jonathan Kent, Pa Kent. He talked about giving up his son to the world." Smallville TM & ©2004 Warner Bros.

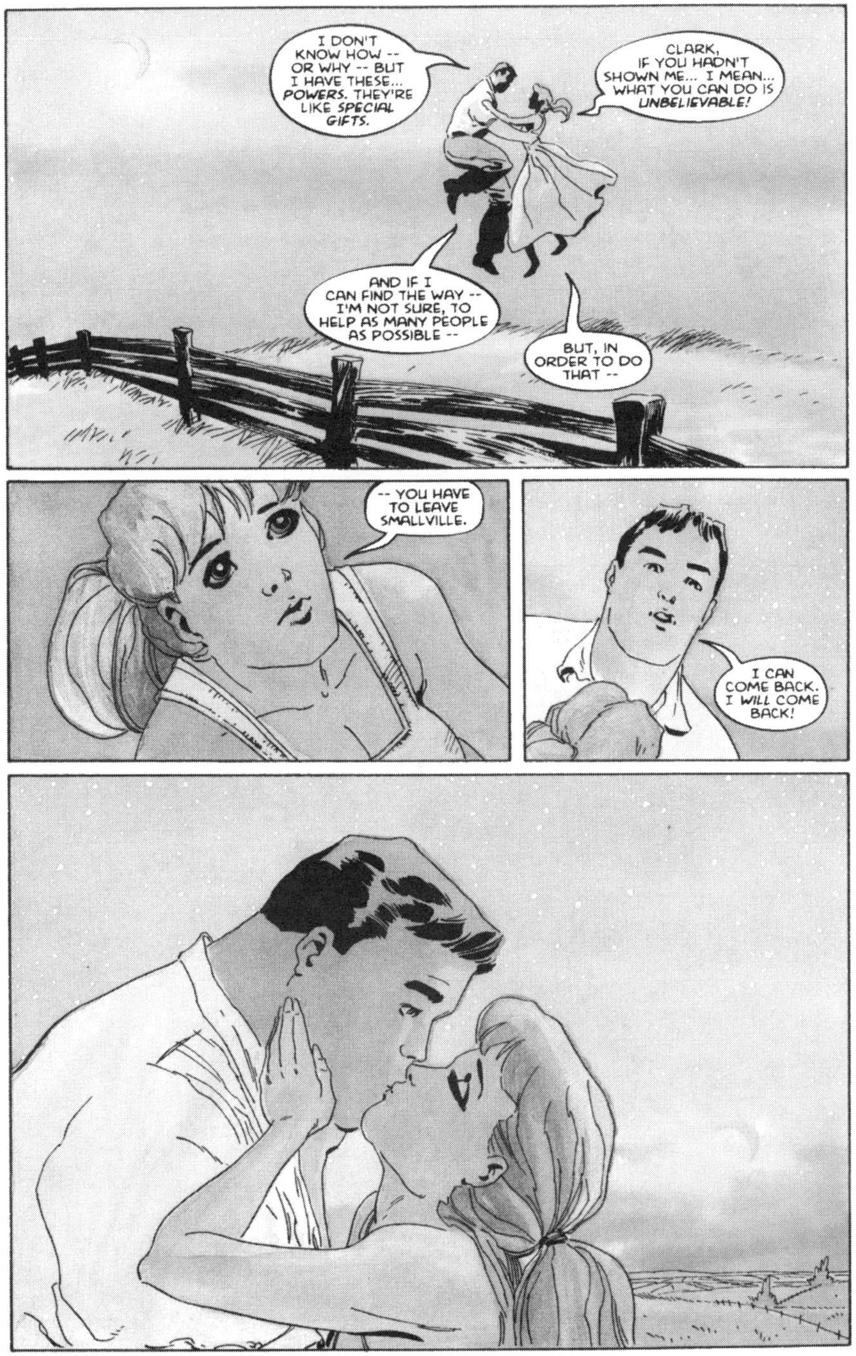
I DON'T KNOW HOW -- OR WHY -- BUT I HAVE THESE... POWERS. THEY'RE LIKE SPECIAL GIFTS.
CLARK, IF YOU HADN'T SHOWN ME... I MEAN... WHAT YOU CAN DO IS UNBELIEVABLE!
AND IF I CAN FIND THE WAY -- I'M NOT SURE, TO HELP AS MANY PEOPLE AS POSSIBLE --
BUT, IN ORDER TO DO THAT --
-- YOU HAVE TO LEAVE SMALLVILLE.
I CAN COME BACK. I WILL COME BACK!

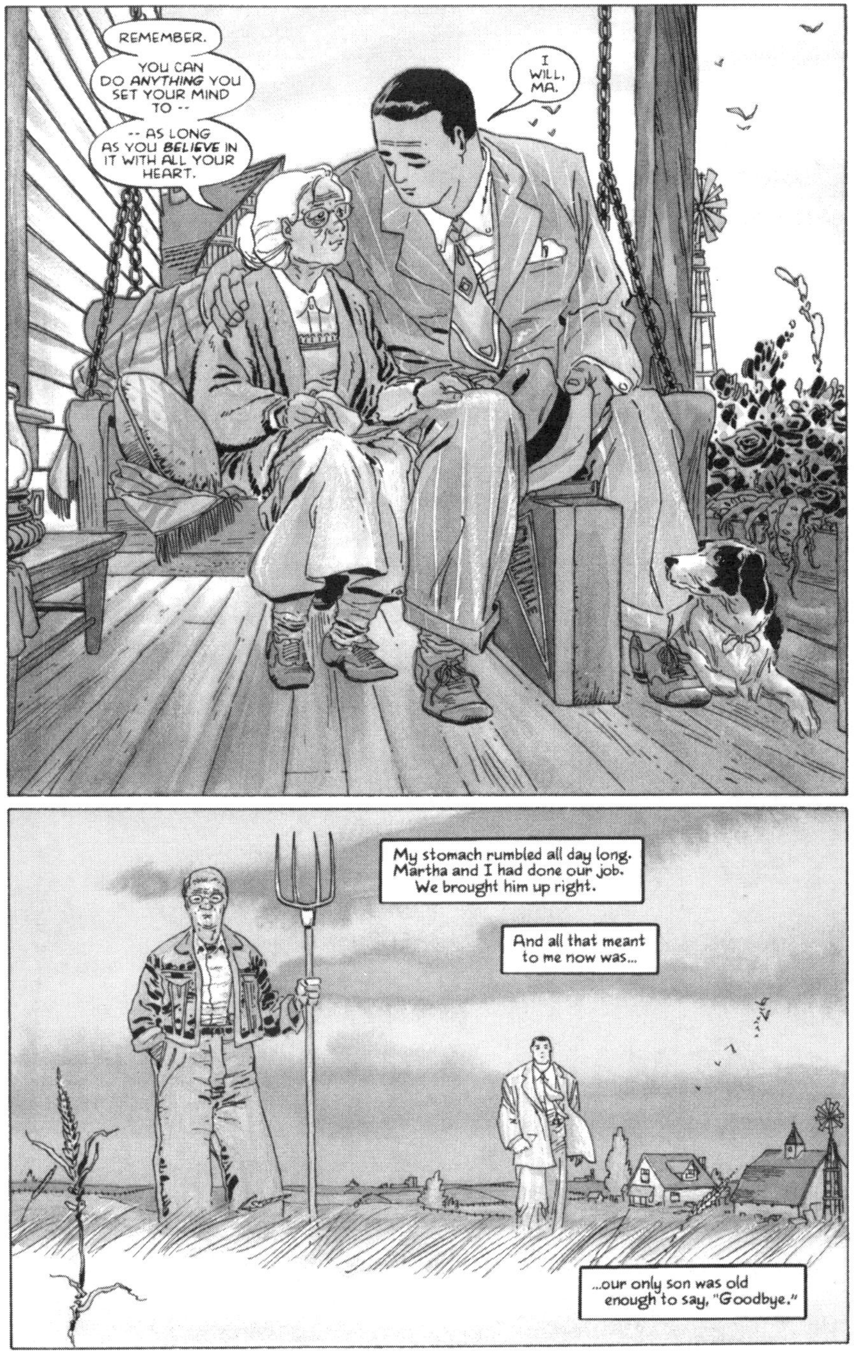
REMEMBER.
YOU CAN DO ANYTHING YOU SET YOUR MIND TO --
-- AS LONG AS YOU BELIEVE IN IT WITH ALL YOUR HEART.
I WILL, MA.
My stomach rumbled all day long. Martha and I had done our job. We brought him up right.
And all that meant to me now was...
...our only son was old enough to say, "Goodbye."

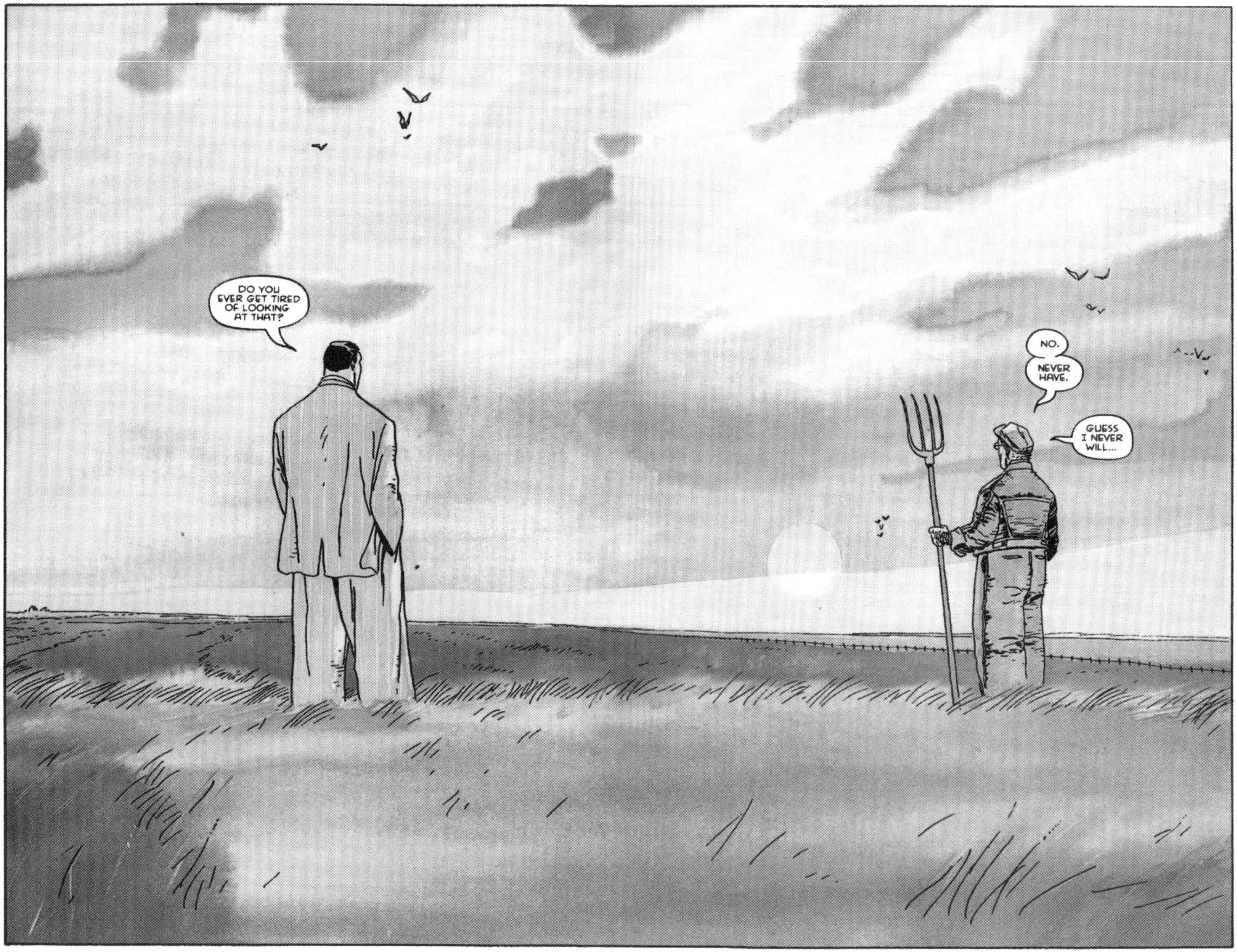
DO YOU EVER GET TIRED OF LOOKING AT THAT?
NO.
NEVER HAVE.
GUESS I NEVER WILL...

A Soldier in the Field

Before breaking into comics, Loeb broke into movies first. He earned his career one battle at a time, learning skills that allowed him to grow and move from one production to another. He has worn many hats–producer, director, even pitchman–but it is screenwriting that first captured his imagination.

JEPH LOEB: Being a teenager who reads comics didn't really have a "cool" factor to it. It was more of an "eughh" factor with my friends and girlfriends. On the other side, my parents had given me a little nine-inch, black-and-white Sony television. And Channel 56 in Boston would run Warner Brothers movies from the 1930s and 1940s every night at eleven o'clock. I soon was completely involved with Humphrey Bogart, James Cagney, Edward G. Robinson, and George Raft. And if you go back and look at that period, they weren't all gangster films–there were musicals, comedies, Westerns…fairly hilarious Westerns. But they were movies that were well-structured, and I quickly caught on that this was clearly a way you could make a living. And if you could tell stories and make it in the movies, that made a lot of sense. So I started to pursue that. I started to try to write professionally at a very young young age–at about tenth grade–mostly without having any idea what I was doing, but there were teachers who encouraged me.

Nothing really happened until I got to college. I went to Columbia University and found out that there was a film school and went there. I had some really interesting mentors in Paul Schrader, who did *Raging Bull* and *Taxi Driver*, and Milos Foreman, who won the Oscar for *One Flew Over the Cuckoo's Nest* and was a production assistant on *Ragtime* and *Hair*. It was a good learning experience. I had tried to write in film school and found it to be a very slow process. I knew that I could make a living out of it, but it wasn't as much fun as being on the set every day and being responsible for a big-time production. Basically, making it possible for the writer, the actors, and the director to realize their vision–everybody, brought together, was personally my first love and the thing I'm always drawn back to, because in many ways that is the purest form of storytelling. You're bringing together all of the elements and controlling all of the elements as you tell the story.

So I went to film school. I made a lot of connections. I came out to Los Angeles. I had written a screenplay in film school that had garnered some attention and got the help of Paul Schrader, one of my teachers and sent it to an agent. The agent called me up and said, "Come on out here." I flew from New York, then I moved. And then nothing happened, as it happens, in Hollywood.

I saw an ad in *The Hollywood Reporter*. It was for an assistant to a producer who was making television shows for HBO. And very early on, they started developing *Tales from the Crypt*. And being the comic book buff, I knew quite a bit about *Tales from the Crypt*. It eventually became the *Hitchhiker*, and that was the first thing I worked on. I worked on the pilot for *Hitchhiker*. I'm not credited on it. And I had a writing partner named Matthew Weisman, and we stayed on for a season of the *Hitchhiker* as story editors. And right around that time, a gentlemen by the name of Jonathan Dana, who was at a small independent production company called Atlantic Releasing that had

Teen Wolf, starring Michael J. Fox, was written, produced, and pitched by Jeph Loeb and Matthew Weisman, the first of their four collaborative efforts in Hollywood. Teen Wolf TM & ©2004 Atlantic Releasing Corp.

nothing to do with Atlantic Records. They had made a movie called *Valley Girl* with Nic Cage, with Martha Coolidge directing. They had made it for less than a million dollars and it made about thirty million dollars. They thought it was a good business to be in, and asked if I knew a story that they could make for about a million bucks? And I said, "Yeah."

I pitched them *Teen Wolf*. And they paid us $4,000. Scale at the time was $20,000. We shot the movie in 21 days. And we were really lucky that we got Michael J. Fox. To be truthful, they said to us, "We'll pay to write the script, and if you can get Michael J. Fox, we'll make the movie." Because they believed that Michael was going to pop. And we wrote the script, got it to Michael, and then met with Michael on a Sunday at the office building, because there was nobody else in the building, and talked to him about it. There weren't any producers on the movie in the beginning, it was just us. And then we picked the director, with Michael, which was a very, very strange way of working. But it was fun, because it sort of made us feel like we were in charge for about a half an hour. And Rod Daniel, who directed *Teen Wolf*, did a terrific job and really understood the humor of it. Michael was amazing.

And right around the same time, we kept going to meetings and we would pitch stories. So we would tell the story, and people would go, "That's a great story! Do you have anything we can read?" And Matthew and I would go, "Yeah, if you hire us, you can read the script!" We were naive in that area, and it wasn't until someone sat us down and said, "Look, you guys need to spec a script as a writing sample." And that's something that I always give as advice: 120 pages

can change your life, so sit down and do it. So we wrote *Commando*, and sold it for a lot of money to 20th Century Fox. And so, while we were making *Teen Wolf*, they were making *Commando*. And the following year, they both came out and were big hits. And when you have two hit movies in the same amount of time, that'll pretty much carry you for about ten years.

I remember being foolish enough to believe that everything we wrote would be made because of the first four things that we wrote, three of them got made. So I just thought that's the way it was going to be all the time. I learned rather quickly that most people in Hollywood make a living writing movies that never get made. I think if I've had any secret to my success, it's that I've tried my best to continually reinvent myself. So I've been a movie writer and producer, did pilots, and worked on television series.

I started my career in comic books while I was still doing movies. Then I got involved in animation and I learned how to do that. Now I know how to do that, so I sort of became a prime candidate to work on Saturday morning. That led to the *Buffy Animated Series*, because I knew how to do that and I was a fan of *Buffy*, and Joss [Whedon] was a fan of my writing in comics. It was all kind of moving together. Then *Smallville* called. There were people who said to me, "Do you think you could go from being a general to being a soldier in the field?" And I said, "You know what? How am I going to find out unless I try it. If I don't like it, I can always leave." It has turned out great. It really is an incredibly fun place to work. I get paid all day long to talk about Superman!

Loeb ventured into the world of animation, directing the *Buffy the Vampire Slayer* animated series for Saturday morning. Concepts by Eric Wright. Art © Mutant Enemy. Buffy the Vampire Slayer TM & ©2004 Twentieth Century Fox.

OFF TO FAO SCHWARTZ

Even though Loeb had written Hollywood features to his credits, he still loved the comic book art form. So when the opportunity to write for comics appeared in the form of the Challengers of the Unknown, *Loeb jumped on board.*

JEPH LOEB: Yes. I broke in unfairly. I didn't pay my dues. I didn't struggle through conventions and wait on lines and try to get to know people. It was through Elliot Maggin that I first became aware you could make money out of writing comics. I was also fourteen at the time, so it didn't occur to me. For someone who collected comics and for someone who loved comics, I was naive as to how comics were made. I knew that Stan Lee wrote them all, and that was basically the way I looked at it. Even though I knew that there were people like Gerry Conway and Len Wein and Roy Thomas and others were running around, I didn't understand what they did. Even though every comic had a caption that told me what they did, those were only names at the bottom of the credits page and I never really studied them. But I met Elliot, and Elliot was the first one to show me what a script looked like. I wrote my first script and sent it to him, and he ended up giving me some very good criticism of it. The Superman story I had written degenerated into the ending of *Spider-Man #100*, literally. My favorite criticism he gave me was, "You can steal from novels, you can steal from plays, you can steal from television. The only thing in comics you can't do is steal from other comics." That was pretty good advice!

But like I said, I was twelve or thirteen. I didn't know what the hell I was doing, but it was fun, and I still have those old scripts with Elliot's notes. I treasure them.

Cut to, years later, I was working at Warner Brothers and the people who were producing the *Batman* movie wanted to develop the Flash. I had a friend who worked there by the name of Stan Brooks. Stan was in charge of the television division, but knew of my love of comics and talked to the guys over on the feature side and said, "Look, if you're gonna get a writer who's written features and knows comics, you should talk to Jeph Loeb." I met with those guys and they then introduced me to Jenette Kahn, who was then the president at DC Comics. The Flash movie never happened. It was one of those things where it just collapsed under its own weight. When it ended, Jenette called and said, "You had wonderful ideas for the Flash, you obviously love this medium. How would you like to write a comic book for me?" It was like Santa flew up to my house and said, "Sorry I missed you this year, but if you want to go to FAO Schwarz with me, I'll buy you anything you want."

I hopped in the magic sleigh and went off. She told me to meet with Dick Giordano, who, up until that point, I had only known as the inker who inked Neal Adams, who was my favorite artist. In actuality, Dick was VP-Editorial and he called me and said that Jenette had said that I was going to write a comic. He asked me what I wanted to do, and I answered, "I'd like to write a Superman." This is the point where my naivete took over, because I thought comics were like in television, in that there were a regular team of people, but that there would be some freelance assignments–that you could do fill-ins and stuff like that. I didn't realize that it was such a closed boy's club, that if you were going to do a fill-in, you generally go to people who

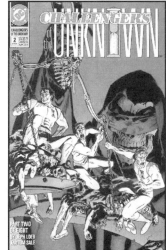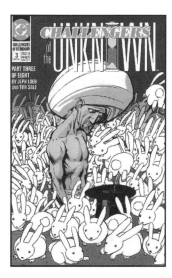

Challengers of the Unknown TM & ©2004 DC Comics

Jeph Loeb first collaborated with Tim Sale on the *Challengers of the Unknown*, an eight-issue mini-series in 1991. It's interesting to note that the covers featured the art of several top illustrators in the comics field, including (left to right) Brian Bolland, Michael Golden, Kyle Baker, and Matt Wagner...

also work in comics.

So he told me that "No, Superman was taken."

What about Batman?

"No."

I said, "Well, before I go through the entire Justice League, maybe what you ought to do is give me a list if there is such a thing?" He said, "Actually, we do, we have a list of characters that are available." So, he sent me a list. I called Dick back and offered, "I really think that I could do something interesting with the Atom." Dick says, "We have a proposal for the Atom." This goes on for like an hour. I pitch a character and he tells me that character–who is on this list–is not available! I'm literally just going down the list crossing names off, and I finally got to *Challengers of the Unknown*, which I didn't know at all. I said, "Well, what about *Challengers of the Unknown?*" There was sort of a pause, and he says, "No, we don't have anything for that." "Fine. I'll write a *Challengers of the Unknown* story." So I went down to the local comics shop and said, "Do you have any *Challengers of the Unknown?*" And there was a box. I think I bought the entire run for five dollars, which, of course should have told me that not a lot of people were interested in The Challs. But that didn't matter. I was going to write a comic book!

At the time, Grant Morrison's *Animal Man* and *Watchmen*, Frank Miller's *Dark Knight*, all these books had come along and by the early Nineties, heroes were really being deconstructed. The idea of four guys who went out and found adventure, which is probably what I would do now, was the furthest thing from my mind. So I told a story about how a bunch of guys who in their twenties had been superheroes, but when they turned forty, looked back on their lives and said, "We won't want

to do this anymore." They go off their separate ways, and good and bad things happen to them, and then something happens that would have to be brought back. It was what we'd call a "critical success." In fact, it was such a critical success that when they got the numbers of issue #6 of an eight-part series, they called me and said, "Do you think you could wrap it up in six?"(laughs) I said, "Actually, I can't, because they aren't even back together yet, they're still off by themselves." So that was one of the things I was grateful to DC for, that they didn't pull the plug, they let me finish it out at eight. What's funny is that I periodically go back and read those comics, it's the only thing that Tim and I have done that hasn't been collected. Ironically, the entire series, with a previously unpublished 12-page epilogue, will be collected this year. The epilogue is very much of its time–Guy Gardner and Ice–hilarious. Some of it, I think, holds up well. Some of it I can look at it and see that I didn't understand the craft yet. That's sort of the point though. I would hope that one would get better as you keep doing it. Otherwise, what's the point? Sometimes it's harder, because you used up all those tricks. Sometimes it's easier, because you've become very, very comfortable with the voices. Kind of like an old jacket.

When asked about his favorite comics work, Loeb has his standard answer, but he also has a soft spot for a certain Blue Boy Scout.

LOEB: My favorite work is generally what I'm working on right now. It would have to be. If I don't believe in what it is that I am doing, this being the best thing that I'm doing, then why am I doing it? But there are certain things that I've done that I have great affection for, mostly because they remind me of a time. Any comic that I've worked on, I

can remember distinctly the conversation I had with the artists that led to the making of every single page, and with Richard Starkings, the letterer, just because he's so important to all of my work.

But when I get down to specifics, certainly in terms of the impact that it had, as a creator, I go easiest to *Superman for all Seasons*. Oddly enough, I just didn't know the power of the character I was working on. I had worked on Batman, I had worked on the X-Men. I had certainly received great success, great financial reward. I had gotten the kudos of the community, as they say.

I had a very different expectation for *Superman for all Seasons* and as it turned out, not a particularly smart one on my part. We were working on the third chapter, and there were four chapters. This was just about when the first issue was about to go on sale. I'm talking about something that was in the warehouse, about to go out to stores the next morning. I had what's best described as an anxiety attack. I called up Tim Sale, the artist and my partner and said, "I've made a gigantic mistake." He said, "What do you mean?" I said, "Look, I've read the first issue a hundred times, and I've read it again today, and nothing happens." He said, "Well, that's sort of the point." I said, "No, no, no... nothing happens. You don't even see him in his costume until page 47. And even then, he just says, 'Thanks. My mom made it for me,' and he flies away. That's not a Superman comic. That's a story of young Clark Kent. Nobody cares about Clark Kent, nobody cares about Smallville." He said, "What do you want to do?" I said, "Well, this sort of gentle, namby-pamby kind of way that we've been telling the story has to go. I think we should start over with issue three, throw out the opening of it, and just have ten pages of him fighting Mxyzptlk and Brainiac and the Prankster and just give the kids the action that they're craving! Let's turn it into an action movie! We could have Lois narrating, talking about, 'As the months went by, Superman had this great reputation,' and this is what it should be." There was a long pause and Tim says, "Why don't we wait until tomorrow and see whether they like the first issue." It was one of the few times I've been very grateful for the Internet. The first issue went on sale in Europe first and then in New York. By the time it came to California, I had gotten over 500 e-mails, mostly from fans who called me and thanked me or had written to me to say that this was the Superman that they remember from their childhood, and that I had really touched something. I can't tell you how many told me that when they read it, they cried. Most of that was simply drawn from the narration from Jonathan Kent, Pa Kent. He talked about giving up his son to the world.

That spoke to my own particular fears, being a recent father myself, of what it would be like to have to give up my own son at some point. It was the first time I was kind of aware of how much Superman is a part of the world's conscience. Beyond all the other characters, it's a story that everyone knows, and they don't even know how they know

it. They've just been told it at some point during their lives, and it's just become part of it for them. They've seen the movie or they've seen the animated series, or if they watch *Smallville*, you can take that "S" symbol, you can walk into a village in China or Afghanistan or wherever you want to go, and show it to somebody, and ask them, "What is this?" And they will tell you "It's Superman." If you put the bat symbol on something, somebody will look at it and say, "It's a bat." They wouldn't necessarily say, "That's Batman." When you have that kind of penetration into the collective consciousness, it's a tremendous responsibility in terms of what you're telling for stories. I'd never, ever, felt that before. The X-Men were far more popular, in terms of sales and in terms of the comic book audience. Batman had a tremendous, loyal following, and a cool factor that Superman doesn't have as well as league of movies that are much more recent. Out of this fear that no one would respond to the way I had chosen to tell the story in *SFAS*, I learned something very valuable about the power of the character in real life terms.

Superman For All Seasons was a labor of love and a project unlike any other for Loeb. A poignant story, Loeb was able to reconnect many fans to the power of the Superman character. In 1999, Loeb was nominated for an Eisner Award as best writer for *SFAS*. Superman TM & ©2004 DC Comics

SMALLVILLE AND SUPERMAN

Loeb has worked on both the Superman continuity for DC Comics as well as the hit show Smallville *for the WB Network. It is his work with the Superman comics that got him noticed by the network, but it is his understanding of the hero that is Superman that makes him valuable to the show.*

JEPH LOEB: I am very grateful that Al Gough and Miles Millar have on many occasions noted *Superman For All Seasons* as one of the inspirations for the show. I was thrilled when they asked me to come on the show. I remember when I first met them, I said, "Look, guys. You've gotta do one of two things. You've either gotta hire me, or you've gotta stop making the show, because I keep thinking of episodes and I can't do anything with them unless I work for you." So they decided to hire me. I think it was cheaper then the years of therapy I would have had to endure. *[laughs]*

The joy of working on *Smallville* is that the audience knows how the story ends. What they don't know is the journey. You're emotionally invested from the moment you meet this guy, because you know Clark is going to be the greatest hero the world has ever known. So any time that he tries to deny that, the audience is yelling at the television set, "No! Don't!" The genius of what Al and Miles brought to the legend was making this friendship between Clark Kent and Lex Luthor, which existed once upon a time, and then was erased from modern continuity (don't get me started). We know that Lex Luthor, like young Anakin Skywalker, is going to grow up and become the greatest villain who ever lived. Every time Lex takes a

step towards the dark, the audience is yelling at the television, "No! Don't!" It's because you care. Because, to be perfectly honest, if the audience doesn't give a crap about the characters, then whatever they do is just noise or eye candy. You're not invested.

Now that we're end of our third season, we've actually told sixty-six of these stories. I'd like to think we have a pretty good sense as to what the characters are going to be doing. Our cast has grown tremendously, both as actors and as people. The kinds of stories that you tell, the emotional weight of the stories, the burden that Clark is feeling, sort of goes beyond the "I'm different because I'm a teenager," the tales of struggling with the real realities of what it is to be sixteen or seventeen. Instead, it's "What the hell am I going to do with my life?" Which is dealing with a whole other level. It's those kinds of passages in life, those things that happen to you, each of those are changes in the human condition. The things that are important to you then and the things that are important to you when you're a grown-up are just remarkably different. It's always fascinating to me that even when you're caught in the period itself, you're thinking, "What could be more difficult than this?" There's your future version of yourself looking back at you, going, "What an idiot you are!" From a high school point of view, the amount of time and energy is spent on whether or not people like you as opposed to what you're going to do in your life, is hilarious. Because once you get to be forty, you realize that as long as you're not bothering anybody, what people think of you is not really important. It's really much more about what you're doing and how you're spending your day and the joy of being alive. There is that thing that I tend to write about heroes, that the

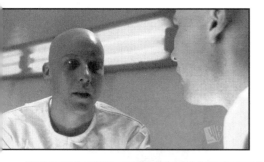

In *Smallville*, Loeb particularly enjoys exploring the friendship of Clark Kent and Lex Luthor. It is Luthor's decent into villainy that drives the series. Smallville TM & ©2004 Warner Bros.

arrogance of youth, that you think that you are going to live forever and then you start to realize you have been here for more days than you have left. It changes your perspective tremendously regarding how you're going to spend the day.

When I think about what Superman's greatest weakness is, it's not Kryptonite, it's not magic, it's not any of the physical manifestations of things you can become weaker from. It's that his heart is made of glass. He may be made of steel, but because he always wants to believe the best in everybody, he's heartbroken all the time. Humanity is constantly, on some level, letting him down. Back in the day, when he had a relationship with Lois that wasn't a marriage, it was much more classically-illustrated in the sense that here was this woman he loved who loved him as Superman and ignored him as Clark Kent. She actually thought Clark was a bit of a boob. Clark was a victim of his own small-town upbringing. In many ways, she saw him for what he was. He was this wonderful Norman Rockwell painting come to life, but I loved that she was very much like Rosalind Russell in *His Gal Friday* who could look at him like, "You're in the way!" That was very hard to do when they were married. You continually had to be challenged as a writer. I remember coming in at the beginning and being told by Superman Editor Eddie Berganza: "Just because they're married doesn't mean they're dead." The challenge however is to the fifteen-year-old reader, I don't think you want to see your mother and father out there making out. How can you make their marriage an exciting part of storytelling within the limitations of what you're given.

Generally, you are hired on a book because it's having a problem. You bring with it a fresh perspective. You're working with an icon, and the audience wants to read something. I've argued, I believe successfully, that in DC comics, all anybody really wants is a really good Superman, Batman, Wonder Woman, Green Lantern, and Teen Titans book. The rest is cream cheese. Over in the X-Men world? They just want two good X-Men titles. They have nineteen of them, not all good. But I remember really specifically that right around the same time, both the Superman and Spider-Man books were suffering. Both had had long-time teams and in editorial's opinion, a change was needed. They brought in Joe Kelly and I [at DC] and they hired [J. Michael] Straczynski on Spider-Man, to sort of say, "Fix this." Both franchises had a similar problem in that the previous regime had gotten to a place where you could say...in an effort to try to reinvent and reinvent and reinvent, they'd taken this really handsome apple tree and put ornaments on it, until finally it had become a Christmas tree. Now, I really liked those stories and I'm not in any way running down those people. The result was still a tree, but you couldn't see the apples anymore. All I did was take the ornaments down. For example, when I came in, Clark Kent no longer worked at the *Daily Planet*. Nor did Lois, nor did Jimmy, nor did Perry White. I had it easy. I put 'em all back to work! People immediately stood up and said, "Ah! This is it! This is what we want!" Meanwhile I watched as Straczynski did essentially the same thing with Spidey. He just dusted off all the stuff that came before it and went back to essentially the core of the character.

Smallville is the tale of how Clark Kent grows up. He deals with issues that average teenagers face, even though he will eventually mature into the world's greatest hero. Smallville TM & ©2004 Warner Bros.

What Is A Producer, Anyway?

Jeph Loeb offers the answer to the mystifying question of a producer's role.

JEPH LOEB: We live in an environment of absolute magic where you can make movies like *Lord of the Rings*, and even commercials for PlayStation, where visually anything is possible. The computer has now made it possible for dogs to chase a man up the side of a building and have it look absolutely real. Or dragons, or whatever it is that your imagination can come up with. It's just incredibly expensive.

As we learn every week on *Smallville,* we try to continue to tell the exciting adventures of young Clark Kent and do everything your imagination allows within the limitations of what the budget and production itself can handle. You have a certain number of days in which to shoot the show. You can't be thinking that it would be great if the United States Army decided to roll into Smallville and quarantine the entire place and put everybody into a giant concentration camp. It'd be a great episode, but who's going to pay for that? How are you going to find the days to do that? There's a reality you need to constantly be aware of, and that's somebody has to make this show.

Many people think of a producer as the one that goes out and gets the money. That's somewhat true, in the sense that the producer goes to the studio to get the money, but it's not as though you're rounding up old ladies in the afternoon like they did hilariously in *The Producers*. You're basically responsible for the entire production. Still, I consider it to be storytelling. You may have to look to the writer in order to know what it is you're telling, you may need to look at the director to how it is that you're going to tell it, but the actual production itself, the coordination of all those elements, falls to the producer. Ultimately, if the picture is over budget or under budget, it's the producer's responsibility. He's the father of the story, he's responsible for all of the people there. I guess the director is the mother, and I guess the writer is the one who is the biological mother since he or she has to give the script away, to beat that metaphor to death.

One of the elements that has always been on my mind is what comics do better than any other art form. It's because they are a truly unique art form. They translate a story through single, two-dimensional images. If they're told really well, you don't need a lot of dialogue or narration, because the pictures are telling the story. There's a lot of mumbo-jumbo about how comics go all the way back to drawings on cave walls. I suppose that that's a way of doing it, but in the strictest sense, stories that are contained on a piece of paper, pulp, sequential art in boxes is very much a unique art form. When you get to the superhero, it's a uniquely American art form, which has now been embraced by the rest of the world. Given the fact that we can lay claim to jazz and McDonald's, I think it's important that there also be something else that we're proud of. That way of storytelling, to me, is very much a cousin to motion pictures and television. Look at storyboards from which the director works, they are essentially comic books. They are two-dimensional panels that take you from image to image, that help the director tell what he has in his head. Those two cousins have been running around in my head since I was a kid. I am very lucky in that I get to utilize both my left hand and my right hand in order to create stories.

As creative producer for *Smallville*, Loeb is "the father of the story." Here, Clark learns from Jonathan Kent that all of his decisions are not necessarily black-and-white and he must be flexible in dealing with problems. Smallville TM & ©2004 Warner Bros.

THE RIGHT HAND

Jeph Loeb learned from movies and production first. From these origins, Loeb learned that the craft of writing should be an organic process, able to be molded and tweaked. In writing for comics he adapted his style to be a collaborative effort with the artists, thus utilizing both strengths to tell the best stories.

JEPH LOEB: Well, I think that when you compare, in terms of the actual writing, both comics and movie scripts and television scripts, they have a single thing in common: they are blueprints. No one reads scripts for pleasure. I mean, you could, but it's not a form of storytelling that exists for any other purpose other than to create another piece of medium. What I've likened it to very often is that you are an architect and you are drawing blueprints. Well, blueprints are great and fun and wonderful to look at, but if they don't build a building out of it, they have no function whatsoever. If you're writing a comic book and no one draws it, or you're writing a movie or a television show and no one films it, then you've certainly gone through an awful lot of foreplay not to be able to close. In the motion picture business, that goes on all the time. It's affectionately referred to as "development." The odds of getting a movie made are like winning the lottery. But television, particularly if you're on a series, you have to screw up pretty badly if they're not going to shoot your show. You're pretty much writing something that is going to get made, so you'd damn well better write it in such a way that it can get made. Which is another area that you have to be very, very astute about. One of the things I think divides people who want to write screenplays and television shows and people who actually do it, are the ones who actually do it understand that someone has to make this thing.

With comics, you actually can get away with pretty much anything. You can say the moon explodes and large chunks of it come raining down on the Earth and you blow up the Sphinx and crack the planet in half and the rivers can run with blood. I can't tell you how well it's going to get drawn, but you are only limited by your imagination and by the talent of your artist. Toward that end, there's no budgetary restrictions. But you again have to be realistic. You can't say, "Ten thousand soldiers with spears and helmets march over the hill and come down upon the city of Rome as they race to attack." Unless you've got three hundred pages to tell that in, it's going to look a lot like you don't want it. That's part of the gift of the storyteller. You have to be able to understand the limitations of the medium you're working with. I don't ever see limitations as something that holds you back. I actually see limitations as, these are the gifts that you are given. If that's a magic lasso and a cape, well, then use them. Don't be standing around going, "Gee, I wish I had a shield."

I really do believe in structure, in particular the three-act structure, the sort of classic storytelling of setting up your story with the classic questions: What does your hero want? What is keeping your hero from achieving that goal? And how does your hero finally achieve it? It gets interesting when the thing your hero wanted in the beginning of the story is not necessarily what he wants at the end and that's all due to how he made the journey. Superman is the perfect example. As a boy, he only wanted to fit in and to a certain extent, be rid of his powers. As a man (or in the third act of the story) he's come to terms with the superhero aspect of his life and finds he can do both (as Clark Kent *and* Superman). Tim Sale has said that I am best when I get very emotional, when I write stuff that's

Tim Sale and Jeff Loeb won the Eisner Award in 1998 for their work in *Batman: The Long Halloween.* Batman TM & ©2004 DC Comics

intended to make the reader feel something in their heart. It's certainly something that I reach for. I know that it's touching me as I write it. Like most cynics, I'm a great romantic, and like most romantics, I'm a great cynic.

Richard Starkings, who is a world-class letterer and a universe-class friend asked me once who do I write for when I write a comic book. I didn't understand the question. He said, "Well, do write for yourself? Do you write for the reader? Do you write for your editor? Who do you write for?" I said, "Well, I hope that I'm writing for everybody." I certainly am trying to make the story reach as many

As a writer, Loeb tailors the type of stories he tells to match the artist's strengths. Tim Sale is an incredible designer of light and shadow, and captures both a dark mood and Gotham City's noir atmosphere in *Batman: Dark Victory*. Batman TM & ©2004 DC Comics

people as I can. But if I had to start with who I'm writing the story for, I'm writing it for the artist. I try, in every case, to work with friends, because I know what their tastes are. But if they're not my friends, we start to become friends, because we spend a great deal of time talking about what it is that they like. Artwork is a completely subjective thing; you either dig it or you don't. I can look at something and think it's good, but when I deal with Mark Chiarello or Tim Sale, who understand illustration in a way that I will never understand, they see something I don't. It's like the old saying, "I don't know if it's good or bad, I just know what I like." If I can get my head around it, and I can see what this person seems to do well, I spend a long time talking with them before we even start the project about what it is that they do well, what it is they like to draw. I try to tailor the story towards their strengths, meaning that if I'm going to write a story for Tim Sale that has Batman in it, it's not going to be the same story that I give to Jim Lee, who has Batman in it. They have different strengths, different abilities.

Now, I can't put that into specific terms, because it's not a formula. It's very much magic. I don't believe in trying to interpret magic, because once you start to interpret magic, it's no longer magic. If you innocently see a magician pull a rabbit out of a hat, you go, "Wow, that's cool! He pulled a rabbit out of a hat! I'll never understand it, it's magic!" Well, if you go backstage and the magician says, "You have to understand that there's a false bottom in the hat, and I've got the rabbit stuck down there, and when I reach in, I lift up the bottom, and then I take the rabbit out," well, it's not magic anymore. It's just science, or something that is very practical. How what Tim or Jim or Michael Turner or Ed McGuinness or any of the enormously talented people that I work with say to me in terms of what they like to draw, how I interpret that, I can't explain.

I'm starting to tell a story that by the time this comes out will have already been printed, which is the reintroduction of Supergirl into the DC Universe. We didn't want to tell the story until we had the right artist. When we found out we get Michael Turner, I knew he was the right artist, because I knew two things: whoever is to draw this arc is going to have to draw Supergirl, and Wonder Woman. Michael happens to draw the most beautiful women in comics. That made sense to me. I knew that when Jim and I set off to write and draw Batman, that where Jim excels is in the details. What we both agreed was that we wanted to tell a more classic superhero story than a dark, moody, film noir story. A dark, moody, film noir story is something that I would tell with Tim Sale in a minute. Jim loves to draw Batmobiles and Batcycles and mechanics. Tim loathes it.

One of the great truths about working as a writer is that you spend an enormous amount of time alone. Anything that will ply you out of your solitude is very much a narcotic. Look at any writer's phone bill, it's quite enormous. Comic book artists, are the same way, unless they happen to be in a studio with other people. They're sitting in some office or basement or attic space, and they're spending all day drawing. Being able to sit on the phone and talk to somebody for any length of time is quite rewarding. That's how working with an artist becomes a partnership. I mean, when it's really rockin' 'cause you're having a good time, then it's great fun, and really nothing thrills me more than when it comes across the fax machine and the computer when the pages are done. I generally get to see them two or three in a bunch, because artists tend not to send one page. They don't want to give the impression that they've done very little work. Two or three pages leave a different impression. The writer, of course, gets to cheat, because he actually turns in an entire script that takes far less time than it does to draw. The writer always gets to go, "I wrote the whole script, why can't you draw the whole book?" (laughs) Even some of the speediest guys I know, it's hard to get a lot of pages done and it takes an enormous amount of discipline. When it's not working, when the pages aren't coming, when the script isn't finished, it can get fairly tense, mostly because it's a constant hand-off between who has control of the baby.

The process has a number of steps. Leaving out whatever step involves the editorial process, it begins with writing the script, which is very detailed in my case in terms of what's on the page. Very often I write what the camera shots are. I do write in a fairly unique way in the sense that I never learned how to write a comic book script that looks like a comic book script; I only used the program that I use for screenplays. Each panel becomes a scene description. Each line of dialogue goes down the middle of a page, as opposed to in comic books, where they go to the left of the page when you type it out. It also helps me when I look at the dialogue down the middle of the page, I actually get a sense of how big the balloons are going to be. What I give the artist is commonly referred to as a full script, but I still see it as a blueprint. My artist reads it, and I've written eight panels and they can do it in three, fine. Similarly, if they see three and they want to do it in eight, that's fine. The only thing I try to get them to do is read the dialogue so the artist knows what the expressions are going to be. If it's a conversation between two people, just realize it needs to be paced. If the artist decides to put one head on the left side of the page and one head on the right side of the page, then the dialogue had better flow from the person on the left to the person on the right. You can't cross balloons. The artist needs to set it up so the dialogue flows properly. Some do, some don't, and it's up to me to come back later and re-jigger the dialogue to have it fit the images.

For the most part, 90% of what I write, people draw because I have thought it out, I have laid it out like camera shots,

and nothing is taken for granted. I really do try and make a page drawable in a day. After the pencils get done, they go out to the inker to get inked, I generally have a copy of them at that point, and at that point I can start to lay out where the balloons are going to be placed on a page. Often once it's drawn, and it's usually within, I'd say, three weeks of when we've started, something else may have occurred to me, in terms of what the scene should be. As long as it flows for the story, I keep 75% of what I've written originally. I'll go back in and fuss with the dialogue and get it all together and the placement for the page, where the balloons go, and do a script

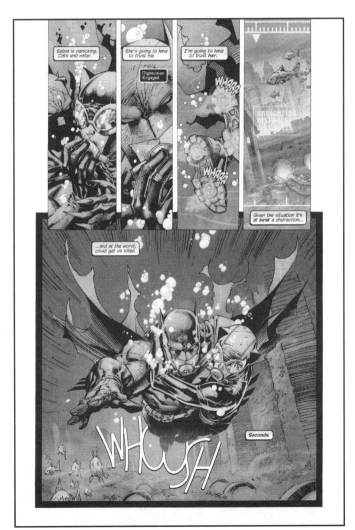

which is only dialogue. That goes off to Richard Starkings, who then letters the book. After that, it's out of my hands. I tend to take a look at it again when it's all done, before it goes off to the printer. That's just because my editors have been very generous with me. But once it leaves me, it goes to the letterer, it generally is the responsibility of the people in production and the editor to make sure that it actually becomes a comic book.

I never really understood, although it's actually quite common and people still do it, the idea of writing full script and then giving it to an artist, and then letting the editor do the placement of the script, and the writer not looking at the art. It seems very strange to me. Obviously, it works, because there are so many people who do it. There certainly aren't many comics where I'm going, "What's going on on this page?" But I just think it's better to go back in and make sure. It's a little bit like in television, going back in for a looping session or ADR to sort of make it work better. Because when you finally see the film put together and you realize there's a big long pause, you better put a piece of dialogue there.

Very early on I went to work with DC and I was with an editor who I did not get along with. When we started working on the story, I said I'd like to call the artist, and he said, "Why?" I told him, "Because I think it's important that we talk about how I see it, where it's going, help him through it." He didn't like that at all and told me, "I think it's a bad idea. In my experience, whenever a writer and an artist talk, the artist gets more confused. If you have something to tell the artist, you can tell me, and then I'll tell the artist." I tried to explain that's not going to work for me. He didn't care. I got

the artist's phone number from somebody else and called him. (laughs) The editor and I had very much a different way of working. I don't know that it's right or wrong, it's just different from the way that I work. I'm lucky enough to have editors who sort of allow me to go the way that I go, and even more lucky that people buy what it is that I write, so that the editors who I do work with don't pull out all their hair. It keeps me working. Look, it's like anything else, there will come a time when it doesn't work. At that point, hopefully, I have enough fail-safe systems, and signed written agreements with various writers and artists that say, "If this happens, come to my house and shoot me in the head rather than make me go on and embarrass myself."

I think when you keep making stories that are intended to be summer tent poles, to use a movie term–and that's sort of where they've placed me now, both at Marvel and at DC–that you're given a lot more leeway. There's a certain expectation that what I'm doing will meet with the financial expectations of the company. That results in their feeling like I can go and do what I do best. I'm lucky to be in the handful of people that get to go and do that. I don't kid myself. I know that there will come a time, and it may be tomorrow, that it all collapses. There certainly are more people out there waiting for you to fail than there are people to cheer for your success. That's just the reality of any artistic field. They always like kicking a man when he's down. Hopefully I will leave the building long before that happens.

"With comics, when you deal with real emotions, you run the risk of becoming sappy and cliché. But I don't shy away from that. You can look at the movies in the Thirties and Forties and it's all about repartee, just bouncing dialogue off two people. That's one of the things I'm most proud of in *Daredevil: Yellow*–it's what I describe as a romantic comedy. Every now and then a comic book breaks into this and I like being able to take that challenge. I lean toward love stories largely because it's too easy [to write] a character to go out and hit something." The covers to *Daredevil: Yellow* painted by Tim Sale. Daredevil TM & ©2004 Marvel Characters, Inc.

THE BUSINESS OF MY CHOICE

Comics have never been as popular to Hollywood as they are now. You can tell stories through comics, television, and movies. But each medium tells its stories in an individual way—the key to your story's success is to understand what makes each medium unique.

JEPH LOEB: A reporter asked Raymond Chandler once, "What do you think of what Hollywood has done to your books?" Non-plused, he replied, "Hollywood hasn't done anything to my books; my books are up there on the shelf." That's really what it's about. It's a hard, hard lesson to learn. Everyone wants to make the best movie. That doesn't mean it's going to look like the comic book. They need to know that *American Splendor* and *Ghost World* are quite extraordinary. The development process is such that they can try and protect the source material as much as they can. But, they made two X-Men movies and the X-Men don't wear their costumes. That's pretty straight ahead saying, "We can do whatever we want." And you know what? They're pretty good comic book movies. I really like them. They're very well-crafted, they're very well-thought-out. They are true, in many ways, to the characters. But they're not wearing their costumes.

If you can't accept that going in, then don't sell your comic. It'll always be yours. No one will ever do anything to it. The best example of that is Bill Watterson could have made, and still could make, more money than anybody has ever made in their entire lives by selling Calvin and Hobbes. People would love to make that into a movie. And a television series. And a cartoon series. And a, and a, and a. But he sits in his house with his two cats and says, "No."

If you owned a property and wanted to see it translated into movies or television, there really isn't a better time. On every level, this field has, for so long, been best exemplified by the Comic Book Guy on the *Simpsons*—loathsome, heavyweight, bearded, unkempt people who hide in their mother's basement. Those of us who have created comics, are now very sexy to Hollywood, because clearly the genre, for now, makes money. You start to include *Star Wars* and *Matrix* and *Lord of the Rings* into that realm, which I do, you realize we aren't going anywhere.

Going all the way back to how they are cousins, one of the best parts about being able to sell a comic book movie is that when you bring in the comics (and in some cases the statues and the posters and the toys and everything else), the people in the studios "get" it right away. They look right at it and go, "This is what he's gonna look like, this is what he looks like when fire comes out of his eyes, and this is what he looks like when ice comes out of his mouth. And he's a man, and he's kind of sexy, and there's sexy girls in there." They "get" it.

I came from that world and went into comics. I didn't go the other way around. I am now seeing my friends going for that world. But some of these people are in for a rude awakening. Writing in comics, you talk to your editor and you say, "I think what I'm going to do in the next three issues is this, this, and this. This is who he's gonna fight." The only thing that you may bump into is, "Well, you can't use the Penguin because they used the Penguin over in *Detective Comics*." "Okay. Well, suppose I could use Two-Face?" "Okay, that's cool. You can do that." You go away, you write the script, it gets drawn, and somewhere between three weeks and six months later, it's on the newsstand. There it is, hello! Television is very much the same way. You write an episode and, depending upon scheduling, probably six weeks, ten weeks later, you're on the air. What you wrote, there it is, you can see it. Ten million people watching. You're at a movie, most cases it's two, three years before it comes out in a movie theater. You don't get that same instant gratification, and you also don't get that same sense that you're going to be there for the whole ride. My friend that's a writer in movies said to me, "All you do in movies, as a writer, is wait to get fired." That's not a great way to work. Because in television and comics, all you do is wait for your story to come out, and hopefully it comes out great.

Part of the oddity of working in movies and television and comics is you tend to hang around people who work in movies and television and comics. You don't get the same kind of immediate reaction that you have from when you talk to old friends, people you knew in high school or in my case, friends who are not in the business who get to say, "It must be so great to work in show business." It's not hard for me to remember how lucky I am. I hope I never take for granted that I'm lucky enough to work in the business of my choice. One of the things that I like about what I do is that every so often, the project I'm working on ends. I get to go out and find something new and it starts all over again. A new group, a new crew, a new story and all the new challenges. That's when the fun begins.

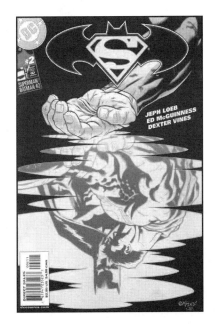

"Now I'm working on *Superman/Batman*. It's just great fun being able to tell the fall of Lex Luthor and the return of Supergirl…stories that really will have an impact on the entire DC universe. And that's not something I really went looking for, but I'm very proud of the work that we've all done. If it has any kind of legacy to it, that's great." *Superman/Batman* #2, written by Jeph Loeb, illustrated by Ed McGuinness. Superman, Batman TM & ©2004 DC Comics

Chuck Wojtkiewicz
on Comics & Storyboards

Storyboards are used to plan the narrative sequencing of visual productions like Websites, video games, and video and film production. Every major commercial, music video, television show, and motion picture relies on storyboards to plan for the camera, the actors and a variety of elements used in production. A good storyboard artist can establish the scene, move all of the actions, and plan for props or effects on the screen.

Chuck Wojtkiewicz has had a long career in comics, but finds the challenges and rewards in storyboarding and pre-producing film and animation (Rockfish, inset) both satisfying and rewarding. His roots are in comics, even if he never knew what was on the covers of what he read.

CHUCK WOJTKIEWICZ: I was one of those kids who always drew pictures, from kindergarten on up. I constantly drew the robot from *Lost in Space*. I thought it was the coolest thing. I just couldn't get enough. I'd build little clay models of it. Teachers finally asked me to stop doing it, but I just wouldn't. My grandfather would crustily remind me, "Artists stave to death, boy!" My dad, who ran a neighborhood tavern, would barter with people for all sorts of things and one guy would come in with shopping bags full of comics that had the covers torn off. Back in the day, magazine dealers could tear off the covers of unsold comics and send them back to the distributor for a refund. Well, the guts of the comics got dumped in recycling with newspapers. This

friend of my pop's worked at the homosote factory in Trenton, New Jersey, where I grew up. Homosote is a kind of particle board made out of newspaper. Well, he'd bring my bartender dad a couple of shopping bags of comics and my dad would slip him a beer or two, I guess. As a result, we were drowned in comics as kids. Thanks, Dad! We didn't know what the hell the covers looked like for the most part, but we loved comics. My fate was sealed at that point.

There was a candy store at the corner by my elementary school; you could go in those days with twelve cents and buy a regular comic book, a quarter would land you one of big ones–specials and annuals. Ah, that old spinning rack! The first book I remember ever seeing and buying was an old Viking Prince comic, believe it or not. He was standing boldly in the prow of his ship and there was this giant, white arctic snake rising menacingly out of the storm-tossed sea before him. I thought, "Wow!" and plunked down my pennies–the first of many. The Fantastic Four really stood out in my childhood. The first book I remember being able to read was *Fantastic Four Annual #1*, "The Sub-Mariner Conquers the Human Race." I've always loved the Four–and Jack Kirby's phantasmagoric art style, and it's just a wonderful thing those characters are still around–so cool. My good buddy Mike Wieringo is drawing them now!

Chuck Wojtkiewicz entered comics as a penciler. The following pages are from original pencils to *Secret Files of the Legion of Superheroes*, #2. "I most enjoy drawing comics about kids. Kids express themselves so dramatically, so effusively–it suits the way I like to act out in my drawings...heck, in everyday life! Here's a selection from *Secret Files of the Legion of Superheroes #2*, in which our youthful charges fight to survive and escape the doomed asteroid on which they've been marooned. I particularly enjoyed this sequence because it had all the challenges a comic book penciler could want: a large and varied cast; a complicated panel layout; a unique setting; and lastly, action to spare. The writers deftly focused on each of the many characters in the successive panels of this, the culmination of the plot. I had to include the primary players and as many of the doughty crew as possible in each panel as they battle (no kiddin') zombie alien apes." Note the detailed layers of each composition–foreground, middleground, background, extreme background–a colorist's dream...or nightmare.

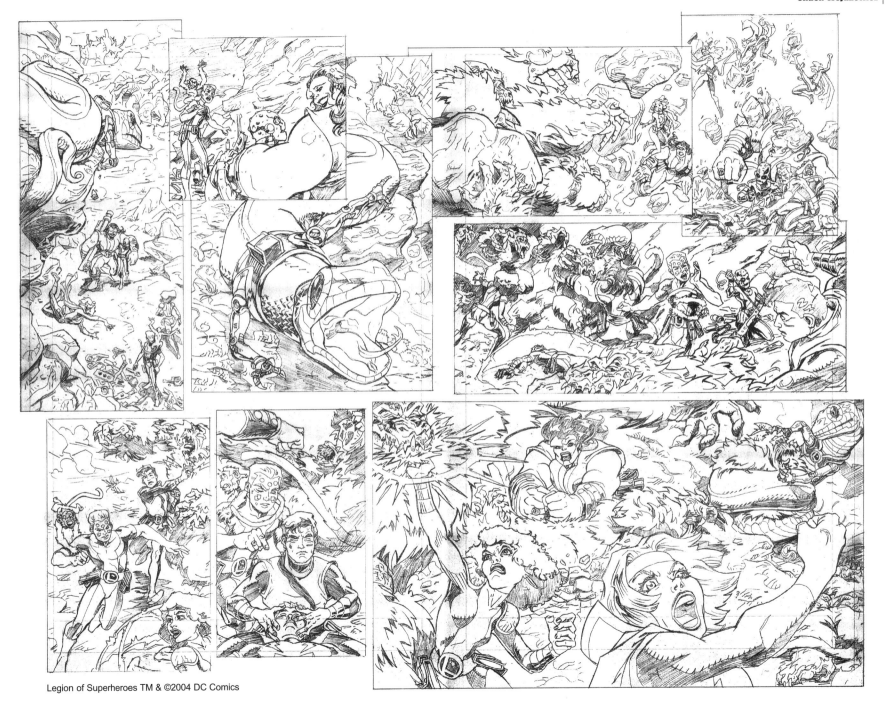

Legion of Superheroes TM & ©2004 DC Comics

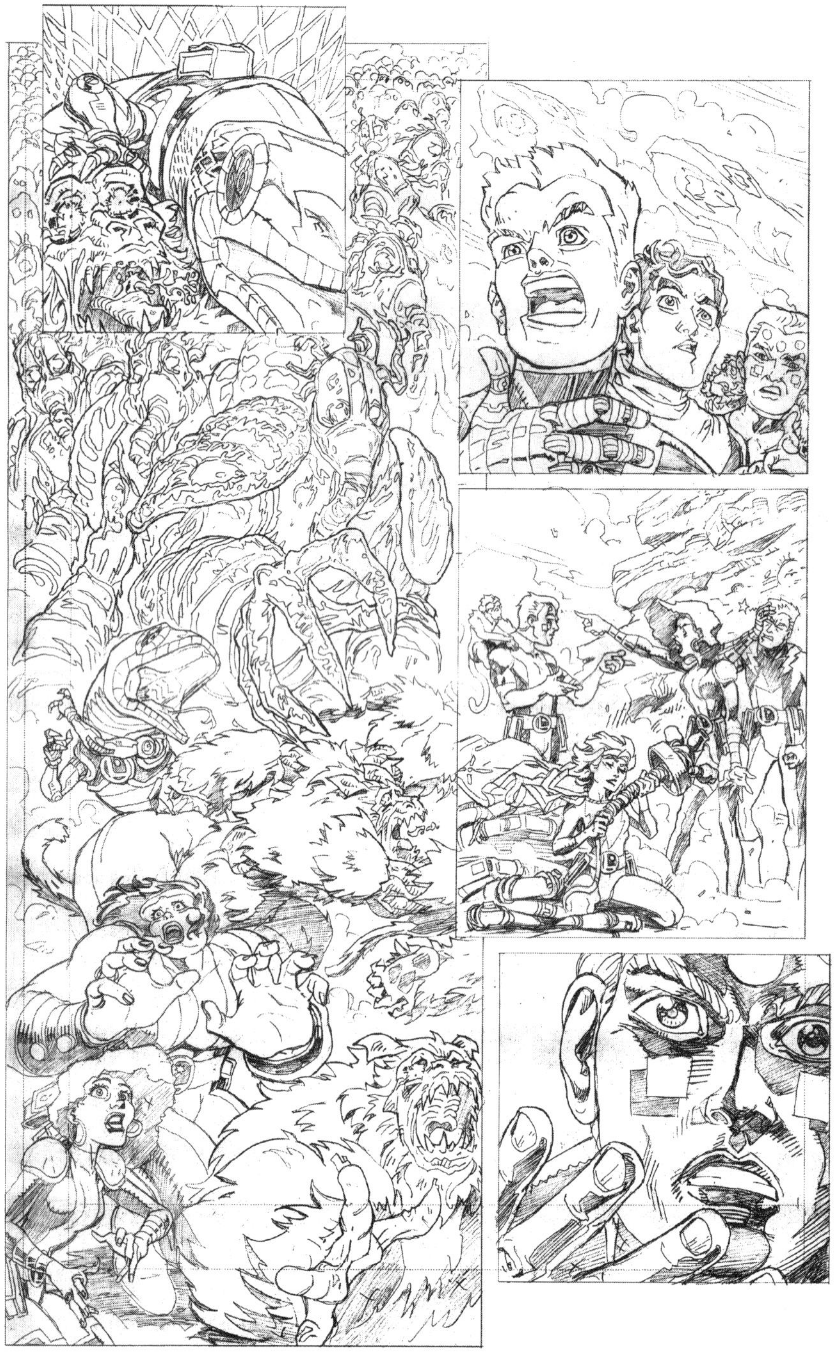

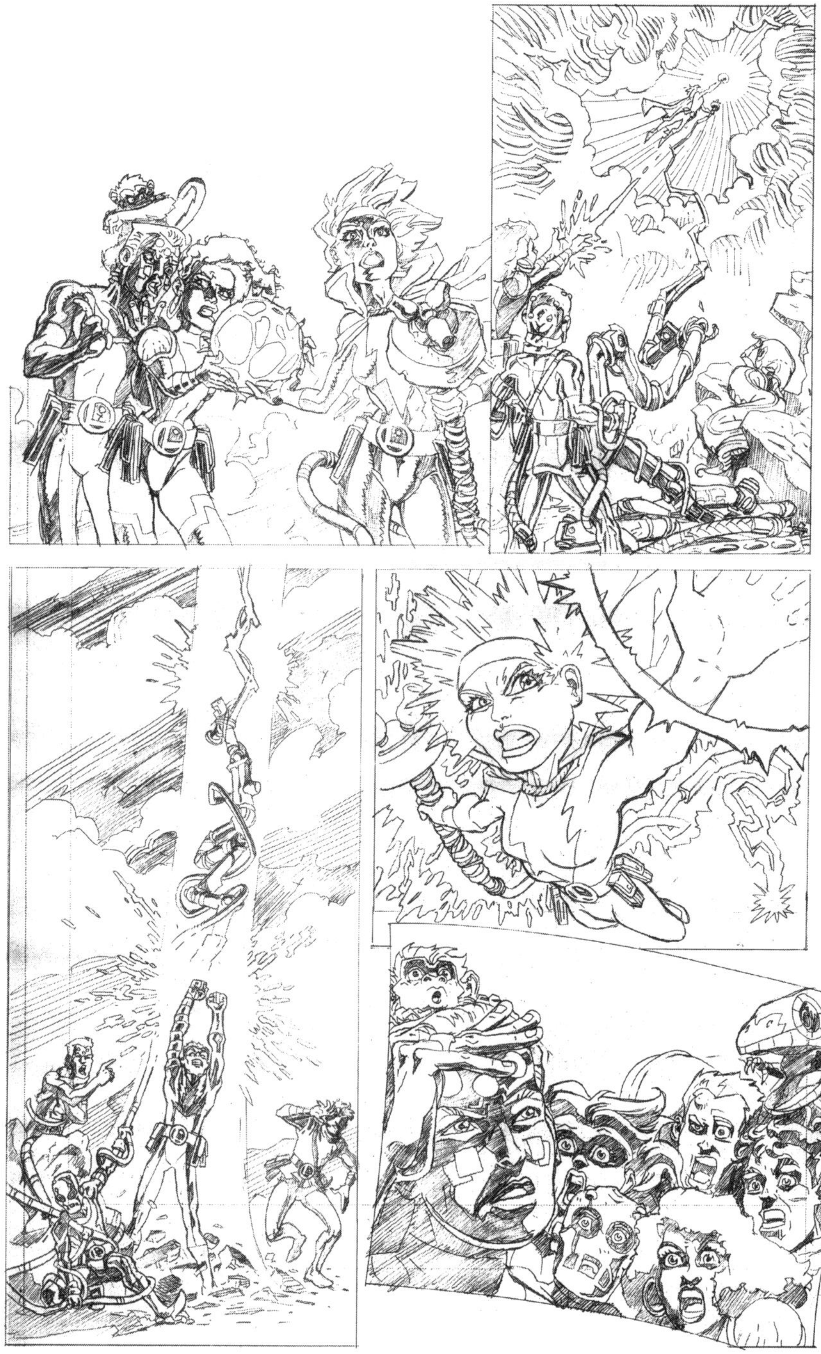

YOU CAN DO ANYTHING

As soon as Wojtkiewicz decided he wanted to draw comics for a living, he found himself networking the conventions to drum up work. Comic cons are a unique phenomenon in that other professions do not hold conferences to bring together industry luminaries to talk shop and share ideas. Cons are great opportunities to test your readiness as an artist as well as build up a portfolio.

CHUCK WOJTKIEWICZ: Y'know, I used to love to draw comic strip characters out of the newspaper when I was a kid. I copied Ryan's "Tumbleweed", stuff like that. And I realized, "Hey, y'know, you can do this kind of thing." Then later on something clicked. I can't quite remember when. I think it was about seventh grade when a friend of mine was drawing funny comic strips about one of our teachers and I started drawing strips as well. As a teen I blundered across a comic book convention…at a mall! As my buddy and I gaped at the legendary Ernie Chan painting a *Conan the Barbarian* cover with some dirty-looking little nubs of pastel chalk, I whispered, "I could never do anything like *that!*" And my friend said, "Sure you can, Chuck. You're really good. You can do anything." What he said! Much later I had the good fortune to meet Ernie and I told him of this pivotal moment. "That's a nice story," he intoned quietly as he sketched away.

I started doing a weekly comic strip in college—I just loved doing it so much. Surprisingly it caught on! I was at Duke University to study Marine Zoology, but I realized that science didn't really appeal to me as a career. So I thought maybe I could go into anatomical illustration—after all, it's a related field that is still "science"—I wasn't cheating my education and my "real world" goals. After enough contemplation of a lifetime spent "drawing guts", I just said, "Screw it, I would hate that." I studied art full time. I determined that I was going to be a Marvel or DC comic book artist. I hammered away until I got good enough (I certainly didn't start out that way). Eventually I got in.

I figured out how to get started by reading magazines that suggested doing sample pages to show The Powers That Be. I went to comic book conventions, showing the pages around, just like ernest would-be professionals do. I showed some samples to William Johnson, who was drawing *Daredevil* at the time. He was a guest at a comic con in Raleigh, North Carolina and he liked them, for the most part. Some guy who was watching and came up to me afterwards—he said, "Hey, a friend and I are publishing a comic book called the *Southern Knights*. I think you'd be really good at it. Would you like to draw the comic?" I said, "Yes!!!" So I did a sample page, then I sent it in. They called me up and said, "Hey, would you like to draw the book?" And I said, "Yeah, I'd love to!" They said, "Good, because the script is already in the mail." Well, there I was drawing *Southern Knights*—my real comics job. Henry Vogel was the guy who was writing it. I can't remember the last name

of David, the letterer (sorry, dude!), who had actually first seen my work. I was a total newbie, and in my opinion, it was pretty horrible fanboy-level art. It's all still in print, and it all still comes back to haunt me at shows when collectors bring up those issues for autographs. "Can you sign this old comic?" I'm always reminded that you have to start somewhere. From there on out, I freelanced as a *true comics penciler.* It was a quarterly book, which was great because I was pitifully slow, and I was getting the princely sum of ten dollars a page for pencils. I worked for these guys for many issues–it was the great black-and-white boom, and then that kind of petered out

I supported myself working a "regular job." I would draw comics at night, weekends, and holidays. After my run on *Southern Knights* I went on and I worked for such luminaries as Solson Publications–drawing a ton of stuff for them–and the pay wasn't much better. I worked for First Comics, I did a few fill-ins on *Dreadstar*. My first big break was with TSR Comics, drawing Buck Rogers, which was *fun*. That was my first full-time gig. I had actually been laid off from my old newspaper job. Buck Rogers came along at the right time, like the U.S. Cavalry. There I was, drawing *color* comics; it was great. I was also going to bigger conventions. Dave Dorman convinced me that I needed to go out to Chicago. After Chicago, I started going to the San Diego Comic-Con. I met Neil Pozner from DC Comics, their submissions editor, and I got a tryout from him. That led to me getting a nice interview with Brian Augustyn and I started drawing the *Jaguar* for Impact Comics. I also worked for Jim Owlsey (now the writer known as Christopher Priest). After the Impact line was closed down I went back to working for Brian drawing *Justice League*, and that was the main bulk of my career at DC.

It was a dream come true. The money was great for a guy living out in the woods of North Carolina. I used to tell people that I had the best job in the whole world, and I meant it! Comics are a good way to go.

Working as a storyboard and concept artist for Blur Studios, Wojtkiewicz still finds himself crossing paths with comic book characters in the most interesting ways (top to bottom): a storyboard for a Batman theme park ride, a picture frame concept for the Spider-Man ride at Universal Studios, and a Hulk concept sketch for a toy commercial pitch. Batman, Joker TM & ©2004 DC Comics. Hulk TM & ©2004 Marvel Characters, Inc.

ARTAMUS STUDIOS

Creating comics can be a solitary existence. Often times, a comics creator works in an attic, basement, or third bedroom turning out an amazing amount of work to make publication deadlines. However, artists with similar tastes and goals can come together to create a studio. In this environment, the creative dynamic can lead to wonderful work and experiences.

CHUCK WOJTKIEWICZ: The studio was a great experience. It was Rich Case who actually approached me with the idea to team up and fight crime, I mean, form a studio. He was sharing space in an artists' co-op with a bunch of fine "arteestes." He said, "Hey, Chuck, you oughta come up here." I hemmed and hawed, wondering about paying extra rent and coming out of my comfortable little shell. But eventually we shook hands and said, "Well, let's get a bunch of guys up here." So I called Mike Wieringo, and Jeff Parker, who was a local, jumped in, and Craig Gilmore, and John Lowe, who I had worked with. And before we knew it, we had a studio full of guys—and left the arteestes in the dust. Scott Hampton, Casey Jones and later, Dave Johnson parked their drawing boards in the hallowed halls of Artamus. It was great fun. It lent us a sense of legitimacy in the industry. We were a bunch of professionals working together, watching each other's backs, helping each other along, and editors and publishers seemed to get a real sense of security with that. We were a regular item on the Rolodex when it came to people looking for artists to handle projects because they knew we had a thing going on. Having the constant artistic input, and the resources of the other guys—their libraries and

such—as well as their varied and awesome talents—it was just great. We also had the networking aspect in full swing. We had access to other artists, editors and inkers and colorists, that kind of stuff. It was a big learning experience, a good time to become a seasoned pro and figure it all out.

We could jump in and at least buck one another up when times were tough, and there were many times when you'd help somebody out in a tight spot with a difficult panel, maybe ink a line here and there, a panel or two. I did some layouts for Mike Wieringo, because he was getting just pasted with work—people still can't get enough of that guy. I was just looking through an old notebook the other day and came across a few things I had collaborated with my buddies on. I put everything in spiral-bound books. Here was my little layout, and there was Mike's finished job. I drew in some of the background elements and it all worked out really nicely—Mike made his deadlines and we all had fun—and got paid. That kind of thing was artistic comradeship at its best.

Wojtkiewicz has the artistic freedom to create many character types in a variety of styles. He is influenced by different genres, including classical art, sword and sorcery, fantasy, science fiction, and manga. Empire Earth TM & ©2004 Sierra On-Line, Inc.

MOVING ON UP

As fun as comics can be, in the end, it is a business. Like any other field, the comics industry goes through good and bad times. During the down times, it is important to note that many comics creators develop a wide range of skills while doing comics. Successful sequential artists can apply their skills to a diverse range of opportunities.

CHUCK WOJTKIEWICZ: When the comics industry had its great big crash, everything went south and sales of comics dropped. Marvel did their ill-omened thing with their own distribution system that killed many comic shops. Work dried up. DC relaunched *Justice League*, with Batman and Superman: the original team, characters I didn't have on my team roster. They cleaned house and all the guys who worked on *Justice League* earlier…well we couldn't get arrested at DC. It was a shame. Later on they killed off or modified all my original takes on characters, which hurt. Well, it's their clubhouse and it was fun to play in it while I had the chance. I eventually went back and I did a bunch of other stuff for them, so I can't really complain.

I started doing stuff related to comics and outside of comics. Because I was pretty good at rendering stuff with an eye to the sculpted, 3-D format, I started doing toy design and souvenirs for the Marvel theme park. It led into doing more varied concept work. My friend Dave Johnson found himself swamped, and he gave me a call one day. "Hey, these guys at a computer animation company want me to do some robot designs, but I can't do it, Chuck. Can you help me out? They want me to get somebody to fill in." I said, "Sure,

let me send them some stuff." And I talked to a guy named Tim Miller at Blur Studio, and it's where I work today. Thanks, Dave!

As time passed more guys moved out of Artamus studio. John Lowe went down to Savannah to study, and later to teach, and Craig Gilmore moved down to Atlanta. He was closer to family, and he got into the animation industry. As comics work petered out, I could see the writing on the wall. I had to make a choice between comics and concept design–concept was fun and paid really well. Comics seemed pretty much closed to me at that point.

Freelance concept design was paying so much better I moved more toward that consciously. I could see that Blur was growing and it was a going concern, so to speak. During a phone call to Blur's *main man*, Tim Miller, I artfully insinuated, "Well, y'know, Tim, if you ever want a full-time concept artist, I hope you will consider me." And he called one day and made me an offer I just could not refuse. At the same time, my wife was fed up with her job and was ready for a change as well, so we made the plunge. It was a painful decision indeed to leave Artamus, because it was my comfortable little home away from home and the boys were my dear friends. As a studio, we were down to four guys, and I thought, "Well, if I pull out, will it knock the whole house of cards over?" It did not, but eventually the three remaining became only two, and now they have closed the studio.

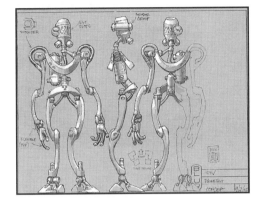

From "The Robot" in *Lost in Space* to his first concept design job at Blur Studio, robots have been a fascination for Wojtkiewicz. Some robot concepts done at Blur Studios. All art and characters TM & ©2004 their respective owners.

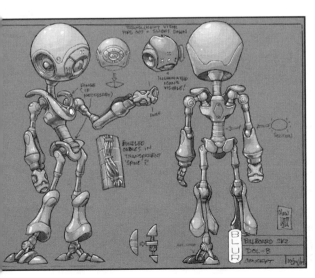

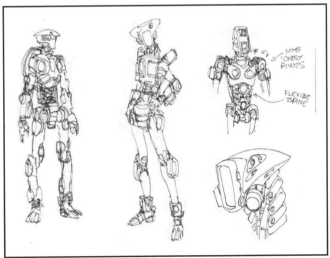

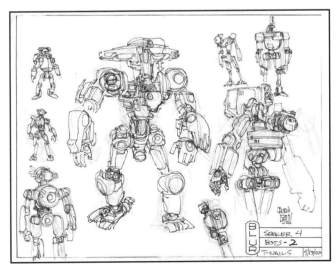

BLUR STUDIOS

Already coming from a successful studio environment, Wojtkiewicz understood what made the experience of working with other artists enjoyable. Blur Studios had a similar environment conducive to artistry and camaraderie, but on a larger scale. Working with creative people trying to do the most creative work possible was an intriguing possibility.

CHUCK WOJTKIEWICZ: Tim Miller, who is one of Blur's principal partners along with David Stinnett and Duane Powell, is our creative director, and he always pitches the studio as run *by* artists *for* artists. We'll turn down work that would not be fun. For example, a major theme park wanted a ride film in 3-D, and though it was a very tempting project monetarily, had a big scope, and would be fairly high-profile, Tim just could not bear to tell us that we would be animating dancing candy bars for six months. He always said that he would rather die than work on *Hello Kitty.* On the other hand, we have guys who really like cartoony animation and we're working on a Disney project. We also have guys who would not want to touch that kind of thing with a ten-foot pole. You can request to not be on a project and Blur'll respect that.

We do a lot of what I like to call the "bloody flying head" stuff for video game cinematics—you know, the sword-wielding barbarian cyborg schtick. There are guys who like to do compositing effects in feature films, combining live action and CG. It's a really healthy atmosphere that way. We don't have any "suits"—non-creative executive types—to muck up the works. On the whole, everybody is creative. Our IT guys are extremely creative in their own right. There are many

bugaboos that pop up in the production of large CG features—our IT guys power through technical glitches and ever-changing production demands like ninja masters. Anyone who watches TV has seen the ever-so-cool efforts of our motion-graphics team.

The Blur experience is like Artamus Studios times ten, because we're now up to 75 people, and we've got people from literally all over the world. We've got a chap from South Africa, we've got a guy from Finland, and others from Brazil, China, Korea, Turkey, Spain, France, Canada, (I'm probably leaving a few represented nations out) and all over this country. Everybody does things differently, and everybody has a distinct creative angle and their own love of the art world. We have a guy whose passion is abstract art and another guy who's particularly into creepy stuff. When you're exposed to all these kinds of things, you get fresh angles. Everybody's a technical expert too, so it's been a great place to learn more about using various software programs—even branching out into using 3-D Studio Max, programs like that. Learning constantly is a wonderful thing.

We do an incredibly different array of things. We do cartoony work such as things for Kids WB network. We do historical video game cinematics, like *Empire Earth.* We do sci-fi, we do fantasy, we do movie f/x. Once in a while, we'll do abstract stuff and product work, commercials for the Sirius radio network, that kind of thing.

My main duties at Blur include creating concept designs of all kinds. Basically speaking, that means coming up with characters, props, and environments for all the work we do. A big, strong influence for me along these lines has always been cartoonist Michael Golden; he is simply a master of 3-D form, and a guy who thinks hard

Due to the diverse needs of Blur Studios' clients, Wojtkiewicz has broadened his artistic style. Some examples of his "cartoony" work (below). All art and characters TM & ©2004 their respective owners.

about the details of scenes and makes things functional and realistic. It's not just a bunch of filler, you get a feeling for an environment, for a character, for a machine. He does wonderful historical research, so you get an accurate German Tiger Tank and not a box on badly-drawn tank treads. Now I've always been a model builder, ever since I was a kid. For my first-grade birthday I got the Aurora Batman model kit and I started building, and I haven't stopped. It was another event where my fate was sealed. Through assembling countless plastic model kits I got a good feel for how things were shaped and what things do what. I've always been curious. "What's that nozzle there for? Why was there a handle right there? What's that big thing hanging off the rear of a tank do?" I would research these details as best I could. And failing that, I would just make it up.

The second main thing I do is storyboarding. Blur didn't always use storyboards. Our computer animation would start out with script, then we'd go to what's called an animatic, which is simple animation using blocky little figures in blocky little 3-D settings that kind of symbolize the setting and the characters. It locks down camera work, timing, and basic movement. Now we've changed our philosophy, because we can effectively bounce storyboards off a client. They take a lot less time than an animatic, and changes are made very quickly and very inexpensively, too. I can whip out simple boards and we can lock things down better with a client early on. A second benefit is that later in the process, say if I draw characters interacting with shrugs, subtle gestures, facial expressions, that kind of thing, it helps the animators when they go in to do the more final work. The blocky little animatic characters have no faces, *per sé*.

STORYBOARDS

Creating beautiful art is never the function of good storyboards. For complex productions, storyboards offer the client an opportunity to interact with the planning at the earliest stage. Without committing to any animation style or visual or special effects, a good storyboard completely outlines the project. Moreover, it paces the narrative so the client can get a good feel for the production and a clear understanding of it. This collaboration allows for joint ownership of the idea.

CHUCK WOJTKIEWICZ: Storyboards are pure storytelling. We've done storyboards that are basically blank-faced characters, concentrating on just the action and the camera angles. We've also done tighter ones that have shown more detail, but it all comes down to basically telling the story of how the final animation's going to go. Often clients hire blur to fully create a piece of animation–story, design–the whole works. The other times, people come in and they have a very solid idea of what they want the job to be like, but their vision may outstrip their budget. Storyboards help us to reach that common ground and get them exactly what they want, at a price they can afford.

Sometimes the client comes in and knows they want something, but they don't know what it is. Good storyboards are a nice visual–and economical–way of showing, just like in a comic book, characters in a setting doing things. It's been a natural transition for a lot of other guys who branched out from the comics industry. What would take an animator several days or a week or more to produce in animatic form can be achieved in a fraction of

To help the 3-D animators with backgrounds, Wojtkiewicz will create detailed environments. Wojtkiewicz solves client problems by using his technical drafting skills and a variety of styles. All art and characters TM & ©2004 their respective owners.

the time through storyboarding. Furthermore, doing changes at the storyboard level is a snap, because you can just swap out a panel, which is very easy compared to changing an animatic.

Let me give you an idea about how we work on storyboards. I'm doing some boards for a video game spot for Midway called *Area 51*. It's a teaser for E3 [Electronic Entertainment Expo]. Once again, there's not much time to do it, because E3 is coming right up. I'm not even sure how long it's going to be, a couple of minutes long, possibly.

I draw the boards really, really quickly in blue pencil with stick figures blocked out just so we can get camera angles, the number of cuts we're going to do, and different scenes. And I'll present them to the creative director and the project supervisor. We'll sit down and we'll discuss what story points work and what could be changed to make the story cooler. And that's where we get collaborative. Somebody will say, "Hey, what if you did a low angle there, because we could do some really good lighting and make it really dramatic." "Okay, well, let's change that." I'll make a note, throw out some sketches, then I'll do some more. Once we get it to where we like it, and to where the budget likes it, I'll go back and then I'll tighten 'em up and run them by the client to see if they like it. Often we'll cut a storyboard animatic, where we just flash the pictures on the screen for the approximate length of the cut as it's going to appear in the animation.

In essence, you can sit down and watch it and you'll say, "Okay, there's a minute of animation, and that's how the pacing is going to go." That's really good for the client as well as us. It's

helpful to the animatic artist, who will have suggestions of his own as he works the 2-D into living 3-D animation—the project continues to grow and blossom. In essence, we can have as many as four people collaborating in-house on the storyboards. We then present it to the client, and another round of changes can usually be expected.

It was a team effort back when I was doing comics, too—a much smaller team. The jobs now can involve dozens of creative artists. I really respect the guys I work with—their talents are amazing—and for the fact that they'll take my drawings and turn them into these beautiful CG models and then walk them around. It still stuns me. Yeah, I have a lot less control; I'm not an art director, *per sé*, or a supervisor on a film, but I do have an awful lot of input. I'm basically Step Two; the script is Step One. I sometimes get to collaborate on that when we write in-house or rewrite a client's script to fit our budget and time. That's enough of the pie for me!

Basic storyboarding's not very different from comics. You're getting a storyline broken down into paragraphs. One of the things in comics was learning how to take a script, break it up into individual comic pages and panels, and make it interesting. The different thing about doing storyboards is that the end product is going to be so much more "hot" a medium, as Marshall McLuhan would say, than comics. The written word is the coldest—the reader imagines all the visuals. Comics supply the visuals that accompany it, but you still do a lot of construction in your mind as you absorb the story. With animation, the story's moving, it's talking, it's got sound and color and lights. To put that script down in 2-D pictures is a different animal—you've got to think about motion, you've got to think about

Wojtkiewicz splits his workload between concept art and storyboards. Having worked in comics, he already understands the importance of pacing, timing, and shot selection in delivering a story. As a storyboard artist, he needs to present a clear visual representation for the live action or animation directors. "The Swarm" storyboard sequence (right and across) was produced to pitch a *Fantasia*-type film set to electronica music. All art and characters TM & ©2004 their respective owners.

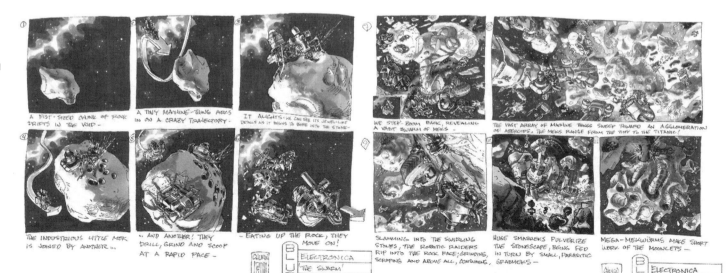

changing lighting. You also think about the pacing. Where do you insert a beat, where do you hold for a moment of tension, how many cuts can you get into a scene before you'd make somebody dizzy from the camera angle constantly changing? Organization is key–just keep yourself and your thoughts organized.

You have to factor in economics, too, because we have not only a money budget (yes, animation can burn money like it's going out of style). You also have a time budget on how much effort you can put into a scene before the deadlines are reached and the work is released. Let's say you want to show somebody dragged through dirt behind a truck. You have to consider the fact that you have to do the effects animation as well as character animation, adding in the flying dust and the bits of rock and so forth. This can be a time-consuming and therefore expensive proposal. Ask yourself, can you cheat around it? Can you indicate action off-page and not show a full figure being dragged through the dirt? A long shot of the truck towing something obscured in a cloud of dust will get the same idea across–and at a real savings of time and money.

Once we get our script/storyboard/animatic act together it means smooth sailing for the rest of the animation process–at least under ideal conditions. We refine our skills constantly. We're proud to say that our clients are pretty happy with what we do. We very often get an awful lot of freedom with our stuff as a result.

Once you get that kind of confidence going with a client and they feel more at ease, we have more leeway to go along and work at the fast pace that we're accustomed to, which can be a

tough one! Big studios do things very, very slowly. People are encouraged to slow down. People tend to stay at Blur, but a few guys have gone on to work at big studios. We've had a couple of guys who have moved on to larger outfits and they say, "Chuck, we don't really do that much in a week." They don't seem to feel very good about that. One of the nice things about Blur is that we do work at a decent clip, and you look back after, say, three months, and we've done a buttload of work. I've filled up a couple more notebooks with page after page of artwork, and we've got a couple more features done, and it's great. You really feel like you're getting your work out there and you're getting to do more cool stuff and for me that's what it's all about. In comics, when you've got that monthly book, it's sweet when it comes out. That's always a red letter day, when your book hits the stands. When you see that commercial on TV while you're sitting at home that night and you say, "Look, honey, look, it's my commercial!" It feels all warm and fuzzy–like zillions of people are seeing it, and the exhibitionist kid within takes a secret bow.

There are many particulars in creating storyboards. Developing the story through pacing and rhythm as well as camera work and framing are the time-honored tools of a storyboard artist. In the battle to stay in lockstep with technology, a good storyboard artist is immune to these advances. They only need pencil, paper, and clarity.

WOJTKIEWICZ: As a storyboard artist, I have first shot at any visual. I'm always amazed that in film storyboard artists have as much sway as they do. Look at Steve Skroce's work in *The Matrix*. He worked

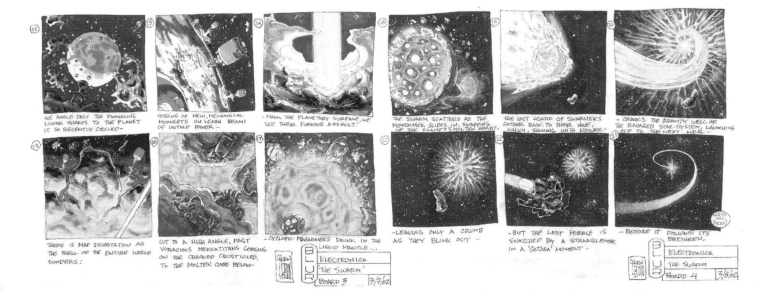

intensely with the Wachowski brothers, But then again, it was his vision that showed through in their film. When you watch *The Matrix*, you can see those Marvel comic book poses that Neo is striking from time to time. It's fantastic. But it's his vision, and it made it all the way through, right to Keanu Reeves' acting. If you watched the last *Matrix* film, not only did Steve Skroce get a great big credit early on, so did Geof Darrow as the main concept artist. Two comic book guys got big credits early on, and I say that's a wonderful thing—those films were all about the visuals and the story-telling involved.

I do miss composing pictures in the differently-shaped frames of comic book pages. It was fun to say, "Hey, let's do a really vertical panel," or "Let's do a really skinny, horizontal panel." In one way, storyboarding is easier because you just get into the mode of thinking in that one frame shape. You do have to consider the fact that the camera is moving, and you can pan up an entire character and do that long, vertical shot. You don't see it all at once, but you do get that impression. I would say it's just as satisfying.

I do think about design as much as I can, but I also get to concentrate more on the rhythm and pacing. I'll often listen to music that I think would be appropriate. You know, if you're doing a dramatic scene, I'll put on some dramatic soundtrack, or I'll put on maybe some martial, marching kind of music, if you're doing a military scene and you want a sense of grandeur. Or you can put on something fun, something bouncy, something calm, something mysterious. I've always done that, I've always listened to different types of music while I was drawing differently-mooded scenes. I still have

to think about composition, but it's a different kind of design, I guess. The frames are all the same shape, but these frames move—and have rhythms.

Every good illustrator thinks through the eye of the camera lens when doing realistic or narrative work. You look at Scott McCloud's book *Understanding Comics*, you see how panels read from left to right, showing action and reaction—and thereby the passage of time—in a single panel. It's a bunch of little pictures put together, composed to tell a bit of story. But yeah, when we're doing story-boards and so forth, you would have to think about the motion of the camera, and you get to do so much more. You can think about somebody walking through a house and passing from one room to another, or from darkness to light. You consider pacing, too, they may start to run, they may fall down a flight of stairs. That sense of motion is always in your head when you're doing storyboards, because it's the nature of the beast, and it just adds not only a really fun aspect, but a real challenge, too, in telling a story. I'll sit down and talk with the supervisor, and ask, "How do you want to do this? Do you want this to be really rhythmic and lyrical, do you want it to be choppy and kind of handheld shaky-cam kind of thing? Do you want it dark or do you want it bright, or what?" It's just that much more information that you've got to juggle while making a story come to life.

I've had to pick up a bit of the vocabulary of cinematography—I really did not know too much of it. Well, I knew a little bit, because you have to study cinematography to do comics, but everybody uses different little terms. Once in a while we'll get a script from a client that'll have some strange, new abbreviation. I'll say, "What is

WE OPEN ON THE HEAVING PROW OF VIKING LONGBOAT AS IT PLIES THE FRIGID WATERS OF THE IRISH CHANNEL. THE CAPTAIN STANDS TALL AT HIS POST, GAZING CONTEMPLATIVELY AT A GLEAMING OBJECT CLUTCHED IN HIS FIST—

WE CUT TO THE OBJECT OF HIS INTENSE FOCUS—A CELTIC CROSS OF SOLID GOLD, BATTERED AND BENT, AND STAINED—WITH BLOOD!

CUT TO A BRIEF BUT INTENSE MOMENT OF BATTLE, AS A VIKING AXE SUNDERS A FARMER, THE SAVAGE SWING SPEWS GORE IN A GLITTERING ARC—

CUT TO THE INTERIOR OF A SIMPLE STONE CHAPEL. WE SEE A HUMBLE ALTAR, LAID WITH THE RICH VESTMENTS OF CHRISTIANITY'S TREASURES—

AS WE FOCUS TIGHTER ON THE ALTAR, FUMBLING, PANIC-DRIVEN HANDS GATHER THE HOLY ICONS, WRAPPING THEM IN THE ALTAR CLOTH ITSELF TO FORM A MAKESHIFT SACK

that?" "I dunno," comes the reply, " Let's just use a pan." You can clue in and use a term you learn from one person, but another will say, "What's a smash pan?" That's when the camera just rockets in on something. People use different terms for that, but as long as you get the gist, that's fine. Thankfully the pictures tell the story! That's why it's vital to always communicate well with your clients, so you can figure out what the hell they're thinking no matter how they verbally express themselves. After all, it's much more practical for me and my pencil to put words into pictures, rather than a team of six guys animating a character to do the same thing.

It's simple, it's hammer and nails stuff. It's time-honored and true, and the software doesn't change every six months. I can just keep going the way I've been going and getting the good results. I do boards really fast. We don't do pretty storyboards, where they're all shaded and colored or anything like that. Yeah, we do things slambang. If I draw a guy running, if one leg's too long or too short, I don't worry about it. The thing that I'm really concentrating on is the actual storytelling, not the beautiful rendering.

It's not like our clients are hiring us to produce illustrations, which is the case with comics. People are hiring us to produce animation, and they want to see the tight render on the finished production—and we give them the very best as possible. The storyboards are a stepping stone as part of the process. The Wachowski brothers sold *The Matrix* using Steve Skroce's well-rendered, beautifully-drawn storyboards—he put a lot more into it because they were using those boards to convince investors to front big bucks. If we ever had to do that, you can bet that I'd be sitting down and doing some tightly-rendered stuff, probably even in color using Photoshop or something like that. As a matter of fact, we have done some color production boards for a Mask theme park feature that ran at the Paramount Park in Madrid. And I did do tighter line art colored in a simple way with Photoshop. They liked the boards so much that they decided to use them as the backdrops in the animation. So you have the character, the Mask, in front of painted backdrops that once were merely boards.

While on the subject, theme park ride storyboards pose their own challenge because a park ride is one long cut. You know the famous shower scene from Hitchcock's Psycho that had how many cuts, dozens or something, in a minute-and-a-half? It was just flash, flash, flash, flash. Well, a theme park ride will go on for three minutes or more, and it's one long camera move. As you're storyboarding those, you have to think of the constant motion of the journey. It's your journey, the camera is audience's point of view. So that in itself is a challenge. And when you modify those, that gets kind of tricky later on down the animation pipeline. You can end up redoing a lot or work to make even a simple change in the story.

The opening storyboards (below and across) produced for a proposed cinematic for the game *Viking: Total War*. Not as polished as his conceptual illustrations, Wojtkiewicz instead concentrates on framing a moment much like a director or photographer. Storyboard artists often have the first shot at the visual interpretation of a narrative by working with just pencil and paper, which is much more efficient than working in animation or film. Total War TM & ©2004 Activision, Inc.

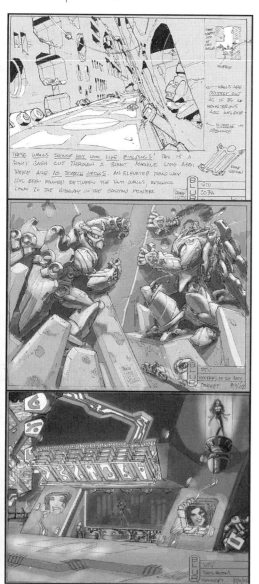

A sampling of conceptual and storyboarding work for the Shania Twain video "I'm Gonna Getcha Good." In planning for movements (above top), narrative moments (above middle) and sets (above bottom), Wojtkiewicz got to play with both technology and robots. Shots from the final video (right). Video images ©2004 Shania Twain.

S H A N I A   T W A I N

Storyboards have been traditionally linked to motion pictures as a way to help plan the actor's actions and scene. When you add visual special effects on top of the process, then storyboards become invaluable.

CHUCK WOJTKIEWICZ: We did a video for Shania Twain, for her song "I'm Gonna Get You Good." The director and his effects coordinator were in the studio all the time and poor little me asked them not to watch over my shoulder as I was drawing. They really wanted to, but I just couldn't be creative that way–that was just a little too much Big-Brothery. In the end we came to a happy understanding and things sailed along. It can be a little difficult, but close cooperation's a really good way to work with folks. The director had done a lot of music videos, but he'd never worked with CG before, and he wasn't really aware of the limitations of the medium. After a while he caught on because he was able to be right there for the process. We worked together really well. We were able to take a great big story and cut it down to fit in the allotted time, and we were satisfied with what we got. And we did it all in an incredibly short amount of time–I had three weeks to do both the storyboards and concept designs. Being able to nail things down at that early stage in storyboard form made it possible for the animators to go ahead and squeeze out three minutes of animation in three weeks' time–no mean feat!.

We can do almost anything given time and money, but with his budget, and more importantly his time budget, we began the job by cutting the story back. We all sat down and we went through it, shot by

shot. We said, "Well, y'know, that's a big, expensive shot, because we'll have all these characters that we'll have to design, model, and animate." So you cut those down, bang, everything gets a little more realistic. We did that, trimming the story but keeping the key parts to make it entertaining and fun. I started my scribbles and we went over those. Tim Miller looked it over and he said, "Okay, this is going to be about ten minutes worth of animation, and we have three minutes worth of time." So we then started throwing away scenes. That means you'd have to bridge different shots differently, and adjust your storytelling to suit.

Once we got that down, I did a final pass over the crude blue pencil drawings with a pen–just a single, deadweight, good old black marker, and tightened them up so that they were pretty readable. And we went over them once again. By that point we had decided that we were happy with the story and the way it was coming out, so we started moving on into the animatic. Once that was done and we had trimmed the tale down to the point where it worked, we had our camera angles locked and the animators could start working. We had a lot of assets that I'd been designing in the meantime, concurrent to the storyboarding process. I'd work for a few hours on boards, then we'd have to wait until we could talk to the director. I use that time to design the big robot and the city and the little robots and all that stuff. With the animatic done, I would look at each cut and do a really quick design over key frames from each cut. It was design on the fly! The road the character traveled on, the various tunnels and bridges–all were fleshed out at top speed from the blocky stand-in structures of the animatic. I'd had time to work out a basic design philosophy for the robotic world our heroine rocketed through, and these quick

drawings helped place and adapt those designs into specific situations. They'd be handed off as I finished 'em to waiting scene-assembly specialists, animators who take the varied elements of the job and knit them together into finished cuts of animation.

CRIMSON SKIES

There are many elements to a video game that can be storyboarded, from dictating scene details, to cut scene animation. Blur Studios excels in animation of all kinds and any preproduction work needed in the field of video game design.

CHUCK WOJTKIEWICZ: We dealt directly with Microsoft on the game *Crimson Skies*. They were an involved client–really hands-on with the animation, though not so much with the concept design; it was the end product that they wanted to tweak. Which is unfortunate with an eye to efficiency, that's the difficult and expensive end of the animation process! They had produced a lot of the storyboards themselves. I did some boards, but this was a case where they had done a lot of pre-production work themselves. We worked on cinematics for several months, investing a lot of time and effort on design and animation, all in close cooperation with Microsoft. They debuted the game at E3, and it was received flatly. I was thinking, "Aw, damn, they're gonna cancel it." However, they knuckled down and did a heroic revision, and it's a great game. I worked on that damn thing on and off for two years! It was intense.

They had neat little maquettes sculpted of the main characters Nathan and Maria. They weren't the greatest sculpts (in my humble opinion), but they were decent. They had busts of all the other principle characters sculpted up to aid them in digitally modeling the characters. It fell to me to create their costumes and physiques. Plucky sidekick Betty, the villainous Khan, the lovable, tragic Dr. Fassenbinder, and Remy the treacherous Cajun (he was a bigger character in the early game)–I got to play haberdasher for them all. Khan originally was a two-fisted pirate type, as well as being the slick, urbane gangster, so I wanted to give him a big-league wrestler look–nixed! The heroes had a secret base on an island somewhere, and a big scene with Dr. Fassenbinder, before he gets ignominiously drilled. I worked on a ton of different scenes destined never to make it to the final game.

I'm an airplane nut. Airplanes are my favorite subject to model–I build esoteric scale flying models powered by rubber band motors as well as grotesquely detailed scale plastic subjects, so this project was a dream come true. My only regret was they didn't let me design any of the planes! Wahh. Maybe with Crimson Skies II...

Working with a mega-corporation like Microsoft carried a certain edge of intimidation. I couldn't help but feel sometimes that the people I were working with faced the enormous pressures of answering to the Mighty Megalith that is Microsoft, and I was a simple freewheeling pencil jockey happily scrawling pretty pictures. My trepidations were unfounded–the folks I worked with had a goal I could identify with easily–we all just wanted to do our best to make a fun and entertaining product. The Discovery Channel produced an hour-long feature about the process Microsoft used to produce three different games, one of which was, you guessed it, *Crimson Skies*... and I'm interviewed–I made it onto the Small Screen!

An airplane enthusiast, Wojtkiewicz infused his aerospace knowledge into the game *Crimson Skies*. He designed characters, airplanes, and locations (below) that greatly inspired the cinematic cutscenes (above).

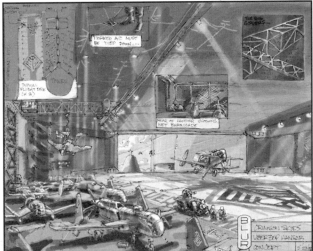

Crimson Skies TM & ©2004 Microsoft Corp.

ROCKFISH

Artists need to work to be happy. Every studio hits intense creative moments, but the top studios keep creativity in-house, even during the down times. The results? In Blur's case, an Academy Award nomination or two.

"What's the story of Rockfish, in a nutshell? A blue-collar guy drives out into the desert of this giant wasteland alien planet in great big-ass truck; he parks; he gets out, and he drills a deep, deep hole. Then he puts a little cage over it, with a seat and everything, and he drops a hook into it. Then it goes down, down, down, down, down. And he's just sitting there fishing in the desert, in the dirt. And eventually something hits the line, and it's the big one that does not get away, and he goes on a wild ride through the desert, being towed by this thing that's deep beneath the surface of the earth."

Frames from *Rockfish*, an animation project conceived, produced, and released by Blur Studios. For Wojtkiewicz, having a high degree of creative input on dream projects is the biggest perk of working in a studio environment. What he learned from working in comics–imaginative storylines, drawing speed, and storytelling clarity–has proven invaluable with his work in conceptual art and storyboards. Rockfish TM & ©2004 Blur Studios

CHUCK WOJTKIEWICZ: Back to Blur being a place run *by* artists, *for* artists; the management realizes that Blur *is* the art and animation team. Somebody could say, "We want to buy Blur." They'd simply be buying a big warehouse full of computers, because the all-important artistic staff wouldn't necessarily come along in the bargain. Like I said, we've got guys who moved an incredible distance to work with us. That's Blur. A lot of animation studios, traditional or CG, will do a big project, or a series, say *Batman: Animated* or *Ice Age* or whatever, and when the series runs out or the film is in the can, a bunch of guys get laid off. So animators, particularly 2-D animators, have had a really unsteady source of employment. They know exactly when they'd be out of a job. We're not like that. We keep people on because they're our team. We recognize that there are rhythms to our workload, as well. There's the big video game push that goes on with E3, and then after that, often there's been some dead space. Well, we don't want to lay guys off and hope to rehire them later–they've got bills to pay, they'll find a job somewhere else. They're really good–how could we replace them? So we do short films. We do our shorts and we keep people busy. We better ourselves, we increase our knowledge base, our skill base–and we develop properties we own–it's invaluable. As a side benefit we promote the kind of work we'd like to do. We did *Aunt Louisa*, which was a humorous two-minute short, very cartoony. We made the next-to-the-last cut for the Academy Awards short animated film category last year, and that helped us get lots of cartoony work. It helped us get the Disney movie that we're working on right now, *Mickey's Twice Upon a Christmas*. We're doing forty minutes of animation for a straight-to-video release, with the balance supplied by the French studio, Sparks. This year we had a competition open to any full-time employee in the studio to submit a short story for the next short feature. The supervisory staff were tasked to read and vote for a winner. And we selected *Rockfish*, written by Tim Miller–it wasn't cheating on his part. He just happens to be a boss, honest!

Kidding aside, it's a good story, a sci-fi tale of a guy on a distant planet, with crazy machinery and a little alien pet, as he stalks an unseen monster. We had a lot of content we really wanted to do–tech, monsters, character work and action. We sat down, hashed out the story, and then we just kicked it out–a bunch of dedicated artists working really, really hard to do the thing we'd all trained for long years to do. We've gotten an eight-minute film out of the deal, and now we're proudly showing it around. We're getting a great response from it. I can just see some cool new projects coming out of it, hopefully a feature film, our holy grail.

We are up for an Academy Award. As a matter of fact, I had to bow out of seeing the presentation yesterday of finalists, from which they'll pick the three final nominees that will be presented at the ceremonies. At least we made the second-to-the-last cut–we did it last year, too!

It was a great project for all of us. First of all, the design work was really fun, because it was our property. We could do whatever we wanted with it. We just worked together, we're a good team, we've been working together a long time. I could pass concept designs off to the model builders and I said, "Hey, make this look better" (which they always do). I was in on a lot of the story development, too. We sat down and hashed out a rough idea, and the story changed vastly from the original kernel while we worked on it and all added our input; it grew from a clever tale to an epic adventure. The back story is that our hero, Sirus Kirk, is helping miners on a distant planet that are plagued by giant subterranean creatures that wreak havoc on their endeavors. He's kind of like a hunter who keeps people safe. Usually the creatures he finds may be thirty feet long or whatever, but he catches one that's 150 feet long. The grand concept is that the desert itself is alive—the dirt and rocks are like geologically slowly drifting coral reefs, teemingly populated by strange subterranean lifeforms. If we'd had a bigger budget and more time, we would have had a lot of little critters running around, jumping out of the dirt, that kind of thing. But, well, it was our own film, and we spent a fair amount of money on it, and we got our story out. I guess if we had a budget and time to do *Rockfish* as a movie, we could really blow the roof off!

SEE THE WORLD THROUGH A CAMERA

Wojtkiewicz has very simple advice to break into the storyboarding profession.

CHUCK WOJTKIEWICZ: The art of storyboarding is envisioning how the end movie is going to look, and crystallizing it into two-dimensional images. A good storyboard artist knows how to pick out the significant scenes and moments in a film and present the most important and interesting shots.

Study cinematography. Get a good feel on how a good movie is made and what makes a good movie entertaining and substantive. Keep your eye on what you think is a hot trend in storytelling, specifically commercials. Also, be aware of history, too, because stuff comes back—everything old is new again on the cinematography end. On the drawing end of the craft, you need to be proficient at drawing quickly. Think about how to express yourself with a minimum of line in a minimum of time—storyboards can often be a speed venture. You don't always get to render things. Be prepared to be part of a team. You've got to learn to set your ego aside, because there is a lot of give and take. Artistically speaking, learn to see the world through a camera. Think about motion, lighting, camera angles and that kind of stuff. As a supervisor, I see a lot of boards that are very unimaginative—the artist is not really thinking about the scene actually becoming moving pictures. The end result of any storyboard, if you're lucky, is that it becomes a finished film, and you are the one who starts it all off. That, my friends, is a wonderful thing.

Bernie Wrightson
on Comics & Concept Art

Concept art is the other half of preproduction necessary in creating motion pictures. Along with story-boards, concept art allows the director to develop a vision that can be shared with the rest of the crew before the first frame of film is shot. Concept art can dictate vision for special and visual effects, wardrobe and costumes, model makers and props masters. A good concept artist can create a visual tone that can be carried throughout the duration of the film.

Bernie Wrightson has been working as a freelance professional artist for over 35 years. He started as a production assistant/editorial cartoonist for the Baltimore Sun *newspaper and eventually found his niche in comic books. He co-created* Swamp Thing *in 1971 and has dabbled with most of the more well-known superheroes, including* Spider-Man, Batman, *and* Superman. *He's expanded his career into book illustration, magazine illustration, posters, prints, and currently finds himself in Los Angeles doing conceptual work and storyboards for motion pictures.*

BERNIE WRIGHTSON: I always had a pencil and paper. I always loved to draw. I think most kids do. Or most kids *did*, before video games. Nowadays young kids seem to be wasting their time on that, but we didn't have any of that stuff. And there was a TV show on Saturday mornings called Jon Gnagy. And it was a drawing show. He would start every show by drawing basic shapes. He would draw a circle and a triangle and a square, and then show you how to three-dimensionalize things and turn a

triangle into a cone, and turn the rectangle into a cylinder and make the circle into a ball. And by using the three basic shapes, he would show you how you could draw anything. I used to watch his show with a pad and pencil and just follow his lessons. I think a lot of kids from that era did the same thing. I know that [Michael] Kaluta grew up learning to draw from watching that show, and Jeff Jones. And later

on, a lot of us took the Famous Artists correspondence course. And we talked a lot about that. Interestingly, nobody I ever met actually finished the course. The reason is that the course was so good that we all started working professionally before the course was ever finished.

Comic books and movies were probably my biggest influences. I watched all the Universal Monster movies on TV over and over and over. I think everybody has a favorite Universal monster. Everybody from my generation, anyway. Some people just fell in love with the Creature from the Black Lagoon, or Dracula, or the Wolfman. I'm just one of the people that fell in love with Frankenstein. Well, I grew up with the movies that I saw on TV. It was a black-and-white TV, so I don't know, I guess I just tended to think more in terms of black-and-white.

I read EC comics and all the other comics in the Fifties. When I was very young, I was all about drawing and reproducing and printing. I would study comics very closely, and I saw that the color was laid down in little dots, and the dots would overlap the different colors and form little patterns. And I don't know, I guess over time I figured it out, that this was the printing process, and this was how you made a soft gray in color, was the little dots of red, blue, and yellow laid down, superimposed on top of one another with just this much white space between.

So for me, comics and movies absolutely go hand-in-hand. I still go to the movies and I'm still a big fan of science fiction and monster movies. So yeah, of course, movies are an influence [on my art]. Nothing has been the same since *Alien*. That changed everybody's ideas about science fiction monsters.

When asked what has been his favorite comic book work, Wrightson mentions *Captain Sternn: Running Out of Time*. "I got to do *Running Out of Time* pretty much start to finish. I wrote it, laid it out, and drew it. I had a lot of help with inking and coloring, because it was such a huge project. But that was probably the most fun, I think, that I've had in comics." In the following pages, Captain Sternn makes a rather unorthodox escape from prison, much to the delight of Mr. Coffers. Capt. Sternn TM & ©2004 Bernie Wrightson

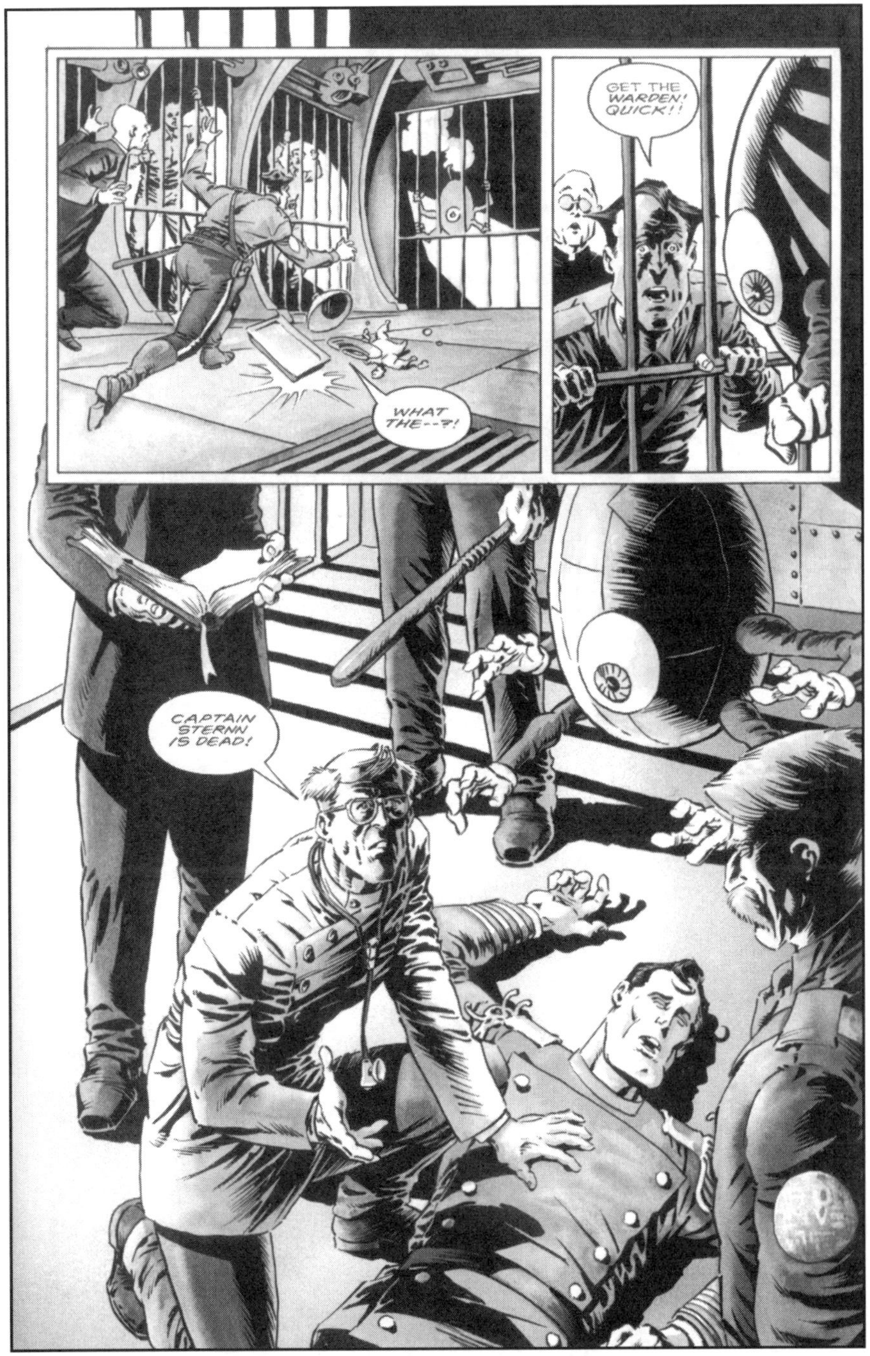
GET THE WARDEN! QUICK!!
WHAT THE--?!
CAPTAIN STERNN IS DEAD!

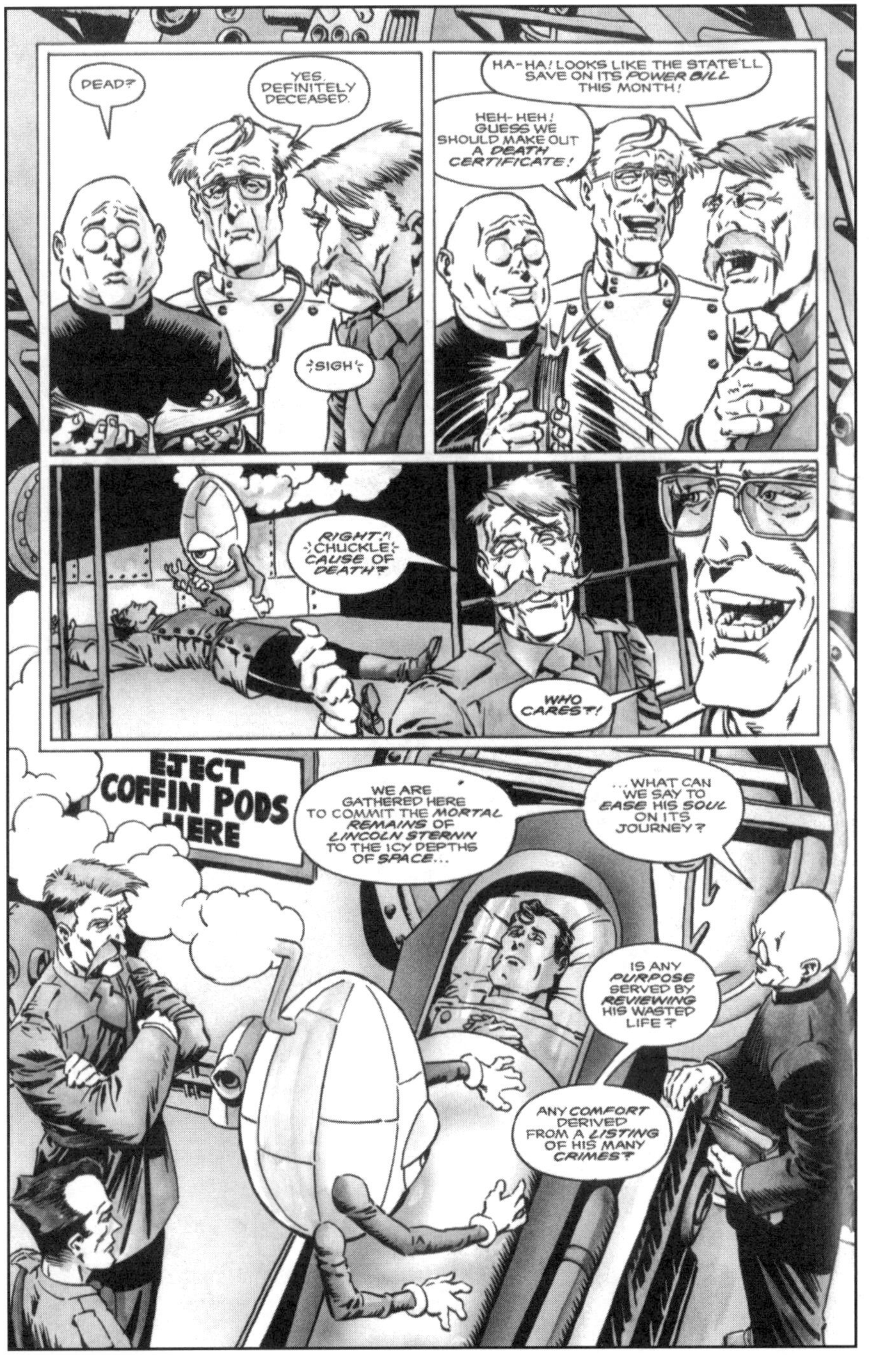
DEAD?
YES. DEFINITELY DECEASED.
SIGH
HA-HA! LOOKS LIKE THE STATE'LL SAVE ON ITS POWER BILL THIS MONTH!
HEH-HEH! GUESS WE SHOULD MAKE OUT A DEATH CERTIFICATE!
RIGHT! CHUCKLE CAUSE OF DEATH?
WHO CARES?!
EJECT COFFIN PODS HERE
WE ARE GATHERED HERE TO COMMIT THE MORTAL REMAINS OF LINCOLN STERNN TO THE ICY DEPTHS OF SPACE...
...WHAT CAN WE SAY TO EASE HIS SOUL ON ITS JOURNEY?
IS ANY PURPOSE SERVED BY REVIEWING HIS WASTED LIFE?
ANY COMFORT DERIVED FROM A LISTING OF HIS MANY CRIMES?

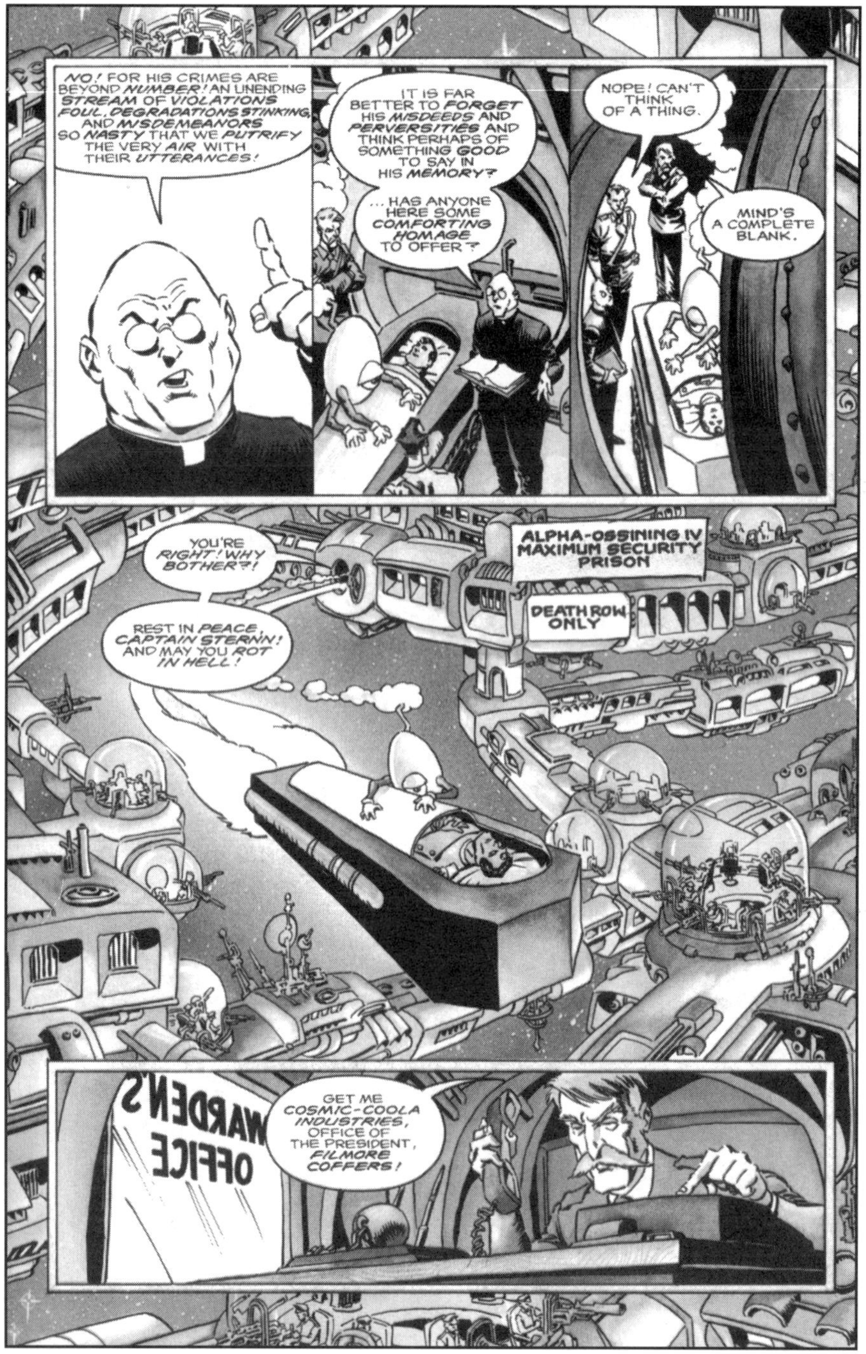
NO! FOR HIS CRIMES ARE BEYOND NUMBER! AN UNENDING STREAM OF VIOLATIONS FOUL, DEGRADATIONS STINKING, AND MISDEMEANORS SO NASTY THAT WE PUTRIFY THE VERY AIR WITH THEIR UTTERANCES!
IT IS FAR BETTER TO FORGET HIS MISDEEDS AND PERVERSITIES AND THINK PERHAPS OF SOMETHING GOOD TO SAY IN HIS MEMORY?
...HAS ANYONE HERE SOME COMFORTING HOMAGE TO OFFER?
NOPE! CAN'T THINK OF A THING.
MIND'S A COMPLETE BLANK.
ALPHA-OSSINING IV MAXIMUM SECURITY PRISON
YOU'RE RIGHT! WHY BOTHER?!
DEATH ROW ONLY
REST IN PEACE, CAPTAIN STERNN! AND MAY YOU ROT IN HELL!
WARDEN'S OFFICE
GET ME COSMIC-COOLA INDUSTRIES, OFFICE OF THE PRESIDENT, FILMORE COFFERS!

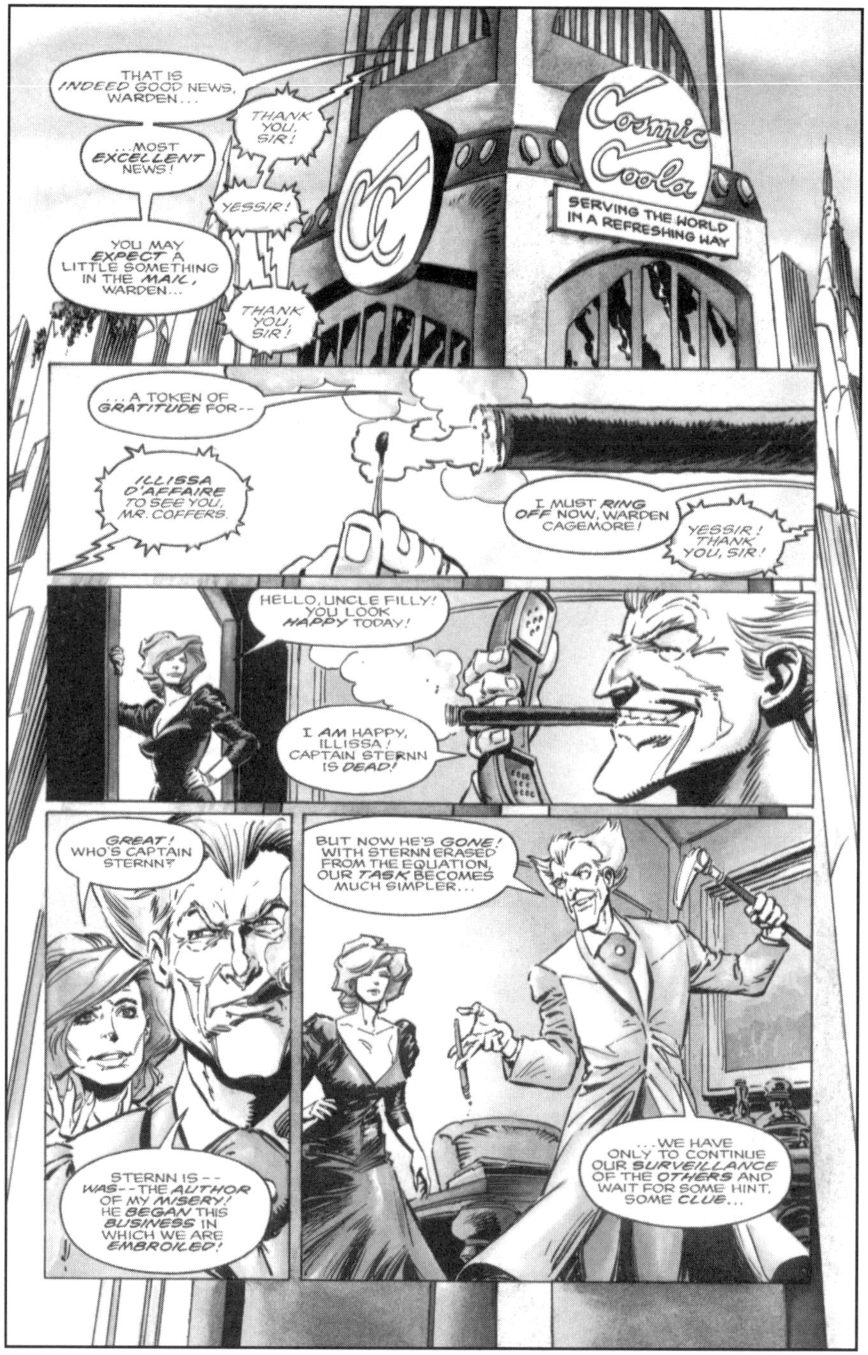
THAT IS INDEED GOOD NEWS, WARDEN...
THANK YOU, SIR!
...MOST EXCELLENT NEWS!
YESSIR!
YOU MAY EXPECT A LITTLE SOMETHING IN THE MAIL, WARDEN...
THANK YOU, SIR!
Cosmic Coola
SERVING THE WORLD IN A REFRESHING WAY
...A TOKEN OF GRATITUDE FOR--
ILLISSA D'AFFAIRE TO SEE YOU, MR. COFFERS.
I MUST RING OFF NOW, WARDEN CAGEMORE!
YESSIR! THANK YOU, SIR!
HELLO, UNCLE FILLY! YOU LOOK HAPPY TODAY!
I AM HAPPY, ILLISSA! CAPTAIN STERNN IS DEAD!
GREAT! WHO'S CAPTAIN STERNN?
BUT NOW HE'S GONE! WITH STERNN ERASED FROM THE EQUATION, OUR TASK BECOMES MUCH SIMPLER...
STERNN IS-- WAS--THE AUTHOR OF MY MISERY! HE BEGAN THIS BUSINESS IN WHICH WE ARE EMBROILED!
...WE HAVE ONLY TO CONTINUE OUR SURVEILLANCE OF THE OTHERS AND WAIT FOR SOME HINT, SOME CLUE...

THE PROCESS OF ILLUSTRATION

Wrightson learned early on that he wanted to become an illustrator. He was inspired by commercial illustration, book illustration, and even package design. He also loved the printing process and found himself fascinated by how art was produced—the printing process, separations, and production techniques. All of these influences came to a head with his seminal work, Frankenstein.

BERNIE WRIGHTSON: My parents didn't understand commercial art; they had no idea of what was involved with commercial art. It was completely out of their experience. My mom was an office clerk and my dad was a steelworker and a bus driver. They didn't even think about the Sunday funnies, that somebody actually sat down and drew these things. They read the comic strips, they liked them, but they didn't think about somebody actually *making* these things. They just happened. I remember one time going to the grocery store with my mom. I was thirteen or fourteen maybe, helping her with the groceries. And I picked up a jar of peanuts. It had a painting of peanuts on the label. And I showed it to my mom and I said, "Okay, see this? This is commercial art. See this label? That's not a photograph. That's a painting. Somebody painted this." And she looked at me like I was an idiot and she said, "Nobody paints *all* of these labels." And I just stopped right there, because it was like, "No, I can't explain it."

My first commercial job was working at the *Baltimore Sun.* My job was mostly retouching photos, which is how everybody in the art department starts. I learned a lot, working at a newspaper, about the printing process and everything. I would go downstairs to where the presses were and I'd talk to the printers down there. They would show me the printing plates, the photographs and half-tone illustrations, how these were photographed and screened to produce the dots. They explained how, if the dots are small and farther apart, the tone is lighter, and if they're bigger and less white space in between, that's how they get dark tones. This was before color, because at the time, the [newspaper process] was all black-and-white printing.

The idea behind *Frankenstein* was that I wanted the pictures to feel like woodcuts or steel engravings or something that fit the era. I wanted something that looked like it could have been done at the time the book was written, using the reproduction techniques of the time. They didn't have color reproduction then, and the illustrations you saw were black-and-white. They were either woodcuts or steel engravings or something like that. So I wanted to evoke that feeling with pen and ink. I never thought of this as a lot of work. I simply loved what I was doing so much.

Years after it's been done, I look back on *Frankenstein* and I'm hard-pressed to recall the process. In other words, I look back on it and it doesn't seem like I really worked on it. It's almost like it just *happened*. The only thing I do remember is that when it was all over, when it was all done, it felt like there was a big hole in my life, because it was over and I wasn't doing it anymore. I don't know, in a lot of ways it was the hole that's never been filled—I've always felt that nothing I've done since *Frankenstein* has been as good. I've certainly not been as committed to or as passionate about anything the way I was about *Frankenstein*. Maybe I exorcised my demons or I used up all my juice or something.

"I was very much in love with these old pen-and-ink artists. I loved penwork. I loved linework. I didn't know any of these [linework] guys, really, until I met Kaluta. He introduced me to the work of people like J.C. Cole, Charles Dana Gibson, Franklin Booth, Norman Lindsey, and all these great masters of pen-and-ink work. All of these guys had been influencing me for quite a long time, even when I was doing *Swamp Thing*. I think over time, Booth became my favorite."
©2004 Bernie Wrightson

LEARN TO DRAW BY DRAWING

Wrightson wanted to be an illustrator, but he developed into a giant in the comics field. This development process was the result of being thrown into the deep end of comics working on stories that were always near to his heart. He worked diligently to understand the skills of a sequential artist, including pacing, composition, and eye movement. In doing so, he developed a diverse fan base.

BERNIE WRIGHTSON: It gets frustrating when I'm talking to kids who want to break into the business. I'm not a good person to talk to because I was extremely lucky. I was in the right place and the right time, and I kind of fell into it. I made a trip to New York and went to the offices at DC and at Marvel. I had some samples, and as I recall, I didn't have any actual comic book pages, just single drawings. Stuff that I liked to draw, monsters and things. And both companies, particularly at Marvel, they were just not interested in seeing this stuff. "Why don't you come back and draw some of our characters." That was kind of discouraging, because I didn't *want* to draw their characters. Drawing Spider-Man just wasn't what I wanted to do. That's not what I was interested in. I wanted to draw comics, but I didn't want to draw superheroes. I still feel that way.

What I wanted to draw was horror comics, and of course, nobody was doing horror comics. So I didn't even try, because that's not what I wanted to do. I didn't want to draw superheroes. So I just continued doing monster and sword and sorcery stuff, and came back to New York a year later for a convention. I had a big portfolio of all my drawings and stuff, and I just started meeting people at the convention. I met Mike Kaluta and Jeff Jones. Kaluta hadn't had anything published, only in some fanzines in Virginia. Jeff had just done a couple of jobs for Warren, a couple of comic book jobs, and I think by the time I met him, he was already getting out of comics and into painting paperback covers. With them I met professionals in the comic book field. We met Al Williamson and Frank Frazetta, and they were impressed enough to show our stuff to some of the publishers and some of the editors, who I didn't even know. People like Dick Giordano and Joe Orlando and Carmine Infantino. It sounded like the Mafia to me. Being from Baltimore, I thought, there's all these tough New York Italian guys.

The first job they gave me was *Night Master*, which was a full comic book. And I just completely dropped the ball. I wasn't ready to do a whole book. It was too much work, I was too young. I wanted to do a good job, and I completely froze up. I did like seven or eight pages of pencils for the first issue of *Night Master,* and it was just awful. Everything was really stiff and overworked. I was just trying too hard. And I brought the pages in, and Carmine Infantino looked at the pages and said, "Okay, you're not ready for a full book

yet. We're going to put you on fillers in *House of Mystery* until you get your chops." They turned *Night Master* over to me after the first issue, and it only ran for three issues. I did the second and third issues. It wasn't really great work, because it was just not something I wanted to do. It was basically a superhero in a fantasy world and everything, but...I just was not all that excited about it.

So other than that, all I was doing up until the *Swamp Thing* series was stories for *House of Mystery* and *House of Secrets*, and covers and single illustrations and stuff. I did two or three page little stories, called fillers, if they had to make up the page count. *House of Mystery* was an anthology book, so the stories were different lengths. If they were two or three pages short, they'd have these fillers in inventory, and they'd just put one of those in. So that's what I did.

Swamp Thing started with the short story in *House of Secrets.* Len Wein and I were both at just the right age and the right point in our careers to do this one-shot, this eight-page thing called "Swamp Thing." Up until then, these fillers, that's all I was doing–I hadn't done a whole comic book. We did this story, it appeared in *House of Secrets*, and the mail that they got on this one story was apparently just phenomenal. All the fans went nuts over this short story, this Swamp Thing story. So DC decided to give him a book of his own. And that was real exciting. It was like, "Finally!" Here's a horror comic. Okay, Swamp Thing, he *is* a hero, but he's a *monster.* So that was a lot of fun. Everything kind of came together.

The biggest challenge for me was just getting the thing done. It was a bi-monthly book. I'd never been a fast artist. I was excited about every page, every drawing, and, on an almost unconscious level, excited about storytelling and the design. *Swamp Thing* is where I began to learn about storytelling. My idea of comics up until then was just to draw the best picture in each panel that I could–I didn't really think about how one panel leads to another, how to pace a story, or how to structure a story visually to just kind of carry the reader along. Storytelling. I would make decisions about whether to do a close-up or a long-shot or an up-angle or a down-angle just based on what I felt like drawing, what I felt would be the best composition for an individual panel. And while I was doing *Swamp Thing*, I began to get a feel for sequential art, and just what works best in terms of moving the story along.

I think storytelling is one of those things that just kind of happened over time. In the beginning, all I was really thinking about was doing the job that I was assigned, turning it around, getting paid, and getting another job. And the idea of getting better at comics was not even a conscious consideration, if you know what I mean. I was really too busy, and I think getting better was just what happened from working all the time. When I was taking the Famous

Artists course, on every other page of the lesson books, they had this little motto printed that said, "You learn to draw by drawing." And I would do the lessons and everything, and I'd read this thing and think, "Oh God, how stupid, 'you learn to draw by drawing.' That's a lotta help. Thanks a lot." But over the years, I've just learned that that's exactly right. Drawing pictures is like playing the piano. You have to practice every day. No matter how good you are, you just have to keep at it.

Illustration is a whole other animal than a comic book or any kind of sequential art. You don't really have to think about how the pictures relate to one another, because the story's being told in the text. The illustrator is decorating the text, or illuminating the text, visualizing it. And you don't have to think about all the problems that you encounter in sequential art.

I'm kind of a straightforward storyteller, and I hope that I can do it clearly, and I hope that I can do it interestingly and engagingly, but I don't really see myself as like a Frank Miller or Neal Adams and people that really push the limits of the form. It's just something that I've enjoyed working in, I've really enjoyed the medium itself as a storytelling vehicle. It's amazing when I hear from a lot of people in different fields telling me that I was a big influence on them. People even from music. I met a guy just recently, he's the drummer for the band called System of a Down, and he said, "I saw your comics and I saw your illustration work, and it changed my life." And I just said, "Wow." Y'know?

Though the nuns at school or his parents at home didn't understand why, Wrightson has drawn monsters since childhood. Through continually drawing what he loves, Wrightson is acknowledged as one of the finest horror illustrators ever. ©2004 Bernie Wrightson

Wrightson was called onto *Ghostbusters* to lend his unique vision. It was his first conceptual design job and a perfect fit. Wrightson visualized the Ghost Librarian (right) from the opening sequence at the New York Public Library. Ghostbusters TM & ©2004 Columbia Pictures Industries, Inc.

GHOSTBUSTERS

In 1983 Ivan Reitman was directing Ghostbusters, *the story of three unemployed parapsychology professors who set up shop as a unique ghost removal service. In those early days of movie making, concept art became a crucial part to the movie making process—concept sketches were often blueprints for numerous departments including special effects, visual effects, props, and costumes. So for a film filled with ghosts, demons and other undead, Wrightson's work in comics prepared him for his foray into motion pictures.*

BERNIE WRIGHTSON: Well, the first movie I did was *Ghostbusters* in the early Eighties. When I started doing concept work, I don't think at the time there was CGI at all. Everything was a practical or an optical effect. And as CGI came in, it just expanded the horizons, and physical limitation ceased to be a factor.

The associate producer on *Ghostbusters* was a guy named Michael Gross, who years before was the art director at the *National Lampoon.* I had done some work for him, but we kind of lost contact with one another as the years went by, and he had gotten into Hollywood and producing movies. And he just called out of the blue one day and said, "Hey, Bernie, it's Michael Gross. Remember me?" "Oh, yeah, what are you up to?" "Well, producing movies now, and I want to send you a script. It's a monster/comedy movie called *Ghostbusters.*" And I said, "Okay, cool!" And that was basically it.

When they started out, they really had no idea what any of these monsters and ghosts and things were going to look like. So they brought in, I don't know how many conceptual artists, to work

on them. It was a fun gig in terms of they gave the script to the artists and said "Listen, do with this what you will. Come up with different designs and give us a lot of variation, and we'll look through everything and make our decisions." So in terms of freedom, it was a lot of fun. I think all of the conceptual stuff for *Ghostbusters* went through a long evolutionary process, where they had just piles of stuff to go through and decide what they wanted, what they didn't. They would take part of something that I did and give it to another artist and say, "Okay, we liked this part of what he did, but do something else with this other part." And vice versa. They would give me stuff that other artists had done and say, "Okay, this is what the other guys did. We like this about it, but we don't like everything else, so see what you can do."

I had never worked on a movie before, so it was a lot of fun to see the movie on the big screen and see something I worked on and say, "Oh my God, I designed that!" or "I had a hand in that!" It was a thrill, it was great.

CONCEPTING WITH PENCIL AND PAPER

As part of the preproduction process of movies, concept art is often collaborative. Any concept must be approved by the entire production team, because the visual style is the initial stage in developing a movie's identity. From special effects to the direction of a movie, the conceptual artist plays a pivotal role, and with today's technology, any idea can be made real. Every production is run differently, depending on the director's vision, but for Wrightson, the process of making abstract concepts physical begins with pencil and paper.

BERNIE WRIGHTSON: Every director is different. The first step that usually happens when I get a job is, "Well, why don't you read the script and just do some drawings." So that's what I do. I'll do some drawings, I'll bring them in. And they'll look at what I've done, and we'll take it from there. They'll say, "This part of it is good, I like this part, but let's change that part, let's try this out." So then I'll take it back and modify and start doing alternate versions.

But mostly, it depends on the people you are working with. Some of the directors are very comfortable with a rough sketch where you can show them something that's very preliminary, and they can take that step from looking at a rough sketch to how this is going to look on film. Other guys just want you to refine it and refine it and refine it until it looks exactly on paper like it looks on the screen.

When I work with a special effects company, I'm curious about how are you going to do this: a guy in a costume? Are you going to build an animatronic thing or something? Almost every time, they say, "Don't worry about that. Don't even think about that. That's not your job. Just design the best thing that you can on paper, and then we'll figure it out." These days, you realize that they can do anything. There are no limits.

With movie-making, there are so many people involved [in production and preproduction]. When I go to a movie I've worked on, if anybody asks, I tell them, "Sure, I worked on that." Maybe somebody sees my name in the credits. "Oh, cool. Did you do everything in this movie?" And I'll say, "No, no." I'll point out the stuff that I worked on.

For *Ghostbusters*, the script initially called for a third incarnation of Gozer the Destroyer, which was to take form after Gozer turned into the Stay-Puft Marshmallow Man. Wrightson continually refined his Gozer III designs to become more cartoony, though the designs were never used in the movie. Typically, Wrightson just uses pad of paper and pencil to do his work (right), but every so often will break out the paints for ideas that are particularly fun (above). Ghostbusters TM & ©2004 Columbia Pictures Industries, Inc.

THE FACULTY

Conceptual illustration is storytelling, and years of creating fantastic characters in comics and illustration enabled Wrightson to further his work in motion pictures. He lists 1998's The Faculty *as the project he felt the most challenged by and enjoyed the most. Wrightson styled the movie with director Robert Rodriguez, balancing individual vision with team goals to produce, literally, a monster.*

BERNIE WRIGHTSON: I really enjoy working with other creative people, and I really like being part of the team. Movies have to be a collaboration. In fact, I think it would make me very uncomfortable if I was the only guy working on a production crew. When you're doing comics, you're pretty much on your own, kind of working in a vacuum. You just sit down and draw this stuff. Then you take it in, the editor looks at it and maybe he makes some suggestions and wants some changes and things, but it's way over 90% all yours.

Concept art is basically the same as doing comics in terms that you're given a script and you're asked to visualize it. There's a few sentences or a paragraph that describes a character or a monster, and you have to turn those words into a drawing.

And when you're doing movies, you're never working in a vacuum, you're never alone. You're in the service of the director. You're pretty much drawing to order. Obviously, you're brought onto the movie because they want you to contribute your work and your look to it. But they have very specific ideas of what they want, and you have to consider that.

The best experience I had was with *The Faculty.* The

monster in *The Faculty* made it to the screen almost exactly the way I drew it. I had a great time working on that. The way it worked on *The Faculty* was they sent me the script, and I read it and flagged all the pages that had the monster. The script was more concerned in what the monster was doing rather than how it looked. So I talked with the guys at the special effects company, KNB. Robert Rodriguez worked with these guys before on *From Dusk Till Dawn* and a couple of other things, so he knew their work and trusted their judgment. I talked with Greg Nicotero—he's the "N" of KNB—about what the monster should look like. Then I had a couple of phone conversations with Rodriguez directly at the beginning, just to try and get a feel for what he'd want.

I did some initial passes at what I thought the monster should look like, then I started refining these drawings. I'd show KNB a drawing and they'd say, "Okay, this part of it looks good, but let's change this other part." And it evolved over a period of time, a lot of discussions and conversations. For the most part, I was pretty much on my own with a bit of input from the other guys.

The drawings then got passed on to the director, Robert Rodriguez. He would find elements in one drawing that he wanted to add to another drawing. So then I'd make another pass, and we'd keep doing this process and narrow it down, narrow it down. And then he was pretty much satisfied with what he wanted, and he handed it back over to KNB. They were the ones who originally hired me, anyway.

It all culminated with me actually sitting down with the effects guys in a conference room with maybe half a dozen people over my shoulder. I sat at the table with a pad of paper, drawing

Stills of the alien from *The Faculty* (top).
The evolution of the alien's design (right).
The Faculty TM & ©2004 Dimension Films

monsters. I had perhaps six or eight people leaning over my shoulder as I was drawing, and as I'm drawing, people are saying, "Oh, make that tentacle longer!" and "Oh, put another tentacle over here!" or "Make those spines sharper!" "Now make those spines longer!" and "Make the mouth bigger and give him more teeth!"

For me it was a lot of fun, because I felt like a police sketch artist, except that I was drawing a monster and just making this stuff up out of thin air, with people throwing suggestions at me. Everybody's there looking at what I'm doing and visualizing something more or something else, and throwing out suggestions, and I was just drawing away. We were trying out all kinds of things. This great group effort was a lot of fun. It was like a party.

And then, I don't know, a month or two went by, and I got a call and went up to the shop and they showed me the finished monster. When I saw this thing in the shop, I was just amazed. And it was beau-tiful, it was absolutely lovely and it looked just like my drawings. This thing was like twelve feet high, twenty feet long and it had cables and everything, the tentacles would whip around, the head would whip around and the mouth would open and close. It was like the size of a baby whale, it was this full-size monster. And Greg Nicotero said, "Watch this." And he stepped around behind the thing, there were a lot of cables and levers and everything. He started pulling these cables, and the thing started whipping the tentacles around and the head is just rocking back and forth, the jaws are snapping. It just came to life! It was just such a thrill to see this monster I designed; they brought my drawings to life. That was great.

So that was the closest anything has ever been to my work, my drawings, as far as transposing that to the screen. When that happens it's absolutely wonderful.

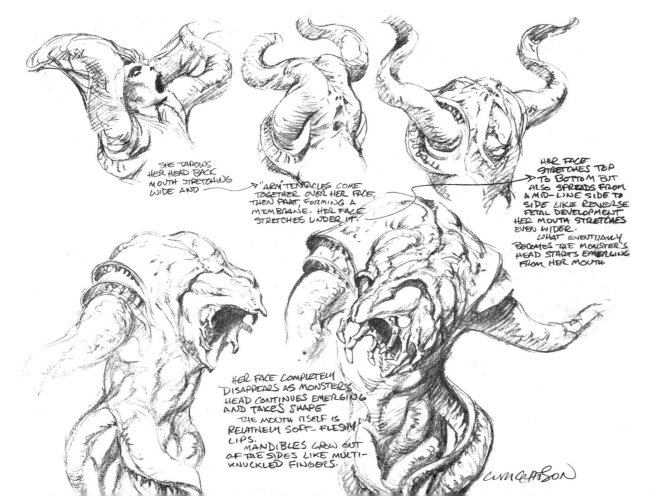

From concept to film, Wrightson's *Faculty* alien design was the closest translation to his vision ever produced. He attributes its success to good communication with all of the principle moviemakers involved. The Faculty TM & ©2004 Dimension Films

SPIDER-MAN AND THE GREEN GOBLIN

Wrightson was brought in as part of the "advance troops" to develop some of the concept art for the blockbuster Spider-Man *for director Sam Raimi and James Acheson, head of the costumes department. Though this was a high-profile production, the conceptual vision was compromised by communication problems between the costume department and the computer graphics department. The decision to shift the Green Goblin's comic book concept from leering mask and costume to the movie incarnation of battle suit and circuitry proved ultimately successful, and Wrightson played a significant part in this.*

BERNIE WRIGHTSON: It's not just one person doing designs, so a lot of times what I do gets handed over to someone else. When they're done with it, it gets passed on again, and it goes all the way down the line until the director or the producers change it so that what I did initially is almost unrecognizable on the screen.

When I was working on *Spider-Man*, I was part of a team with three or four other artists. We just worked all day. We were designing costumes, designing the look of the Green Goblin. Because it's Spider-Man, there wasn't really much to do about Spider-Man, because you do him the way he looks in the comic book, or else it's not Spider-Man anymore. But the Green Goblin, you see the drawings in the comic, and they said, "Okay, let's play around with this and try some different things." We worked for

somewhere between six to eight weeks just on the Green Goblin. We tried everything. We tried every look that we could think of, a lot of really creative stuff. I thought we had some really great-looking stuff. Then our time was up and we all left. And when the movie came out, I don't know what happened, because the Goblin in the movie looks nothing like what we were doing.

When we were working on it, we were working under the umbrella of the costume department, and the costume department has its own union. So the people in the costume department could not communicate with the people in the make-up department, and none of those people could communicate with the props department. So we were pretty much in the dark the whole time that we were working in the costume department. The communication was very bad on that job. We had no idea if they were thinking about the goblin wearing prosthetics and having make-up, like a face and expressions, or if he was going to be wearing a mask, or anything like that. We had no idea what that little winged thing he stands on was going to look like. So we were guessing on a lot of this stuff and just doing the best we could with the little information that we had. It makes you wonder sometimes how movies even get made.

(Counter-clockwise from top left) The final Green Goblin design from the movie *Spider-Man*.

Two Spider-Man costume concepts.

The Goblin-ettes, inspired by the 1996 comic, *Spider-Man: Legacy of Evil*. Spider-Man, Green Goblin TM & ©2004 Marvel Characters, Inc.

(Counter-clockwise from top left)
The evolution of the Green Goblin. The costume evolved into a more circuitry/armored look. The initial sketches drew from the comic book look, with the Goblin's eyes and face being less mask-like. Green Goblin TM & ©2004 Marvel Characters, Inc.

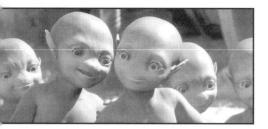

GALAXY QUEST

Yet another career high point for Wrightson was working with Stan Winston on Galaxy Quest in 1998. In the movie, the alumni cast of a cult space TV show have to play their roles as the real thing when an alien race needs their help. The possibilities of drawing aliens in many forms and shapes proved to be a dream come true. And surrounded by one of the more creative environments in Hollywood, Wrightson was able to enjoy this experience.

BERNIE WRIGHTSON: One day, Stan Winston just called and said, "Hey, I'm a longtime fan of yours and I hear you're doing movie work now. Would you like to work on this science fiction comedy?" And I went to his shop to meet him, and it was wonderful. He was working on one of the Jurassic Park films when I went over there, that was one of the other jobs they were doing. So I got to see some of the full-size dinosaurs in progress, and that was really cool. And sure enough, Stan had books and comics and things that he asked me to sign. It was cool!

Now like I said, since concept art is really a collaborative process, my drawings keep getting passed down the line, changing every stage of the way. However, having said all that, the few times that something actually makes it more or less intact, it's great! It happened on *Galaxy Quest* with the Little Blue Guys that look like little babies with shark's teeth. That was almost exactly what I drew.

Well, the Little Blue Guys, they were kind of a no-brainer, because I drew them exactly the way they're described in the script. They're supposed to look like babies with shark's teeth when they

smile. So just reading that, there's not much room for playing around with that: "Okay, this is what it's supposed to look like" so they made it to the screen virtually unchanged from the drawings, from the original designs.

And the Rock Monster, well we went through kind of an evolutionary process with him. Some of the early stuff I did, Stan and I talked about it, and he wanted it to look like the Thing from *Fantastic Four*. So I did a lot of drawings that looked kind of like that and brought those in. Stan looked at them and said, "Gee, this looks *too* much like the Thing." So we took it from there and the Rock Monster just kind of evolved.

With the villain, General Sarris, they had already had some other artist working on that, so I did a few variations on that. I can't remember exactly what I did and how much of what I did got incorporated into it, but that was a very collaborative character. A lot of people worked on that.

Stan Winston is just a wonderful guy. That's what most of the fun is, for me, working in the movie business, is just being able to meet and work with these really wonderful, creative people, whose work that I admire so much, and who apparently like my work, too.

The Little Blue Guys from *Galaxy Quest*. Wrightson kept true to the script, which called for little blue babies with shark's teeth. Galaxy Quest TM & ©2004 Dreamworks SKG

GALAXY QUEST #25
WRIGHTSON

The Rock Monster had its origins in comics from the Thing in the *Fantastic Four*. The original concept art (above) and the final movie CG character (below). Galaxy Quest TM & ©2004 Dreamworks SKG

BE STUBBORN

Wrightson's has always made career choices that allowed him to draw the things he wants to draw. The fact he has been able to create a career primarily drawing monsters and aliens is a testament to his stubbornness. Being known for designing both creative and innovative creatures, many opportunities do knock on Wrightson's door, but it's not all due to luck. He loves drawing, is exceptional at what he does, and has built his formidable reputation by drawing what he loves.

BERNIE WRIGHTSON: For the most part, I've been able to do just what I want to do, which I realize a lot of other people don't have that luxury. All I can really say is, I've just been tremendously lucky.

A lot of my career has been just pure luck; I've just happened to be in the right place at the right time. A lot of those venues just don't exist anymore. When I got into comics, I met these people at a convention, and we were all just out on the floor, just wandering around. And I'd show my work to somebody, and he'd see another guy walking by and say, "Hey, Dick, come on over here and take a look at this." You just don't have that anymore. Now, if you go to a convention and you want to show your work, you've gotta stand in line for three hours with all the other people who want to show their work, and the editors are all sitting at a table evaluating artwork; it's just a completely different thing. There seems to be a lot more competition now. When I got into it, there was just a handful of us who even thought we wanted to draw comics for a living. I go to conventions now, and it just seems like there are hundreds of people with their portfolios. But when you get to *do* a comic, you're the

director and the prop master and the designer and the lighting guy and everything else. And wow, what's better than that?

I lucked into concept work, too. My feeling is that I've managed to be around for a long enough time that a lot of people have noticed my work. A lot of the people that I've worked with in the movie work, they're about ten or fifteen years younger than I am. They were just the right age to be kids reading comics, when I was drawing *Swamp Thing*. So a lot of people that I work with, they know my work from when they were just kids, so I guess that's an advantage of being older.

I have no idea how to approach getting into [concept work]. The work I get is pretty much all word-of-mouth. I don't do promotional work or send out portfolios or things like that. Sometimes I'll hear about a job from another artist who's already working on a show or he knows about it, and he says, "Hey, these people are looking for artists." And they'll give me their number or I'll take their number and give them a call. Usually these people are familiar with my work before I go in. Sometimes I'll run into someone who's never heard of me. They've got into movies through some other route than comics and illustration or whatever. They don't know the artists. And I'll have to show a portfolio, and they like it or they don't like it.

Most of what I've done in movies is in design for creatures for monsters in science fiction or horror movies. The monster for *The Faculty*, work for Stan Winston for *Galaxy Quest*, and *Spider-Man*. I did storyboards for *Reign of Fire*, which was a dragon movie that kind of came and went. I've done conceptual stuff for a lot of movies that

Dragon designs for *Reign of Fire*. Part of the job of being a conceptual illustrator is visualizing as many ideas as possible to give the director options. Reign of Fire TM & ©2004 Touchstone Pictures

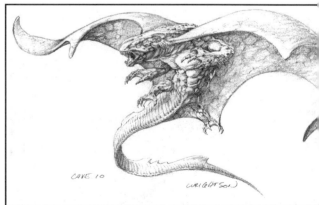

never got made, because that's just the way it goes. It goes into pre-production and then they pull the plug on it, and the whole project just fizzles and dies for whatever political or financial reason. It's just the nature of the business. There's a lot of good stuff that hasn't been made. They decide that it's too expensive or…who knows what they think? I don't have a clue who makes these decisions, but you can't let that stop you from drawing.

To do [concept art] for a living, you really have to love to draw, and you have to want to draw whether anybody's buying it or not. Otherwise, there are a lot of *other* kinds of jobs out there, y'know? There are a lot of opportunities in art, so find something you *do* love. Otherwise, what's the point? And I've always felt the more that you're able to do, the better, just in terms of surviving.

Mostly I tell artists just to be stubborn and pursue your dreams. My parents never really understood what I wanted to do; they never got it about monsters and why I was just fascinated with monsters. But they were really good about it in the sense that they backed off after a while, and didn't try to force me to do something that I didn't want to do. Occasionally, my mom would say, "Why don't you draw some flowers, or pretty mountains with a river running through it or something?" And I actually did a couple of paintings for her like that, mostly because I didn't know if I could do it. But I didn't get too much of that business of, "You're wasting your talent. God gave you this gift, and here you are pissing it away drawing monsters with their heads chopped off." I got that mostly from the nuns, thank you very much.

For me, I just wanted to draw what I wanted to draw. If nobody wanted to buy it, I probably would have drawn it anyway.

Because illustration is a relatively inexpensive and quick way to produce the visual elements of a movie script, conceptual illustration is often used to pitch movie scripts. However, when used as part of preproduction, there is never a guarantee that the movie will be made. Many wonderful ideas simply never get made. This time-travelling concept sketch (left) is an example of work created for a movie that never got made. ©2004 Bernie Wrightson

John Van Vliet
on Comics & Visual Special Effects

Visual special effects combines live action movie making with animation. This discipline is complex because there must be a balance between technology and artistry. Storytelling often determines the success because visual effects must always serve to further the story, not undermine it.

John Van Vliet is one of the visual effects wizards working in Hollywood today. Movies he's worked on read like a Best Of list, including The Empire Strikes Back, Raiders of the Lost Ark, Tron, Stargate, Mortal Kombat, *and* X-Men. *Even though he professes an inability to draw, he has created magic on both paper and screen.*

JOHN VAN VLIET: Oddly enough, I don't think I saw my first movie until I was twelve. Going to the movies was not something my family did. So when I saw my first movie, I was so absolutely blown away at seeing something that big and it made a pretty huge impression. Media awareness was not practiced in our house as we were not allowed to watch TV past seven o'clock or allowed to have comic books in the house. Once I had access to them, suddenly it was like, "Wow! What have I been missing?" Maybe that made them so much more important to me as I didn't grow up with them as "wallpaper", taking them for granted. But in spite of the lack of access to the media, as kids we always had tons of construction paper, woodworking stuff, pens, paper, and all of the basic art tools. I would hazard a guess that early creativity was encouraged by not being exposed to polished, pre-packaged entertainment. So by the time I did get access to visual entertainment, the basic tools were already in place. Maybe it was just a happy accident that it turned out that way, but I always thank my mom for bringing all that construction paper home.

Early on, I liked to draw. And I continued to draw as I grew up. I kept pushing the drawing edge not only because I really enjoyed it, but because people were always so fascinated by it. And when you're a little kid, anything you can do that makes people go, "Hey, look at that," gets you really jazzed. Looking back, I realize it was a sort of sublimi-

nal encouragement. But the bottom line was, drawing pictures was always a lot of fun. I will never say that I'm that good at it, because if I were, I'd be a painter or portrait artist.

It didn't really occur to me until much later that not everybody drew stuff. And it didn't occur to me until many years later that a lot of people don't even think in terms of pictures. When that finally became clear to me, it was astounding. But it took me a long time to figure out that people actually had a different thought processing method than what I was using. When I finally started to work with and comprehend computers, I saw some interesting analogies and came to the conclusion that people are probably born either to think in terms of an image-base or "text" database. In a computer, a file of text is a whole different format from a picture document and conveys information in completely different ways. Each one has its assets and liabilities, and neither one is appropriate for all information relaying purposes.

An early influence was Frank Thorne, who used to draw *Red Sonja* and *Tarzan* in the mainstream comics world. For years I went to school with his daughter Wende, but never realized that he was her dad. And one day someone said, "Is your dad Frank Thorne, the comic book artist?" And she goes, "Yeah, that's him." And I was like, "Oh my God! We have a deity in our midst". To me it was more impressive than discovering that we had a Nobel prize winner living in our neighborhood. So I went over and introduced myself to this amazing fellow, who graciously allowed us unwashed rabble to pester him at length. I'd watch this professional artist draw and it was (and still is) really intimidating—I don't think I could ever draw like that. I can aspire to it, but when you watch a professional sit down and knock out X amount of pages per day and not even break a sweat…that's talent. When I draw, it's excruciating. If I had seriously tried to depend on drawing to make a living, I have little doubt I would be starving and living in a cardboard box under a bridge somewhere. So while I enjoy drawing, I harbor no illusions and realize it would be a foolish way for me to attempt to make a living and that I should pursue it purely for the pleasure.

John Van Vliet can be found drawing in his sketchbook during his movie work. Sometimes, it's a way to pass the time during the tedium of movie-making, but it is also an interesting way to voice his thoughts or record moments. "Doing visual special effects is not as creative as you think. Yeah, you gotta make decisions, you gotta figure stuff out, but bottom line: you're there to make someone else's creative vision work. And if you do a really great job, then it's their creative vision and they were smart enough to hire you to help realize it. That's just part of the process. If I'm frustrated on a show because I'm being asked to do stupid, non-creative things, I'll relieve the stress or tedium by working on my own drawings. On occasion people ask me to draw something for them and generally I'll say, "You know what? I'm drawing this for me." If I have to take instructions on what to draw, then it's no longer fun. So I guess we'll just call it self-help therapy."

The Evolution of Animators.

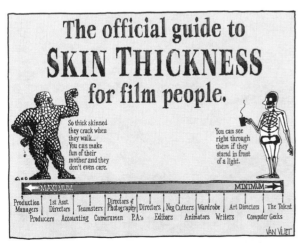

Deadline Excuses Through The Ages

The Magic Journey
of
Demo Tapes

Your special tape, full of hopes and dreams, begins it's magic journey.

Federal employees will hand deliver your tape to the studio of your choice...Along side that big shipment of magnets someone ordered.

A secretary at the studio will press each tape to her head to determine which one has a "good vibe". Those that are selected will be sent to someone who will actually view them.

An assistant of questionable taste and judgement will view your tape and mock it unmercifuly.

Any tapes that do not threaten his own plans, schemes and fragile ego will be sent on to the boss.

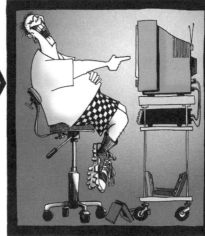

Your tape goes to the studio skeet range where the producers go to relieve the stress of writing large checks to themselves all day. Any tape they miss, will be viewed.

From Training Manuals to Damned Bears

Van Vliet enlisted into the military, and his superiors recognized a talented visual communicator. It was in the Air Force where he developed storytelling skills and it was these skills that eventually lead him to the California Institute of the Arts in Los Angeles, California.

John Van Vliet: One of the jobs I had done in the military was to create training aids. We basically took text from incredibly dull training manuals and attempted to put it all into a visual format to keep pilots on the ground interested. Pilots, especially combat pilots are a fairly dynamic bunch of people and generally the last thing a pilot wants to do is sit behind a desk and read about flying. While generally bright, they have a low threshold of boredom, so we had to make the material somewhat entertaining.

I had seen Will Eisner's military training comics around, but that was mostly an Army/infantry thing. Y'know, it was like "fun ways to strip down an M1 Carbine." But it was famous material; it stuck in everyone's mind and everybody knew about it. So here was a process to relay information that was proven. My stuff was downright primitive compared to his work, and I would say that was a hell of a shadow to be working in. But it was the same type of thinking: "How can I take this rather dull thing we have to learn and put some fun into it?" And we certainly did.

After my four year tour of duty was up, I got out of the military. I ran into a fellow named Peter Kuran that I had grown up with in New Jersey, who, of all things, had gone out and ended up working on the first *Star Wars* at Industrial Light and Magic. I had been interested in animation for a long time, and I basically said, "Where in the hell do you go to school for this sort of thing?" He replied that he had attended Cal Arts and that it was the best place he knew of. After researching it a bit, I concurred with his opinion and applied, got accepted and went there the following fall.

The Disney character animation program at Cal Arts was sort of an island of wholesomeness isolated in the midst of this ocean of debauchery. Cal Arts took great pride in the fact that they were this real avant garde, new wave group, producing free-thinking (and often just plain bizarre) out-there kind of art. This of course attracted some pretty out-there people, who in a different era, may have been institutionalized, or earlier, burned at the stake. Somehow in the middle of this whole new-wave tangle was the Disney animation program...Which was this odd juxtaposition because here's all these kids who their whole life had aspired to embrace the Disney ideal and go work there. They showed up looking like the most wholesome kids you ever saw, and then the next classroom over, there's the rest of Cal Arts. It was like "Ozzy Osbourne" and "Leave it to Beaver" occupying the same channel, just kind of weird and somehow amusing. My draw to the Disney program was because I'd always loved cartooning and at the same time, also had a great desire to make films, so it seemed like a natural connection.

Once I was actually in the Disney animation training program, it became obvious that the studio work we were being trained for was not one where too many of us were going to be asked to do anything that creative. I remember early on wanting to animate this crazy stuff, and the instructor came in and brought down this huge stack of extreme key-frames of Brer Bear for *Song of the South*. I'm going, "Well, what about monsters and fires and explosions and things?" And this instructor gives me this tired look and goes: "Just draw the bear, kid." And I go, "But what about–" "Just draw the bear, kid."

So I drew that damned bear and I hated every last frame of it. And in the middle of it, I remember this moment of terrifying clarity when I realized that the only thing they're really interested in is training us as in-betweeneers to work in the galley. And that's when I started to realize that I have to look a little wider. Naturally I started gravitating to the effects end of the animation as there were a lot less rules and it wasn't such a rigid process. There was this great animation stand, and I remember asking the main instructor from Disney: "What kind of film stock are you running? What can I do with this stand?" The reply was:"You don't need to know that, just draw the bear..." But I figure it was my dime that I was spending, so I pushed a bit more on the effects end, and pretty soon was doing split exposures and shadows and tinkering with camera moves on the artwork.

There was one teacher, Ken O'Conner, who used to be in layout and effects. I think he was originally from Australia and he was about two days older than God. He was so thrilled and delighted that anybody even cared about this stuff, he just started showing me all these tricks. He was an amazing source of information, though I sort of got the impression that this was not part of the normal curriculum. When I eventually started working at ILM, I would routinely contact him to ask his advice on effects problems and he was always happy to offer advice.

Over Christmas break everyone had gone home. While I stayed there to work on my little animated movie, someone knocks on my door and I open it up and it's this guy Peter Kuran again. I showed him what I was working on and we talked, gave comments and some advice, then left. A couple months later in the middle of my second semester, he sent me a letter saying, "Hey, I've got this job up here working on *Star Wars* 2 in Northern California. Are you interested in dropping out of school to come up here to work?" My reply was of course affirmative, but the reaction was more of, "Well, duh!"

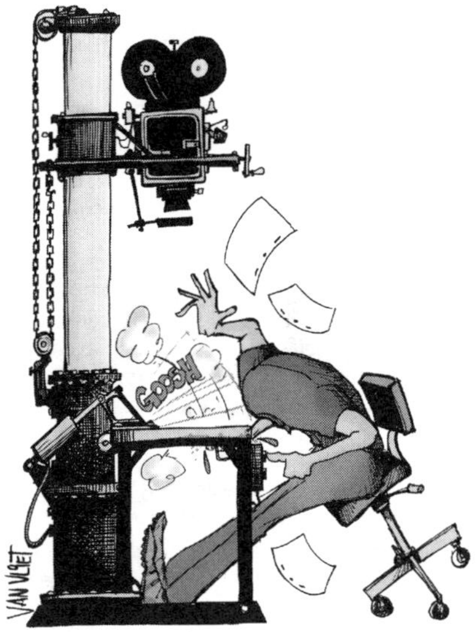
GOOSH
VAN VLIET

Van Vliet has many fond memories of the faculty, and the students he met at Cal Arts. His memories of the animation camera (above), however, still gives him chills. "I look back at Cal Arts and in a very small span of time, they had some very heavy hitters go through there. Tim Burton was still there in the senior class, and John Lassiter would emerge to reinvent the animation process with computers. Rick Heinrich who has picked up an Oscar for production design was in my class, as was Joe Ranft, who has become one of the best animation story guys in the business (now working at Pixar). Gary Trousdale, who directed *Beauty and the Beast* was there, and Brian McEnte who did some marvelous work on *Ice Age* for BlueSky. There is a long list of Cal Arts alums that ended up in really key positions in the business and it would take me forever to name them all. All I can figure is somebody must've dropped something interesting in the water supply up there for a couple of years. It was, and continues to be a pretty astounding group." ©2004 John Van Vliet

VISUAL COMMANDOS

Creating visual special effects for motion pictures is a production within a production. As an effects supervisor, Van Vliet makes a director's vision reality, and because every director has a unique vision, the task can be a difficult one. Here, Van Vliet explains the nuances of working within the tribe of a Hollywood production.

JOHN VAN VLIET: There are two extremes of the spectrum. When I go onto a show the director could know exactly what he wants and is such a control freak that everything is planned out and every shot storyboarded. The other end of the spectrum is a director who doesn't have a clue and is a potential train wreck waiting to happen. Sometimes I get called for short sequences within a film and sometimes I get the responsibility for the visual effects of the entire picture. Let's just look at some typical scenarios…

Ideally the director will say, "I have some ideas and storyboards here, go with this." I would look at what he had and then pick his or her brain to try and get some clues to their thinking process so I can second-guess them later when they are too busy to be available. I would take that material and try to build on it, taking his or her ideas and then modify them to get all the component parts that I need to construct a viable visual effects shot that still leaves an opportunity for the director to modify to his tastes. But that's working with a guy who's got a picture in his head already, is comfortable delegating his vision and not easily frightened by the unknown.

Other situations are you get a director who has few (if any) pictures in his head, so you need to create something from nothing and hope it's what they might want. This is a situation where the

blank page can be either the most terrifying thing in the world, or the most exhilarating. When you confront that blank page, you have an equal opportunity to go out there and really hang yourself or really shine.

Usually we land somewhere in the middle of that range and then it's more of a whittling contest. You show material to the director and go, "What do you think of that?" And the director goes, "Ooookay. Well, how about this and how about that." And you translate his ideas and incorporate your own to make it work. You go back and forth a lot and it is a process that takes a lot of patience and energy, but in the end, it's a lot of your own input and you can often steer the construction of [the shot] to get something that's going to give the best results with the most options.

Of course, then, you can always get into that dreaded situation where you get a director who does not have any picture in his head. This happens more than it should and we always wonder how in the hell this guy ever got a job directing a picture since the operative word here is "picture". Then you're stuck in that horrible, expensive limbo world where you hear those scary words, "Just keep showing me stuff until I see something I like." That's when the producer rolls his eyes into the back of his head, your crew has a fit, and somebody has to call the studio and say, "Better bring more money!" It's not a happy thing.

But serving the director is what we get paid for. The thing that's really tough for a lot of people coming into the business to understand is that when you do a feature, we're all there primarily as support for that director. He's the person they hired to have a vision, and we crew people are the team that is supposed to get in there and offer whatever talents and skills we have to help him fulfill that vision. If the director's favorite color is pink, which I might detest, and they want pink in their vision on screen, I'm going to try as hard as hell to make that pink work. Even if I think it's the biggest flaming turd I've ever seen, I'm going to do everything I can to make it work. Yes, it is tough to swallow sometimes, and yes, I have created my share of flaming turds at the behest of directors. I may have to make them, but at least I don't have to put them on my demo reel.

To serve the director, you need to be responsive; learn to second-guess what he wants, figure out how he's thinking (presuming he is thinking), and gear yourself to get him what he needs before he knows himself. To make this work on the scale that is needed for production work, you can't do it all yourself, so you need to find people who are reliable, are good for their word, think fast on their feet. You're looking for a commando team where you can throw anything at them and they'll figure it out fast. Especially if you're working on a live-action set and you don't have room to stop and go, "Well, we're going to have to completely rethink this." It's often, "How can I save

The Scorpion fight scene in *Mortal Kombat* climaxed with Johnny Cage wounding Scorpion; lava flowed out and caused Scorpion to catch fire and explode. To accomplish this, Van Vliet ironically convinced the director Paul Anderson to avoid cost-prohibitive CG work for Scorpion. In the end, several Scorpion puppets were built, plumbed for dispensing both propane and fluorescent "lava". Van Vliet sums up working with pyrotechnic effects: "Any time you're with pyro guys that all have their fingers, you know you've got a winning bunch." Mortal Kombat TM & ©2004 Midway Amusement Games, LLC

this right now?" Because, depending on the size of the show, you could be chewing up anywhere from ten to twenty to thirty thousand dollars an hour.

Doing effects work is sort of like bomb disposal. If you do it right, everybody comes up smiling; if you do it wrong, you're dead. There's almost no room for error, because from a production standpoint, there's no time for it and from a business standpoint there's so little profit margin in it. It's a very labor-intensive business, the expense is quite high, and just about everything you do is a prototype. You routinely have to guess on how efficient your creativity is and more times than I like to think about, consider luck as a component of the process. As a business model, that's a really lousy thing to gamble on.

Be a director? I have no desire to be a director. I've worked sets where I was doing second unit direction and there's so much to go wrong, that there were times I was grateful just to have film rolling thru the camera. You've gotta really, really want to be a director. If a guy says, "Hey, I need you to go do this shot today," I'll go do it and that's fine. But I'm not willing to die for the opportunity to do so and I know there are plenty of people who are. Now if you're talking about directing animation, that's a whole different story, because you don't have to deal with cranky actors who throw fits and won't come out of their trailers. If an animated character is really annoying, you just erase him. Animation direction is fun, because you don't have the pressure of the huge crew sitting there waiting for a decision right this second, where if you think about a problem more than a moment, you just blew another twenty thousand dollars. It's also

wonderfully safe (unless an irate artist attacks you with his pencil) compared to a live action set. My partner once said, "The great thing about animation is, you can make a mistake and nobody dies."

Animation, to me, is the purest form of movie-making, and I think most of the movies we will see in the future are going to be a form of animation. Part of what makes seeing a film special is the opportunity of seeing something that you don't normally get to see. If you film something that you can't get in reality, then it's so much more magical to watch. If you're filming things that don't really exist, or are too dangerous or practical to do for real, you're getting into visual effects. And if you start to introduce characters, you're getting into animation. Watch the *Phantom Menace* Star Wars sequel; in spite of the story problems with the movie, the thing that was the most remarkable was that this was the beginning of the new age of movies. It was essentially a digital backlot picture. An important percentage of the characters were not real. And we're going to be seeing a lot more of that as the technology improves. To me, that's the best utilization of the medium. We want to see things we can't normally see. When I was in film school, one of the instructors said, "If you can film it, go film it. If you can't film it, animate it." That seemed to be a pretty good rule of thumb.

If you're just filming a couple of talking heads, then you've just got big-screen TV.

"When you get involved in a show that's union-based, then your team has to be very, very careful. If you're on a heavy union show, the camera operator only runs the camera, the focus puller only focuses, the script girl only does script. As visual effects geeks, we do everything. It's good to be a jack-of-all-trades, but you've also got to be incredibly diplomatic, because a live-action crew is generally a bunch of guys who work together *all* the time—and it's more of a *tribe* than a crew. And if you piss off the tribe, they will hurt you. So be very respectful and don't mess with them.

"Effects is notorious for making things run very slowly, because they have to get so much more stuff. When I bring a team in, they are not necessarily from the live-action school of thinking, so they don't understand that a show's crew is under pressure to deliver X amount of pages per day and if they don't get them, they're behind schedule and there's hell to pay. That's the reality of filmmaking. I have to go in and guess how many hours of work it's going to take to make a director happy."

The finished Scorpion scene (below). When plate photography was finished and composited, Van Vliet enhanced the practical "lava" and added more frames. Mortal Kombat TM & ©2004 Midway Amusement Games, LLC

Star Wars: The Empire Strikes Back pioneered many of the visual special effect theories still employed into today's movies. Because *Empire* was pre-computer graphics, Van Vliet and other animators animated lightning, lasers, and explosions using optical effects and animations. The Hoth battle scene (above and right). Star Wars TM & ©2004 LucasFilm

CREATING MAGIC FOR ILM

Before the digital age, the book on special effects was being written while productions were in swing. Van Vliet's first professional credit after Cal Arts was Star Wars: The Empire Strikes Back. It was on this job that Van Vliet was thrown into the deep end of the pool, and he loved every minute of it. Even facing stacks of animation work, he knew he was working on a project that was special. Industrial Light and Magic proved that as long as you can imagine your story, you can commit it into a film. Visual special effects grew up with this mantra.

JOHN VAN VLIET: When I went to work on *Empire,* they put me in the animation department whose main job was to fix things. If they shot something with the blue screen, rarely is the blue screen big enough to cover the whole thing, so you have to go in and garbage matte everything, which is basically making big hole-in-the-wall mattes. And then, because things are always in a hurry, there would be some times where they didn't have a chance to use a blue screen, so that means you have to go in and hand rotoscope every frame to pull a matte. And sometimes the blue screen was just badly shot, because they were in a hurry or somebody was sloppy, so you fix that. There's just a million little things where you had to have some animation skills to be able to figure out how to create hand drawn mattes so they don't wiggle all over the place or "chatter" and look ridiculously bad on the big screen. That was the bulk of what the animation department was intended to do, and it was a huge amount of work.

Our animation department was run by a fellow mentioned earlier, Peter Kuran, who was a very, very bright guy. He had some animation training as well as general film making, so was very innovative and had some really great tricks. He pushed the department to try and come up with new techniques, and a lot of things we tried out there became industry standards later on. We were putting in light sabers and lightning and all the laser battle stuff with energy bolts flying all over the place. When you watch the snow battle with all of this laser fire flying back and forth, every time you see one go ripping by one of those walkers or a speeder, you'd see light reflection on the background or vehicle. Every single one of those frames was hand drawn and air-brushed animation. We were literally sitting under the animation cameras with airbrushes, squirting ink through hoses and coating the lenses and our lungs with paint. So besides handling this huge workload of optical repair work, we ended up also doing what we like to call "the pretty stuff."

Looking back, I think that *Empire* was probably the most fertile arena ever in which to develop and grow visual effects and animation. There was a lot of technology that was beginning to mature and nobody had ever attempted to try things like what was being attempted there. More than once, we would try to figure out how to do something by looking at solutions from the past and realized that no one had ever tried it before. Sometimes there was not a lot of knowledge to draw on, so we were making stuff up as we went along.

After Star Wars: The Empire Strikes Back, *Van Vliet and his fellow tribe members found themselves migrating to the next blockbuster—Raiders of the*

Lost Ark. *This motion picture challenged not only Van Vliet's effects knowledge, but his animation training as well.*

VAN VLIET: *Raiders* was a difficult picture to work on. Spielberg and Lucas partnered up to do this show and naturally came in to do the work at ILM. Initially, it was thought that the whole end sequence with all of those scary ghosts might be handled primarily with effects animation. We heard a lot of references to "Night on Bald Mountain", which was a pretty tall order and frankly, the animation department wasn't ready to do it, because this was a huge job. We started doing tests, and I think management at ILM had no idea how much work was involved in animation, because we had made the work we did on *Empire* look so easy. But full character animation for that length of time was just something they hadn't comprehended. So we did test after test after test, and at the same time, out on stage they're testing techniques as well. Ultimately the solution was a hybrid process using a rag ghost on a stick. Originally I built this rag ghost and I said, "I need to shoot this for a model to get a look, because we have to know what this thing looks like before we can animate it." We did test after test after test, with some promising results, and some results that weren't so promising, and some results that were terrible. But at one point, one of the guys from the model shop picked up the rag ghost and said, "Hey, wait a second…" and put it in the giant cloud tank and swished it around. Richard Edlund, who was the visual effects supervisor on the show recognized what was happening and we were on our way. It was one of those situations and environments where what I call the "collective intelligence"

flourished. You have a series of small steps, mistakes, and successes and a bright guy at the top would be like Edison—he'd pull all the good stuff together and make something great out of it. All the things that happened brought us to the rag ghost in the tank and a guy like Edlund pulls it all together, and makes it all work. For that ability he was rewarded with another Oscar for his collection.

The final ghost stuff actually looked great. Nobody had seen anything quite like it. My role ended up animating a lot of the mattes to make it look like these ghosts were moving and curling in around the live action characters in 3-D space. Whenever the ghosts touched the Nazis and were crawling on them, there were four or five scenes where I animated this ectoplasm crawling over their bodies. My favorite shot in the movie was when the camera pushes (zooms) in on the crate where the Ark is hidden in the ship. As you get closer to the crate, something happens inside and the Ark starts burning the swastika off of the crate, presumably because God had some issue with swastikas. They were going crazy out on the stage trying to figure out how to do this. I remember watching dailies and was basically like this little kid going up to Edlund, going, "Can I try that?" And he was like, "Yeah, right, okay." So I went in and I animated the burn. It's one of the perfect examples of effects animation because it's invisible–it looks like somebody burned the thing.

It was a push-in, match-move shot, and it was a real pain in the ass. It took me a couple of weeks to do it, and nobody knows it was animation. To me, it may be the most rewarding shot I did on the show.

Van Vliet's hand-animated burn from the cargo ship scene (above).

From the Island sequence inspired by Disney's *Night on Bald Mountain*. The ghost and fire effects won *Raiders* an Oscar (below) Also, an actual conversation from the set of *Raiders of the Lost Ark*. Van Vliet can often be found scribbling fun moments like this in his sketchbook while on set. Raiders of the Lost Ark TM & ©2004 LucasFilm

SCULPTING VISION AND TIME

Like comics, the art of making movies involves a production line. A visual special effects supervisor has to be flexible and conduct research in order to match the director's visual sense. Once vision is understood and established, then it must be maintained, even if that means standing up to the director. Of course, you could always go through the editor...

JOHN VAN VLIET: There are some directors that are delightfully stand-offish, and just say: "You know what I need, go get it." And you hope to God you know what he needs and can go get it. Then there are the other guys at the other end of the spectrum who are such control freaks, they can't let go of anything. A director is a special kind of person, some are truly geniuses and some are idiot savants and a few are just idiots, but I won't tell you which ones are which because I would like to keep working.

Some of them can be terribly insecure about their position and feel it is a display of weakness to admit when they don't some aspect of the production process. You then have to be very, very careful, so you don't wound their delicate egos while at the same time trying to maneuver them into not making an expensive (or dangerous) error. I had this one show where there was this guy who had a very sensitive ego, and I had to reassure him that I was going to be his loyal soldier and do whatever he needed to be done to get the shot, and he felt much better. But when we got out on the set, I notice that he's moving a locked camera around and doing things that basically could have ruined hours of shooting. I had to go stop him and of course he

immediately goes and throws back that statement, he goes, "I thought you were going to be a good soldier and do as you're told," blah-blah-blah. My response was: "I will be your good soldier, but sometimes a really good soldier has to make sure the general doesn't shoot himself in the foot." He was not happy with that answer, but I got my shot.

I've worked with all different kinds of directors, and some were the most incredibly visionary people I've ever met in my life, and some of them seemed like they had paper bags over their heads. Directing is incredibly difficult when you consider that you're trying to take written text (like a script) and turn it into ninety minutes of pictures that are interesting, compelling and entertaining. It's the art of storytelling where you have to work with the three segments of film: *Art*, *Technology* and *Business*.

What a lot of people don't understand, is how difficult it is when you're trying to focus on getting individual shots done and you still have to pull back and think wide/global thoughts about the integrity of the story and then put your brain back in macro-focus to deal with the details. I like the lens/focus analogy because most people think like a lens works... If you push it in tight enough to see all the detail work, then you don't see the wide shot and lose sight of everything else. Being able to maintain close focus and still be able to maintain that wide vision of the entire integrity of the story is like having two brains running at once. When you see somebody who can do that, and does it consistently...well, you realize what a special person they are; it sort of blows you away. You also understand why they get to do interesting things with large sums of money. I've been very fortunate in that I've been around some people like that.

Available Light Ltd. was a special effects company co-founded by Van Vliet and Katherine Kean. Available Light was a proving ground for new methods and techniques for effects animation and was immediately pressed into service handling overflow work for the major effects houses. This enabled the fledgling company to earn credit on such pictures as *Ghostbusters*, *Who Framed Roger Rabbit?*, and *Willow*. Available Light was also responsible for all of the dark spirit images and many of the animated beings for *Ghost*. An example of traditional back-lit animation done by hand (below). Ghost TM & ©2004 Paramount Pictures

When I get assigned to a show, the first thing I'll do is go rent his other features. and see what his style is and try to see how he thinks. You can generally start picking up common denominators in his visual sense. There was one director who had done a lot of television and when I looked at his feature work, I realized he'd never really broken out of TV thinking even after he had gotten onto the big screen. He would always go back to comfortable, simple shots that were set up for TV. It seemed the only time he really broke out of the TV thing was when he had a really strong director of photography on his arm. So I learned from watching his work, and sure enough, when we got out in the field that's exactly what he did.

When I do my preliminary meetings with directors, it helps me a lot if they've already gotten into the storyboards, or generated concept art because that tells me where they're going and what they are thinking. The more I talk to the guy, the better chance I'm going to get to pick things out of his head. So it's an exploration to try to figure out what they want, and hopefully they're going to be open enough that as the movie is built, you are in there–you can go into the cutting room and watch what they're doing and match the flavor of what they want. It's really important to me to have access to the cutting room and the editor. After the director, the editor is director #2, because he's the guy who's actually sculpting time. And he's often the unsung hero on a lot of these movies. I've watched really good editors weed through miles of mediocre film and extract an astounding picture, which is an amazing thing. Most people don't understand how much input they have.

So like I said, the editor is literally sculpting time. And if you have an editor and director who have developed a good dialogue, then you get truly great stuff. I watched that happen when we did *Ghost* with Jerry Zucker and Walter Murch. Jerry was a comedy director and had never done anything like *Ghost* and he had Walter, who is one of the best editors on the planet. They just "clicked" and they made this amazing picture which became the sleeper hit of the year. It was just one of those things where everything was in perfect balance. Not bad for a "little" picture.

Since *Ghost* was produced before CG, the dark spirits were created by filming stunt actors in white costumes in stop motion to create ghostly blurs. These elements were then reversed and composited with the final footage. Ghost TM & ©2004 Paramount Pictures

X - M E N

The X-Men are arguably the most popular superhero group in comics today. For most comic book fans, seeing how close a movie matches their beloved comic books is always a dicey proposition. With most failed comics to movie attempts, Hollywood disregards the source material. But on the X-Men movie, sometimes the source material was not enough to capture the grandeur of Storm or the nastiness that is the Toad onto celluloid. Comics and motion pictures are visually two different mediums, and the most seasoned movie-maker understands how to make the most of their medium.

JOHN VAN VLIET: I didn't get hired directly by the production, but one of the vendors on the show, Cinesite of Hollywood. Cinesite had been assigned a number of sequences on the film, including the Storm effects and the tongue work on the Toad. Over the years, especially in the years prior to computer animation, I've been one of the animators who figured out how to draw electricity that meshed well with live-action backgrounds. In effects animation, it was one of the last things that was still drawn (I think it's finally over now as I'm told, they finally got software that does it). But at the time of *X-Men*, they were having a lot of problems with it, so I was asked to come in and provide electrical elements to be composited down there on site. They brought me in and the first scene I did was Storm being choked by Sabretooth. It went together reasonably well, and everybody was happy. Short story! The director was happy, Fox was happy, and the check was good, so I was happy.

At that time in the show, the electrical effects were supposedly motivated by whenever Storm got upset, bolts from heaven would come down and she would start initiating these discharges around her. So that kept me busy for quite a while.

I became involved with the 3-D work on the Toads tongue at around this point as they were looking for someone to act as the animation supervisor. Cinesite had a whole roomful of extremely talented artists trying to animate this Toad tongue, but there was a bit of a continuity problem. My initial mandate was to " just go in and work with these guys and make it better". Never one to turn down interesting work, I happily went in and we further developed some of Toad's particular (peculiar) actions with that astounding tongue of his. The artists were really about 70% there, so I was more sort of helping people along and directing on the thing. In spite of the production deadlines and pressure to produce, we really had a lot of fun with the Toad tongue. We would do little things like when he jumps onto the floor, whips his head around, and then drag his tongue across the rug, "Yeah, now he's got lint on his tongue!" It gave the character a lot of subtle "style" and really underscored what an interesting devil-may-care wise ass that he was. I found him so interesting, I was sad to have to fry him later on in another scene.

The most interesting thing that happened on the show was Storm with her lightning on her hair, because they asked me to go and animate this stuff around her eyes; that's what the director wanted, because it was what was in the comic book. This was one of the times when an image that works as a still frame doesn't always work in motion. A lot of people have a tough time understanding that problem and I have had the same issue come up many times on other shows. But all these guys were looking at the comic book, and there's Storm with the very graphic lightning around her eyes, "Well, that's what's in the comic book, so we have to do this!" And they kept doing it, and it looked, frankly, pretty stupid. And I remember looking at it, going, "You know what? No matter what I do here, even if I'm the best lightning-drawer on the planet, it's still gonna look pretty stupid." Their reply was "Well, just go ahead and do it anyway and make it work." And what a surprise…it looked pretty stupid. Then they're looking at me like, "Well, you're deficient. You are obviously doing it wrong!" And I'm going, "Guys, this is a design problem. Okay? What works well in a still is not–" And they're still looking at me like, "Well, you're deficient." In discussions I remember telling them, "If you want something to look like she's got electricity coming from her, you've got these wind machines blowing this great white hair against this black costume and dark set. If I was the designer on the show, I would be using an asset that we have here, work the electrical stuff into the hair and it'll probably look great." And they were like, "Nah, just make the eyes work." So I went back and, as instructed, worked on the eyes. In the meantime, I took one of the shots and took the liberty of animating the electricity coming off of her hair as I had described it.

I gave the scanned animation art to Kevin Elam who was our effects producer at Cinesite and told him, "You know what? I feel so strongly about this I went and did it. If you like it, I will charge you for it, and if you don't like it, it's free. But I leave it up to you to try it." Kevin looked at it and said, "Well, let's try it." Bless him. So we composited the animation and suddenly the eye sparklers just didn't matter that much. They're still in there, but they're pretty minimal and they still look rather unimpressive. But the hair stuff is what everybody went crazy about. And suddenly that's in all the trailers, all the promo stills. If I had a nickel for every duplicated shot of Storm and her lightning hair, I could probably retire forever. On every show I like to look back to see a golden moment, where there is one thing that I'm most proud of on the show and on *X-Men*, it would be that hair. There was a rare opportunity for creative input, and the support of the organization I was working for, so it all synced up and we all came out happy.

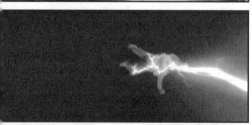

(Top to Bottom) The Toad gets hit by Storm's lightning bolts. As animation supervisor, Van Vliet worked on the Toad Tongue.

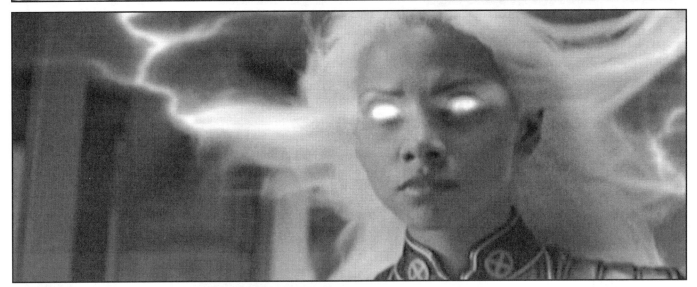

Van Vliet's involvement in *X-Men* grew into providing additional design concepts and animation elements for Storm's lightning (left). Elements were generated by animating under a traditional rotoscope camera and scanning the art into the computer. Final composites were assembled at the visual effects company Cinesite. Storm, Toad TM & ©2004 Marvel Characters, Inc. X-Men movie ©2004 20th Century Fox.

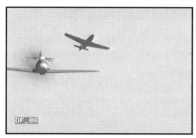

HART'S WAR

Storyboards are a wonderful tool used to visualize a scene. For complex action, there are times when a director needs more. Animatics, or pre-visualizations, show animation and movement at real time—24 frames a second—and were used in Hart's War.

JOHN VAN VLIET: Movies and 2-D images are not the same. I ran into one show where they had some of the most incredible, beautiful storyboards I'd ever seen. There's this one storyboard artist named Kevin McCarthy... His artwork has the grace and beauty of Japanese brush paintings; he did the boards for *Hart's War*. Kevin illustrated these particular actions for the aircraft, giving them exactly what they asked for. When they handed me the boards and said, "This is what we want," I remember looking at them, going, "Well, this is great, but you've got an airplane running two, three hundred miles an hour, and with this camera angle you're going to see it for half a second or twelve frames, eighteen frames, tops. And it's all going to be blurred out, you're not going to see or recognize who the bad guy is or the good guy." And they were just like, "But that's what we want." So we put the shot together and they go, "Hey! Everything's all blurred out! We can't tell who's who!" That's when you go, "Well, duh." (But very quietly)

Trying to comprehend what an image looks like with the element of time added is such a huge leap for most folks not involved in animation. (As animators, we sometimes forget how difficult it is since we do it all the time.) Because of this time problem, I always encourage my clients to allow us time and money for pre-visualizations (or sometimes called animatics) early on so they know exactly what they are asking for. A lot of studio people think it's a complete waste of time as it doesn't directly show a professional looking result up on the screen. But we did it on *Hart's War*, and while they will never say anything, I saw subtle changes in their approach after that. So I think when they saw what they were asking for, it did make a difference. For what it costs to assemble a shot today, it's better to find out what's not going to work on a pre-visualization than to find out later with the actual production.

Speaking of pre-visualizations, the first time I worked on them was up at Lucasfilm. They were planning the big snow battle scene and they gave us all Joe Johnson's storyboards. They handed us all his pages and said, "We want you to do a quick and dirty Saturday morning style cartoon so we have something to slug in for timing." (This is 1979, so we animated it all by hand.) Lucas understood the time issue, because he came from an editing background where part of your job is to sculpt time. I feel this time/image comprehension is one of the things about him that made his work so successful. But the reason I bring up this little bit of history was the actual storyboards. Those particular storyboards blew me away because they were so well thought-out that I started to realize that they were almost extreme key frames for animation. At one point I said, "Okay, let's try a little test here." And I went up to the Xerox machine and enlarged them, pasted the art onto registered animation paper as extremes for all of these wild action moves on the various flying speeders and those big walker things. Well, those little drawings animated really well and "We do have animation extremes... Okay!" Joe actually understood the time thing and his sense of timing helped that snow battle on the planet Hoth look so dynamic. When you get to work with somebody who "gets it," it's such a treat.

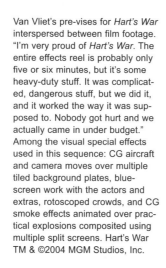

Van Vliet's pre-vises for *Hart's War* interspersed between film footage. "I'm very proud of *Hart's War*. The entire effects reel is probably only five or six minutes, but it's some heavy-duty stuff. It was complicated, dangerous stuff, but we did it, and it worked the way it was supposed to. Nobody got hurt and we actually came in under budget." Among the visual special effects used in this sequence: CG aircraft and camera moves over multiple tiled background plates, bluescreen work with the actors and extras, rotoscoped crowds, and CG smoke effects animated over practical explosions composited using multiple split screens. Hart's War TM & ©2004 MGM Studios, Inc.

THE TWO EXTREMES OF DISNEY

Walt Disney was a huge influence for Van Vliet. He originally enrolled into Cal Arts to become a Disney animator. He worked on the classic Tron, *Hollywood's first CG movie. His favorite effects experience came from Walt Disney's* My Favorite Martian.

JOHN VAN VLIET: *Mary Poppins* and *Sword and the Stone* were my two big influences, probably as they were the first two movies I ever saw on a big screen. Of the two, I think *Mary Poppins* probably had more impact because I was always wondering how they had done some trick. It was live action, with animation and special photographic tricks to create an entire alternate universe for Mary's world.

I think the next big influence was the 7-Up commercials. The Robert Abel Group did it, and one of the people responsible for that visual insanity who was this guy named Richard Taylor, who I ended up working for on *Tron*. As a kid, I recall seeing these just fabulous images with this crazy buoyant color, and going, "This is so wonderful! I want to make that stuff!" I guess there has always been some attraction to strange fabricated universes. (But that is probably a result of growing up in New Jersey.) Little did I know I would end up working for this Taylor years later on *Tron* at Disney. If that isn't some sort of a weird "Dream come true" story, I don't know what is...

After I started on *Tron*, I privately started to think that maybe we really didn't have that good an idea of what we were doing. We were up to our asses in artwork and tests one evening when Harrison Ellenshaw, who was one of the effects supervisors (and also one of the producers), looks at me and mutters, "If I had any idea what this was going to involve, I would never have done this." I replied, "I may of agreed with you." At that point, all we knew was that we were going to have about 15 minutes of computer animation and the rest of the *Tron* universe had to somehow be created using backlit animation with giant photographic cels. Disney took a huge chance on that picture and as we now know, it didn't pay off financially in the way they had hoped. But it was the first CG movie and for better or worse, it will stand out there in the darkness as the first one.

Working at Disney at that time was a bit of a challenge as their attitude was pretty much an "us versus them" towards any outside interlopers (such as the *Tron* crew). Ron Miller, who was Walt Disney's son-in-law, was running the studio and his previous experience was playing football. Going from a football player to a studio exec was tough on everyone... But this fellow named Tom Wilhite manages to surface in there and is smart enough to figure out they needed to move in a new direction. He was a really bright guy, and through his leadership, a number of new projects started and this is how *Tron* was born. Sadly his whole group became the enemy to the old Disney guys. This

political hostility ended up costing Disney dearly because when *Tron* did not perform well at the box office, their attitude was: "Great! Now we can get rid of these people and get back to doing nothing."

And they did just that. Under the *Tron* project, Disney essentially gathered the best and the brightest of this new process of digital film making and had actually built a working production pipeline. They had everyone who knew anything about this and had them all in one place, which was essentially a ten-year lead from the rest of the planet on this technology. Then everybody and everything was just gone. And it was like the big flush valve had been hit. If they had kept them and done some development work, they could have been doing *Jurassic Park* style work years before anyone else was ready.

One of the things about Walt Disney that was so amazing was he managed to take the creative production of a movie and figure out how to assembly line the work and made it cost effective. In many ways he was like Henry Ford. Up until Ford's time, every time you bought a car, it was essentially a hand-built car. It cost a gazillion dollars, and nobody except rich people could afford it until he managed to discover the assembly line process. Now, the idea of making a movie by drawing every frame, when you think about it, is one of the dumbest ideas in the world. Because drawing every frame is just nuts. But Disney managed to streamline the process enough where it actually was viable. And he made a lot of money, and certainly impacted the culture.

I think, because he did it so well and so profoundly, the magic of that delivery is still producing responses today. There are not that many pictures from that era that are looked back at with such strong memories, but almost all of the Disney pictures get an immediate reaction. People, when they think of Disney, they still have this sort of rosy glow, "Oh, yeah, *Bambi! Dumbo! Cinderella!*" When did they do these? Fifty years ago? My God, that's emotional staying power!

The saddest thing about Disney right now is there's been such a brain drain over there, and when you go in any of the Disney stores and you look at the products up on the wall that are selling, it's often not theirs. It's Pixar products, because the biggest brains are working outside the studio. And that's sad, because they used to be creating their own dreams, and now it's basically sub-contract work. But that's the way a lot of the studio system is running right now.

Of all of the shows I've worked on, the show I'm most proud of, that I had the most fun on, was [the remake of] *My Favorite Martian*. It's a fluffy little Disney movie, and I had the greatest time ever. The director, Donald Petrie was a real sweetheart who knew when to let us go loose and go crazy. And the studio actually gave us enough money to do what we wanted to do. We had some pretty crazy stuff, everything was pretty tongue-in-cheek. This was when I was still running Available Light Ltd. And we got a chance to really stretch—and I was able to work on the show with a fairly compact

"Like I said, *My Favorite Martian* (below) is a fluffy little Disney thing, but everything worked. It worked the way it was supposed to because we had a director who trusted us and he let us do our thing. We got to be incredibly creative."

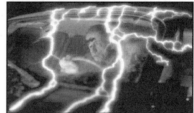

My Favorite Martian TM & ©2004 Walt Disney Productions, Inc.

crew, all really dedicated, smart people. It was our first big 3-D project, and we got an enormous amount of work done with a minimal crew. Watch the movie credit rolls now, and you're seeing hundreds of names go by: "Guy in charge of bringing water," "Tech Director #46." Everybody's gotten so specialized. But *Martian* was still back when we were happily naive and thought we could run the planet, and I don't think we got more than twenty people on the show doing the entire thing. If you were to take that job to a major facility now, they would probably take hundreds of people to do it. But that was in our time when we all wore many hats and enjoyed trying on new ones all the time.

Coffee and the Story

Breaking into the field of special effects demands an understanding of visual story-telling. To Van Vliet, if you can tell stories with pencil and paper, then you have a shot. A healthy love of java doesn't hurt as well.

JOHN VAN VLIET: The way we look at it is, there is basically no problem that you can't solve in post [production], given enough time and money. But producers, being who they are, they rarely want to spend that kind of time and money. If you need to completely reconstruct a scene, sure, you can probably do it, but it's probably going to cost you $150,000. And is that smart? Probably not. Yes, you can fix anything, but you can't afford it. And a lot of times on shows, when they do something that needs to be fixed, they should have known better. And what sort of gets

me is when you're reading the trade journals on how they did this on the shot, and you're looking at it and going, "If this was not a hundred-plus million dollar show, these guys would have been fired for wasting money." Because sometimes you just don't need to do it.

There's a famous matte painter, Rocko Gioffre who I was in a meeting with. Somebody was discussing doing something foolish with CG and Rocko, to illustrate a point said, "You know, if I want to see a really realistic image of an egg hitting a wall and slobbering down after the hit, it seems a whole lot smarter to go get a camera and throw the egg at the wall." And the director suddenly had this look on his face like, "You know, he might be right!" Sometimes everybody gets so enamored with their technology that they just forget that sometimes there's some real simple solutions there.

The big problem is, where do you draw the line? I always tell everyone that successful movie making is the magic triangle–the three points are art, technology, and business. And if any one point gets heavier than the other, then you lose the balance and it doesn't work in one way or the other. You can have the greatest looking picture in the world, and the art and technology work great, but if it costs you five hundred million dollars and nobody wants to see it, then your business side is deficient. And if the business side gets too powerful, you can make the cheapest movie in the world that's incredibly cost-effective, but if it's duller than owl crap, nobody's going to want to see it, so you've lost money. So you have to balance out when it's a smart time to do that.

With visual effects now, the definition is real fuzzy. When Pixar put out *Toy Story*, there was some interesting discussion, espe-

Digital animation was still in its infancy when *Stargate* was made. However, there was a heavy workload of over 110 visual effects shots, so creative thinking was instrumental in stretching resources. Roland Emerich displayed a great design sense. The bulk of the VFX work was accomplished with optical printers and traditional hand animation (below left).

Experimentation was needed to produce feature-quality imagery without going through the largest facilities. The pulse (below right) was created by a hybrid process of traditional animation art scanned and then digitally filtered. This unorthodox process ushered in the "desk-top" studio. Stargate TM & ©2004 MGM Studios, Inc.

cially come Academy Award season: "Okay, is this animation, or is this a visual effect?" When you watch *Jurassic Park,* is that now an animated movie, or is that a visual effect? Where do you draw the line here? And there's sort of informal lines now, where a visual effect will be when you drop animation on top of a live-action background and try to make it integrate instead of trying to create a whole new world. The movie *Final Fantasy* could be considered an animated movie instead of a visual effect. But if I took the same characters from *Final Fantasy* and put them into a live-action background, that would make them visual effects. Like I said, the boundaries are a little fuzzy, maybe even a little rubbery.

The biggest danger to the story right now is the technology, because they get so crazy with it that you sometimes forget why we are here. Visual effects can be pretty damned overwhelming, and more than once, we've all had to stop ourselves and go, "Okay boys and girls, let's stop for a second. Why are we here in this shot?" And if everybody goes, "To make cool explosions!" You go, "Nooo." Yes, that's the fun part, because we just love to do that stuff. But the story part of the movie is always in danger, because it is a delicate flower, and it can be crushed with too much manure.

I'm going to quote John Lassiter: "Stories and characters outlive technology." So, no matter how much tech stuff we get and how many cool toys, it's still really, really important to understand basic storytelling. For my purposes, it's always been important to have basic drafting skills to sit down, take a piece of paper, and while the director, the DP, the special effects guy and the production designer are all hanging over my head, draw out something and in five seconds say, "I need to do this to get there." I have just communicated in five, ten seconds, what it would take me an hour to talk about.

I think it's important to have some basic art skills, even if they're not well-developed and mine certainly aren't. Just understanding depth, timing and the really, basic stuff will put you way out ahead; you don't have to be Rembrandt. There's plenty of people who don't draw, but they have enough eye-hand coordination and comprehension of the process that they can get something on paper. That's how it works for me.

Someone e-mailed me the other night saying they're doing composite work in Tennessee for TV and "Oh, I want to move to Hollywood, and I want to do this and I want to do that." And I wrote them back and said, "You need to ask yourself why you want to go to Hollywood, because if it's for the money, you're gonna be disappointed. If it's for the glamour, you're gonna be disappointed. If it's because you want to live here, you're definitely gonna be disappointed." This is really hard work and you're going to be basically slaving in a dark room all day. But if you just really,

really want to make movies, then yeah, you put on another pot of coffee and you blast through. It's an endurance contest, it really is. If you make a movie without a coffee-maker, you're insane. The stronger the coffee, the better. You can take away everything else—the format changed, we're all going digital—the only thing that still remains in every facility is coffee. If you don't have that, you might as well fold it up and go home.

I've got over twenty pictures with my name on them now, and that and a buck will buy me a cup of coffee. I'll be honest, there's some [work] I'm not very proud of, but there's also some I'm very proud of. There's this addiction to the creative process and, like any addict, you'll do anything to get your fix. I will put up with all kinds of hell just because every now and then I get in a situation where I get to actually be creative and make something really cool that's worth it. Then you look back and go, "God, I made something...I made something from nothing." And when that opportunity presents itself, you grab it and it's just the greatest rush you can get. And when you've got an imaginative team of like-minded people around you, you feel like you've got this invincible creative juggernaut. There are few grins as good as that one.

As an independent effects supervisor, designer, and some-time cartoonist, Van Vliet is especially known for his lightning, laser, and other light-based visual special effects. Stargate TM & ©2004 MGM Studios, Inc.

Bruce Timm

on Comics & Animation

Of all of the sequential art forms, animation is probably most similar to comics in the way both are produced. Cartooning, sequencing, visual development, style, scope, and pacing are skill sets that overlap in both fields. It's no coincidence that many animators had aspirations to become cartoonists and that many comic book artists found their way into animation.

Though he created precious few flip books growing up, Bruce Timm has made his mark as producer of ground-breaking animation. Comics inspired him early on in his life—they launched his imagination and inspired his love for art in general. Not a classically trained artist, Timm nonetheless drew from this childhood inspiration to develop his love for the animation.

BRUCE TIMM: I was definitely into comics, even from an early age. I was a child of the Sixties, so I watched a lot of TV—a lot of monster movies—and read comic books. Money was always fairly tight in our household, so we rarely got comics on a regular basis. Another problem was availability. Distribution was pretty spotty back then. So it was a combination of not having a whole lot of money and that the places that sold comic books were a little bit out of my bike range. But when I was twelve or thirteen, some of the local stores started carrying comics on a regular basis and I was getting more money for allowance and lunch money, so I basically starved myself or dug through the couch on a regular basis trying to find loose change to feed my comic book fix.

My first hardcore exposure to superheroes as a genre was the Adam West *Batman* show. I was at the perfect age for it, five or six when it first came on, so I didn't realize it was camp or that it was a spoof. I took it absolutely seriously and I thought it was the coolest thing on the planet. I was a hardcore Batman fan from then on.

I kind of got into animation as a fluke. I wanted to be a comic book artist when I grew up; that was my life goal. I learned how to draw from copying comic books and drawing, drawing, drawing all the time. I had enough awareness of my own limitations even though I was the proverbial "best artist in my school" and everybody was telling me, "Wow, you're going to be a millionaire because you're the best artist ever!" But I could look at my own stuff and compare it to the actual comic books and go, "Well, I'm not quite ready for comics." But as it happened, I was very fortunate living out here in the San Fernando Valley, where the animation industry was based. Filmation Studios was about ten miles away from my house, so one day I got tired of working retail and really wanted to draw for a living. I went in and applied over at Filmation. Didn't get in the first year that I applied there, but I did the second year. Kind of off and on for the first couple of years, but then pretty soon I was working pretty steadily in the animation business.

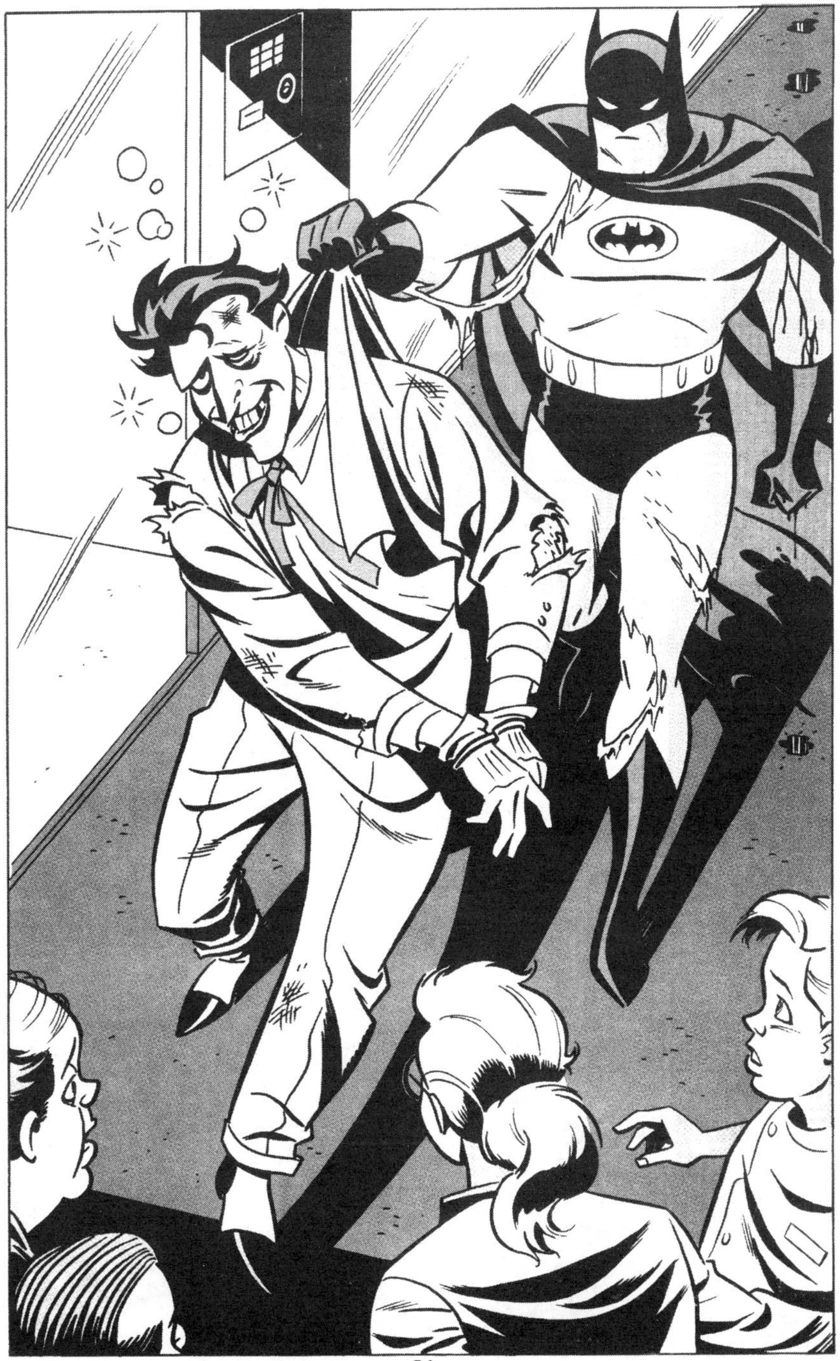

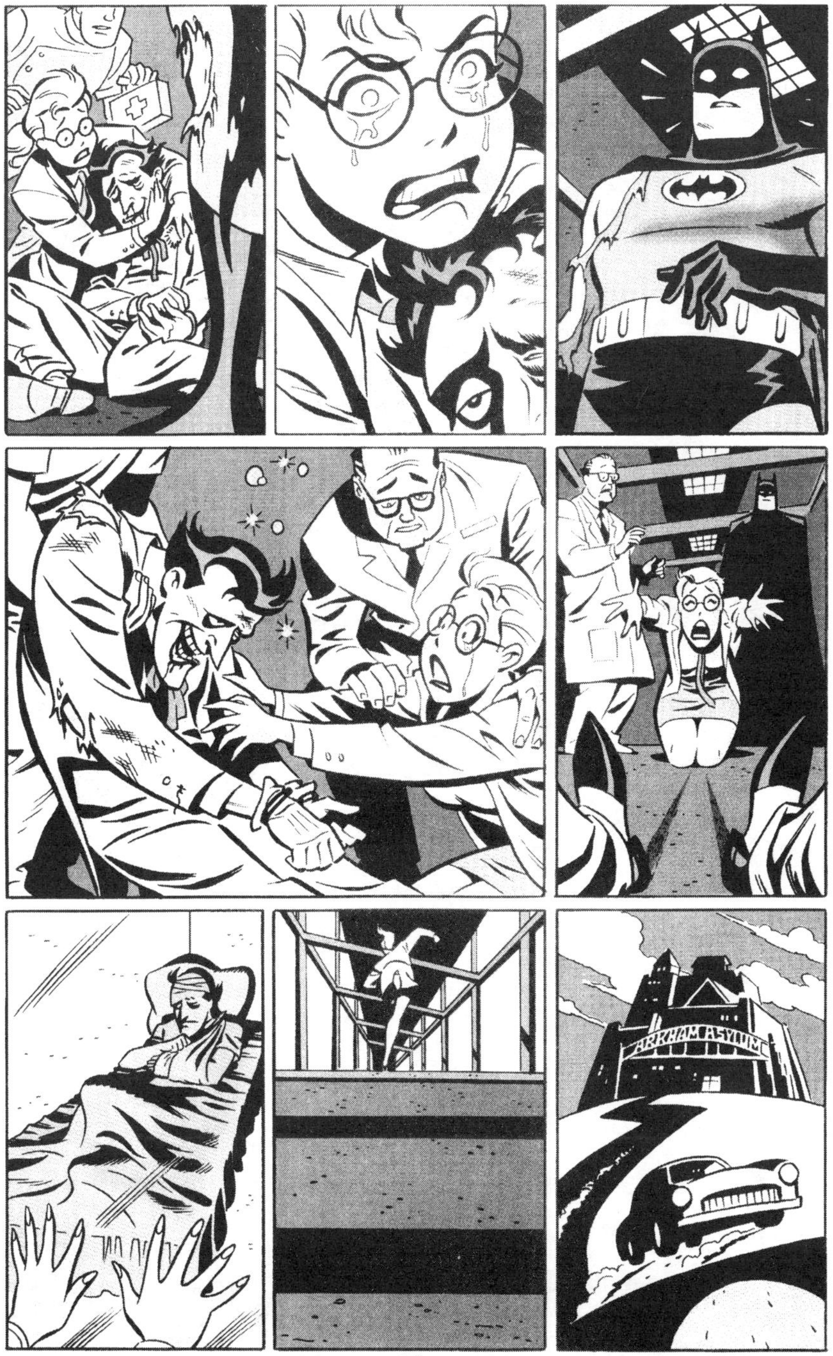
ARKHAM ASYLUM

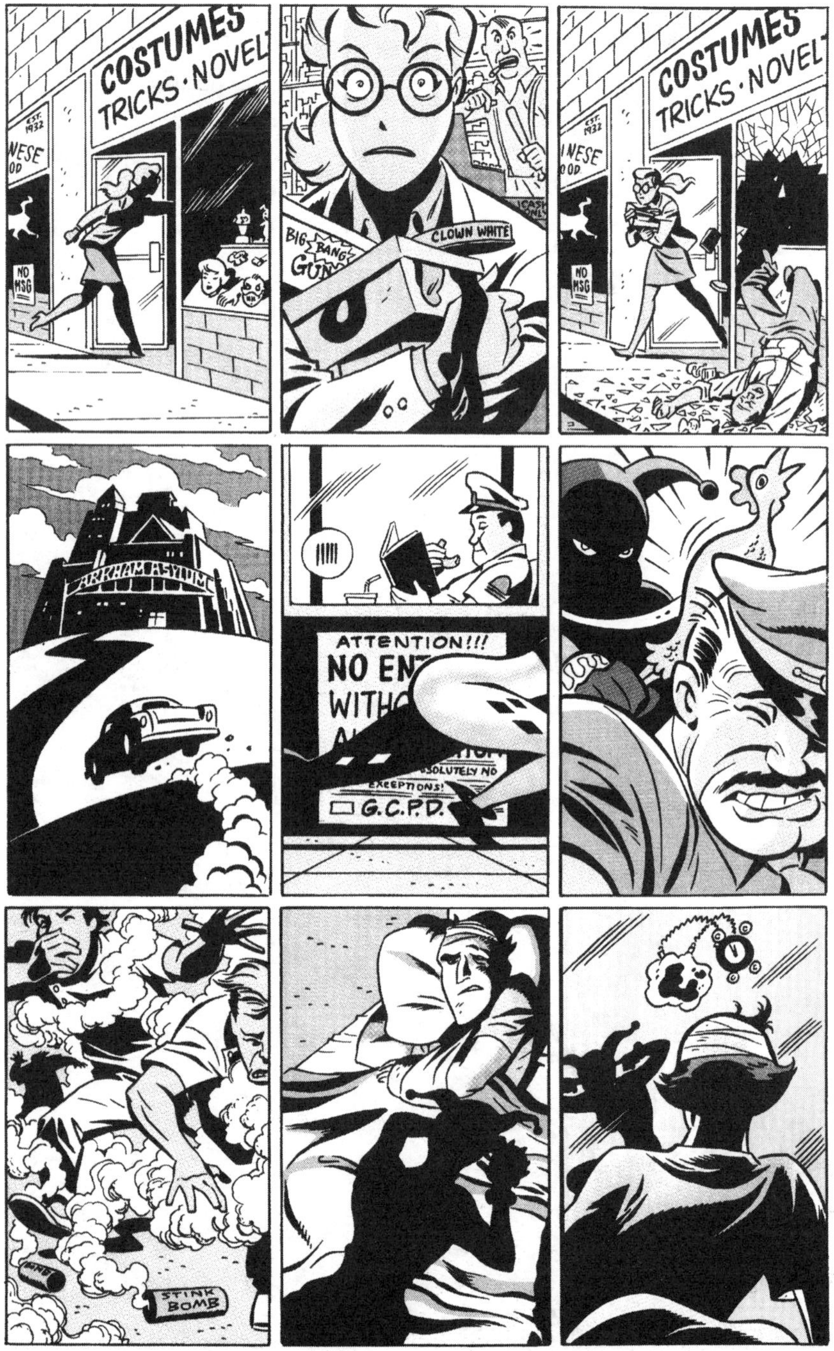
COSTUMES
TRICKS · NOVEL
EST. 1932
NO MSG
CLOWN WHITE
BIG BANG
ARKHAM ASYLUM
ATTENTION!!!
EXCEPTIONS!
G.C.P.D.
STINK BOMB

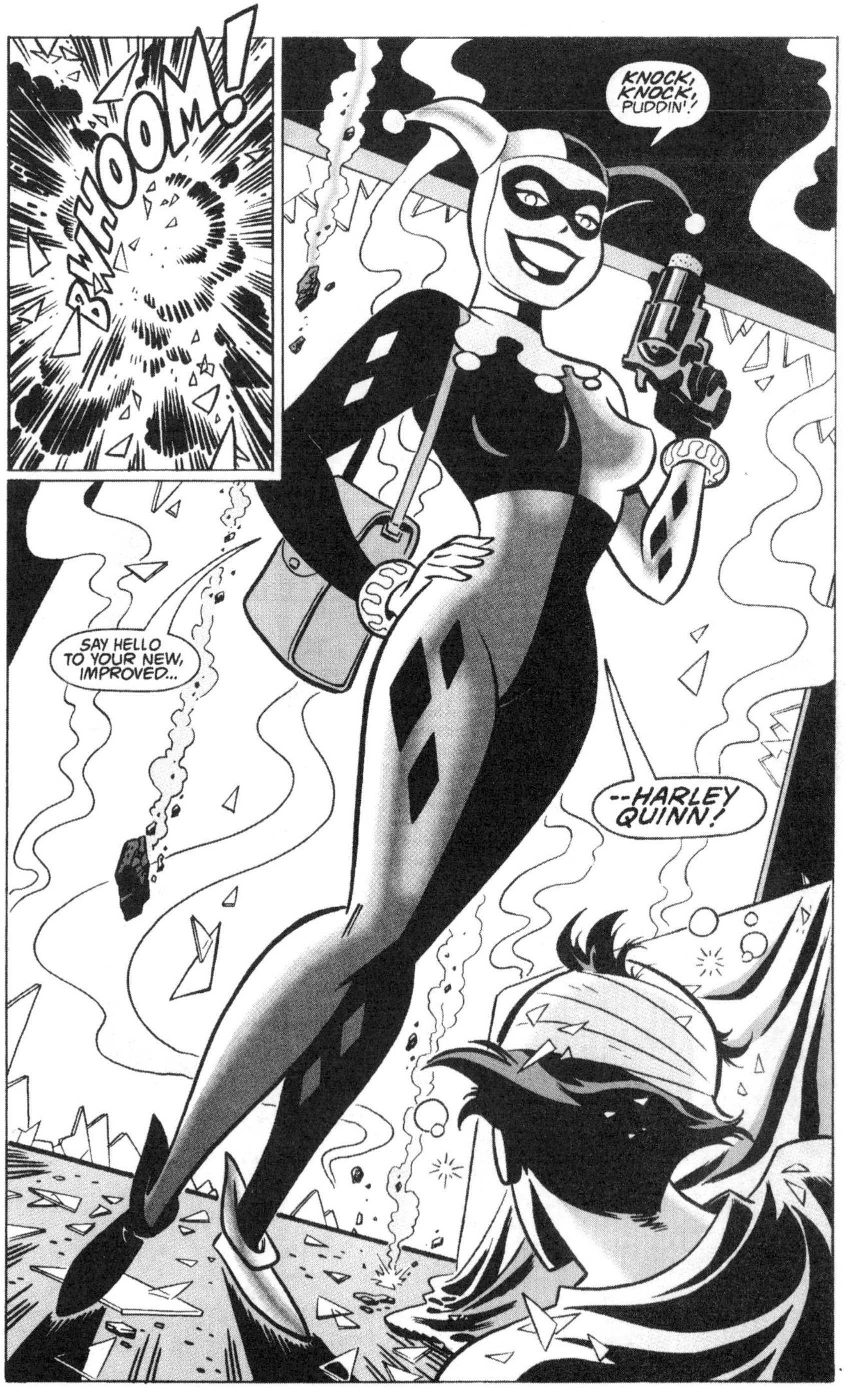
BWHOOM!
KNOCK, KNOCK, PUDDIN'!
SAY HELLO TO YOUR NEW, IMPROVED...
--HARLEY QUINN!
34

BREAKING IN

The 1980s proved to be a fertile proving ground for artists breaking into the field of animation. Artists had the chance to become familiar with all aspects of animation production, from storyboards to pencil tests, timing, and keyframing, unlike the specialization that happens in today's market. During this time, animation was more production oriented and less driven by inspiration—this before Disney's reemergence as an animation powerhouse with The Little Mermaid, *before Pixar and* Toy Story, *and before the popularity of showing animated features in theaters. Within this backdrop, Bruce Timm developed his skills in a narrative field designed for the small screen with tighter budget constraints: Saturday morning cartoons. But these restraints helped Timm develop his vision and philosophy.*

BRUCE TIMM: The first show I worked on was a show called *Black Star,* which was actually a very similar show to *He-Man,* but it was a year or two before. From there, when that show was over, I went over and worked at Don Bluth Productions on *The Secret Of NIMH,* did some assistant animation on that. I went back to Filmation after that and worked on the *He-Man* show, and then kind of bounced around. That was typical back then in the business, and actually still is. You go where the work is, and it's pretty rare that you stay in one place for a long period of time. So I kind of bounced around the industry; I worked at Filmation off and on, and Marvel Productions and Don Bluth.

Animation companies were constantly looking for bodies to fill the seats to get their shows done, so I took the basic test. The typical entry-level position back then, at least in the TV business, was layout. And layout back then for Filmation, and at other studios, was

kind of an in-between stage, in between storyboards and animation. What you would do is you would take the storyboard drawing and do an enlargement of it at the actual animation paper size. You would blow those drawings up, do a tighter version of them, place the characters in the scene compositionally, notate all the camera directions, and lay that all out on pieces of paper. Sometimes you'd have to draw a new background as well, and then they would ship that off to the animators and the background painters and use your drawings as a guide for their animation.

So the first year I tried out their simple test. They gave me a couple of storyboard panels and the model sheets and had me do it, and obviously my work wasn't good enough, because they didn't hire me. But the next year I tried it again, and I guess I just squeaked in under the radar. I mean, literally, looking back at my drawings from that period, they're abysmal; they're really horrible. But the standards were a little lower back then, I guess. The state of animation generally was pretty poor all across the board. Even Disney—they weren't at their height anymore—was kind of a moribund period. This was before the big Renaissance with *Who Framed Roger Rabbit?, The Little Mermaid,* and all that stuff. So these were the dark times.

Just from getting my foot in the door and hanging out with other artists and finding out how the system worked and everything, it quickly became apparent to me that you really shouldn't get locked down into one specialized field in the business, because you never know what any particular studio at any particular time, what kind of artist they're going to be looking for. Especially back then, the business was so seasonal. Really the only market for TV production back then was

While working at Don Bluth Productions, Timm learned many fundamental art theories. Character silhouettes help distinguish personality and individuality. Timm applies this concept to the members of the Justice League. Justice League TM & ©2004 DC Comics

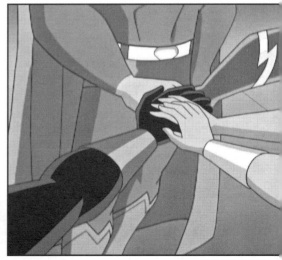

As producer of the *Teen Titans*, he continues playing with shapes. However, he also plays with the Japanese animé language to further diversify his style and storytelling. Teen Titans TM & ©2004 DC Comics

the Saturday morning shows on the three networks, and they would only order thirteen episodes per series. Typically what they would do is hire a bunch of people to come in to work all summer long and get the shows done. Then once the show was over, you were laid off and had to get other work. There was very little feature work back then; there were very few other animation markets. There were commercials and stuff, but even that wasn't steady work. So I realized early on that I'd better not box myself in as being just a layout artist. It helps to have a variety of skills, especially when you're going out looking for work. So that's exactly what I did. I did layout at Filmation; I learned the mechanics of how to do layouts, got a little bit of knowledge there. When I went to go work at Don Bluth, I did assistant animation, which wasn't actually animating. I was basically doing clean-up drawings from rough animation. And I quickly realized that that was not what I wanted to do.

I learned the skill of it and I learned more about animation and about how many drawings it takes to move things–just the basic fundamentals of it just from going over other artists' work. And I'd have to go shoot my own video tests. When I was done with my scene, I'd have to go shoot it on a video test machine and see it and make sure it all worked properly. So, again, I just picked up a little bit more knowledge. I didn't get into doing storyboards until much later. One of the first storyboards I did was on *Beanie and Cecil*, I think, in '88. Oh, and in between all that, when I worked at Marvel productions. I worked on the *G.I. Joe* show, and I ended up doing a lot of character design there, so I had one more skill to put in my resumé. It's just good to have a variety, to diversify.

STAYING IN

Animation is known as a volatile field with high turnover, short deadlines, and cancelations an accepted constant. However, a renegade desire to make animation fun again prevailed and Bruce Timm knew that he was hooked on the medium. Even if it meant turning his back on creating comics, Timm knew that he was part of something just as meaningful and ultimately satisfying.

BRUCE TIMM: All the time that I was working in animation in those early years, I still wanted to do comics. In fact, for a lot of the people that I worked with, that was their ambition, too. And it was a tricky thing, because when you worked at Marvel Productions you thought, "Aha! Marvel Productions! They're connected to Marvel Comics!" But there was actually very little crossover between the two divisions of the company. Marvel Productions was out here on the West Coast, Marvel Comics was back on the East Coast. There was very little connection between the two of them.

People actually told me that when I first started working there. "You're not going to get a job at Marvel Comics from working at Marvel Productions. If you're going to get a job at Marvel Comics, you're going to have to do it just the way everybody else does. You have to go to conventions and show your portfolio or send in your samples." So that's what I did. I would go to the conventions and show my work. And it never was quite good enough to get work. If I'd kept at it, chances are one day I probably would have gotten in there. I came close a couple times. I got a couple inking tests from Marvel at one point, and I eventually did end up doing some coloring

for a couple of the companies. But never quite got my foot in the door as penciler or inker. So in the meantime, animation was a fairly steady gig and became my bread and butter.

The problem for me in the early years, I was jazzed to actually be drawing for a living–it was so much better than working at, say, K-Mart or something, where I actually did work for several years. At the same time, nobody was pushing me to excel. The standards of the industry were so low, and at Filmation, particularly, they discouraged you from doing great work. They would say, "Okay, you're spending too much time on this drawing, just get it done. It doesn't have to be great, it just has to be acceptable." That was the standard. So the only yardstick that you had to better yourself was comparing yourself to other artists in the business. And there were a lot of other great artists working there; I would look at their stuff and say, "Wow, this guy is really good. Hopefully I'm going to be as good as this guy someday." But they weren't pushing you to excel. At Don Bluth it was different.

Don Bluth actually got me fired up. He was the one guy in the business at that time who was trying to reenergize animation. That was his big mandate. He had had this big walk-out from Disney in the early Eighties because he thought that Disney had given up on pushing the animation envelope. So he and a bunch of his friends, top animators at Disney, walked out and started their own company and tried to revitalize animation. So that was exciting. That was one thing that I got from Don, getting filled up with the fervor to look back on the old classics and say, "Wow, that stuff was really great. Hopefully animation will be that good again, if not better." But because I was kind of stuck just doing assistant work there and I didn't really have

any other skills within the Disney-ized kind of structure that Don had in place, I really had no way of bettering my position within that kind of framework. Later Don did try me out as a story-sketch artist, but I frankly wasn't good enough yet, and so, it was back to assistant work.

After that, the first show that really got me charged up about the possibilities of animation was when I worked on *Mighty Mouse* with John Kricfalusi. He was really quite the visionary. I'd known him socially for a couple of years just through friends of mine that I knew at Filmation, who were friends of John. We'd go over to his apartment, and I would look at his stuff, and it was so unlike anything that was being done. Well, obviously. But what was really cool about it was that you could look at John's stuff, and as radically "out there" as it was, it still had fundamental, classic, Tex Avery/Bob Clampett stylings to it. It was like, "Wow! This is retro in a cool way," but at the same time it was very modern and very fresh. It was kind of frustrating, because you just knew that John's stuff was so bizarre that he had no chance of ever getting it sold, because everything was so conservative back then. I mean, really, these were the days of *My Little Pony* and *Go-Bots*, right? It just seemed inconceivable that something as off-the-wall as John's stuff would ever fly.

So when Ralph Bakshi actually put him in charge of the *Mighty Mouse* show, it was like, wow, the stars are in alignment or something; it was totally cool. So I went to go work for John on *Mighty Mouse*. And John's a very charismatic figure and he really knows how to inspire people to do better work. I became an extremist at that point, I totally fell under his sway. That was the first time in the business that I actually got really, really excited about coming to work in the morning. I would stay there way past midnight sometimes, getting the stuff done,

Bruce Timm and Eric Radomski directed *Batman: Mask of the Phantasm* for theater release in 1993. An animated motion picture event comparable to the finest Disney adventures, *Mask of the Phantasm* is among the best Batman movies to ever hit the silver screen. Batman TM & ©2004 DC Comics

just because it was so exciting. It was like a key had been turned. My work made a quantum leap in quality in the few months that I worked at Bakshi's. It was like, "Wow, these are the possibilities. Go for it." That was really exciting. I kind of felt at that point, yeah, that animation's what I want to do. And a year after that, John had had a falling-out with Ralph, so John wasn't doing the second season of *Mighty Mouse*. He got a deal to do the remake of the *Beanie and Cecil* show over at DIC, so I went to go work with John on that. And it was like the complete opposite of what had happened on *Mighty Mouse*. On *Mighty Mouse* we had all this freedom, and on *Beanie and Cecil*, ABC was really clamping down on John. They didn't want John to do the show in the first place, but the Clampetts kind of insisted on it. They said, "If you're going to do *Beanie and Cecil*, John's our guy." So eventually ABC caved in. But they just caused holy hell for John from day one. So *Beanie and Cecil* was just a mess, and at the end of that, I was really disillusioned again.

My hopes for what could be accomplished in animation had been elevated so high, and then kind of been crushed so badly by the *Beanie and Cecil* experience that I thought, "Okay, I'm never going to really put that much of my heart and soul into it ever again, because it's just too painful." After *Beanie and Cecil*, some of the guys who'd been working for John and were waiting for John to get his next project going ended up over at Warner Brothers, working on this new show, *Tiny Toons*. So I went over there. *Tiny Toons* was kind of a fun show, it wasn't quite as exciting for me as working on that first season of *Mighty Mouse*, but it was similar, in a way. You could do some kind of crazy stuff. And it paid really well. So that's where I happened to be when the Batman thing happened.

LESS IS MORE

The Batman Animated series philosophy of style developed out of necessity. As Bruce Timm learned the craft of animation, he became acutely aware of the stiffness that detail could create, specially in adventure cartoons. Developing the Batman style was a conscious departure of the unnecessary detail of animation in an attempt to make things more streamlined. The Batman Animated style, freed of a tedious visual style, allowed for striking character designs, grander stories and immediate fan and critical acclaim. Batman: the Animated Series won both an Emmy and an Annie award while ushering a new benchmark for animation.

BRUCE TIMM: When I first got into the business, I pretty much specialized in adventure cartoons, the *Black Star* and *G.I. Joe* and the *He-Man* shows, because that was where my interest had been leading as an artist. I was never even really interested in doing funny animal type stuff or comedy stuff until I started working for John. And it was interesting, because after working with Don Bluth doing assistant work, and the tedium of having to draw drawing after drawing after drawing, I was very fundamentally aware of the amount of linework that goes into it to make animation work. Every single line has to be drawn thousands of times.

So I tried to apply some of the stuff I'd learned at Bluth's on *G.I. Joe* and I kept getting slapped down. Everybody kept saying, "No, no, no, no, no, no. We don't want that simple stuff, this is a big budget show." By the standards of the day, I guess it was. "We've got those Japanese guys overseas doing animation work, and they do a really good job with all that detail." And the toy company wanted all the detail, too, because we were doing the show basically in conjunction

with Hasbro. They wanted the characters to look exactly like the toys, and they wanted the vehicles to look exactly like the toys, and they were loaded with crap, just detail everywhere. And I would do it reluctantly because I just knew it wasn't really serving the needs of animation. But I was just a wrist, y'know; I did what they paid me to do.

Working for John, where it was all about stripping down extra detail and really concentrating on shapes and composition and all that stuff, it was like, "Yeah, okay," this was something I could apply even to adventure cartoons. I had been on my own doodling, trying to combine the lessons I'd learned at Bluth's and working with John towards adventure cartoon stylings. So when the Batman thing came up, I went back to my desk and just did a bunch of Batman drawings, and it just all kind of melded, all my influences to that point kind of melded. I looked at that and said, "Yep, that would work." And fortunately, other people looked at the drawings and saw the same thing and it took off from there.

I had hoped that our Batman show would have an impact, because I certainly knew that nobody was doing anything like that at that point with adventure cartoons. So I knew that it would make a splash just by its uniqueness, at the time. And I knew that there would be some people who would be radically opposed to it, as there had been in the past. People would look at it and say, "Oh, that just looks like a cartoon. That doesn't look real." But at the same time, I knew that it would help the animation. I knew that it would allow us to do fuller, more fluid animation, because you didn't have to animate all the crap that was all over the characters. I mean, I kind of had an idea that it would make a splash. At least, I hoped it would. But I certainly couldn't see how much it would influence such a wide variety of artists both in animation and in comics after that. Comics were really an afterthought for me at that point. I didn't even think about DC doing a spinoff comic based on the animation; that was gravy.

When the Batman show came along, there was a resurgence of interest in animation all across the board. That includes the Disney features like *The Little Mermaid* and *Beauty and the Beast*, which were like a shot in the arm. John's *Ren and Stimpy* started airing while we were still in production on the first season of Batman, and it had even more of an impact on the field than *Mighty Mouse* had several years earlier. Also, anime became really popular right about the same time that Batman did. When I look at comics now and I look at people who are doing kind of an animated riff in their styling, I can't tell if they're doing me, or if they're doing anime, or whatever. In a way, what's wild about comics is that you look at some of these artists now who are doing mainstream comics, people like Mike Oeming or Carlos Meglia, or even Joe Madueira, and ten, fifteen years ago, they would never have even gotten close to doing a mainstream superhero comic, because people would have looked at it and said, "Oh, your stuff's too cartoony. Maybe we'll give you a Plastic Man comic or something to do or something like that." But not a mainstream comic. People have become more open to variety of styles these days, and like I said, it's a combination of the popularity of the Batman show and anime and even the Disney movies and stuff. It's kind of a neat thing.

Even though I had always admired the more "realistic" comic book artists, John Buscema, Neal Adams, Jim Steranko, Frank Frazetta, and Dave Stevens, and people like that, when I would try to

There is no Rogues gallery more dangerous than Batman's. Timm understands the psychology of form, and Batman's foes come in all shapes and sizes. (Left to right) The Joker, Harlequin, Man-Bat, Mr. Freeze, the Riddler, Two-Face, Bane. Catwoman, Scarecrow. Killer Croc, Clayface, Poison Ivy, the Penguin, and Ra's Al Ghul. All characters TM & ©2004 DC Comics

do stuff in that kind of style, I kept coming up against the fact that I'm not a very good artist. Now, I don't say that self-deprecatingly. I mean, literally, I'm not a draftsman. I never went to art school; I learned how to draw from copying comic books, so I don't have a solid foundation of the art basics. To this day, perspective is a mystery to me! I learned how to fake things. My knowledge of anatomy is very limited, as is my knowledge of perspective and how to draw a background. You look at my work and the backgrounds are usually pretty minimal, because I hate drawing them. I like drawing people. I don't like drawing anything other than people. Cars, vehicles, backgrounds, forget it, I hate it. But you gotta have it, so I gotta do it.

So at a certain point I realized the more realistically I tried to draw, the weaker my drawings were. If I can't do that, how do I make my art better by drawing less? Again, it was kind of a combination of things that I learned at Don Bluth's, fundamental art theories about straights against curves, line of action, silhouettes, negative space, things like that. And from John, I learned how to push and exaggerate your drawing to give it more impact. So kind of combining those two trains of thought and stripping down all the stuff that gets in the way, all the musculature and the wrinkles on the clothing, to try to strip that down to its most fundamental form. Also, art deco illustration was a big influence on me, something that I got really into around the same time that I was working for John. I got into art deco and old WPA posters and stuff. I would look at these really strong, streamlined, iconic drawings and realize how simple and stylized they were, but still very dynamic, and try to put that approach into my work. So it was a way of literally making less more.

MAD LOVE FOR COMICS

Ironically, by being such a visionary in animation, Bruce Timm inspired many artists in the comics field. Not only was there an explosion of more "cartoony" comics, but DC Comics launched Batman Adventures, *a comics spin-off from the television series that is still being enjoyed today. And then finally, the inevitable happened, Bruce Timm had the opportunity to realize a childhood dream by working on the Eisner Award-winning* Mad Love *in 1994.*

BRUCE TIMM: We'd been meeting off and on with DC Comics from very early on in the development of the Batman show and onward. And I think it was at a San Diego Comic-Con convention where Paul Dini and I were having lunch with Denny O'Neil, who was the group editor of the Batman titles at that time; we were just chatting about other different stuff. And the subject of us doing a comic came up. I don't know if Denny initiated it or we did, but Denny just said, "Yeah, anytime you guys want to do a comic, let me know, we'll do something." So Paul and I went, "Great!" We didn't get around to actually doing anything until it was towards the end of the first run of the Batman show and we had a little bit of time on our hands. I was having lunch with Paul one day and he mentioned that he had figured out what the Harley Quinn character's origin was. It turned out that she was originally the Joker's psychiatrist. And I went, "Wow, that's a cool idea and interesting twist! Hey, let's do that as a comic!" So that's where the basic idea of it came from.

And we mentioned it to DC and they said, "Yeah! Great! Do it!" So it was really cool. If it hadn't been for the Batman show,

For *Batman: Mad Love*, Timm relied on a 9-panel grid. Pulling the panels and laying them side by side, this page can be read like storyboards. Bruce Timm and Paul Dini created the popular Harlequin who now exists in her own title for DC Comics. Batman, Harley Quinn TM & ©2004 DC Comics

it would have been much harder for me to break into comics. But because of the Batman show, it was just kind of like, "Okay, here you go, *carte blanche*, do what you want to do." So it was like, "Okay, that's the way to go!" I tell people all the time that I'm so fortunate. I happened to be in the right place at the right time with the Batman show. Again, the stars were in alignment. In retrospect, all those times that I would go to San Diego and show my portfolio and not get work in comics, as depressing as that was at the time, that was the best thing that could have happened to me. Who knows what direction my career would have gone in if I had actually gotten into comics. Chances are I'd still be just inking comics or something today.

Mad Love was pretty satisfying all around. The awards and accolades were totally gravy. I certainly didn't think that far ahead. We just did the book for fun, we thought it would be really fun, and I'd always wanted to do a comic. I had done some comics before that for Mattel, those little He-Man comics, but nothing on the scale of an actual comic-book-sized comic, certainly not with that kind of page count. In fact, *Mad Love* was three times the length of a regular monthly book, so it was quite a lot of work. But it was a lot of fun, and it was super-exciting to actually pick that comic up off the stands. It's like, "Wow! There's a comic book that I did!" That was really neat. In a way, that's all that I wanted to get out of it. But word of mouth got around about it, and we got really good reviews in a bunch of different places. Then the next year at the awards, for the Eisners and the Harveys, it's like, "Holy crap, I wasn't expecting that!" It was very satisfying.

But drawing *Mad Love* was totally intimidating. You're sitting down and looking at a blank sheet of paper and saying, "Now, start drawing your comic." That was one of the problems I had earlier when I was trying to get comic book work: I was always intimidated by the interesting panel layouts that the hottest artists had. I would look at people's work and they would have these wild, interesting panel layouts, I guess going back to the Neal Adams type influence. So I always thought that would be the yardstick that everybody would be measuring me by. So after working on the script with Paul and then actually sitting down to start drawing the damned thing, I was kind of stuck for a day or two. I made a couple of false starts trying to get the story roughed out.

Then I found this *Legion of Superheroes* comic that Keith Giffen had laid out, and I noticed that he had stuck to a really rigid, old-fashioned nine-panel grid. And I looked at it and I was reading it and realizing, "Wow, it's almost like a storyboard. If I don't have to worry about making the page layouts splashy and interesting , I can just concentrate on telling the story in this rigid format…" It was similar to doing a storyboard, as I said, and I had a lot of experience doing that at that point, so that really freed me up a lot. So I basically took one of Keith's pages out of the *Legion* comic, and traced off the grid exactly. I xeroxed that a zillion times and used that as my template for roughing the story out. And from that point on, roughing the story out took no time at all. I roughed the whole story out in about two weeks. So that was a lifesaver.

It was interesting, because, like I said, when I look back now at most of my favorite artists, they usually aren't too worried

about page layouts. Yeah, I love Steranko, Neal Adams, and all these guys who do these really wild, innovative things with the page layout. But Kirby for the most part stuck to a really rigid either six-panel grid or the three-tier grid, like John Buscema, a lot of those guys. So that's ultimately what it's all about to me; it's not about making pretty pictures. Pretty pictures are great, but it's all about storytelling to me. Literally, in comics and in animation, that's my bottom line: how to tell the story, interestingly and in the clearest possible way. Clarity and storytelling, those are my two fundamental things. Everything else is gravy.

Comics Vs. Animation

Even though many of the skill sets used to produce a comic directly applies to animation, there are still fundamental differences between the two storytelling mediums. Bruce Timm is a hands-on producer, fielding different responsibilities from episode to episode and show to show. He wouldn't have it any other way. Not only does it keep him sharp, but he is able to develop an arsenal of problem solving skills for almost any situation. More importantly, he is telling stories. Even if these stories utilize drawings like comics, animation is not an individual effort—it requires a team of artists, writers, actors, musicians and directors to produce animation, and Timm deftly orchestrates these elements to tell his stories.

BRUCE TIMM: There are strengths and limitations to each medium. The obvious thing is that, yeah, in animation you've got real actors saying the dialogue out loud, and sound effects and music and images that are actually moving. And, conversely, there are still things that you can do better in comics than you can do in animation. Again, the craft level of some of the better mainstream comic book artists have gotten so high-caliber that they can do these massive, widescreen adventure epic movies in 2-D form that would cost hundreds of millions of dollars to do filmically, even as animation. To read some of the comics like *The Authority* or whatever, they are like these huge epics. So comics are still the best medium for that kind of unlimited budget, grand scale adventure—it's one of those weird things.

There are things that work great in movies that people think of as comic book styled movies that strangely enough don't translate very well to comics. The prime example is *Star Wars*. When *Star Wars* came out, that was the best comic book movie that had ever been made. It looked just like a comic book on the screen. You had wild sets and interestingly-costumed characters doing heroic things. And when you see it on the comic book page, it's like, "Enh." Because one of the great things about *Star Wars* was that it moved. That was one of the first times when you saw a space battle, where the ships were acting like World War II airplanes. And that just doesn't translate to the comic book page. The Millennium Falcon and the Star Destroyers look great in motion but they look dull and static on a comic book page. *Buffy the Vampire Slayer*, to me, is the same kind of thing. When you look at the show (which I *loved*, by the way) it's a comic book. It's a total comic book premise, and it has a lot of comic book tropes in it, but it's done in street clothes. It's a street clothes

Storyboard artists working in animation must exhibit a keen sense of timing and cartooning. Often times, storyboards can be turned into extreme key frames for in-between animators to work from. (Below) Examples of Bruce Timm storyboards from *Batman: the Animated Series* episode "The Laughing Fish." Joker TM & ©2004 DC Comics. Art ©2004 Warner Bros. Animation

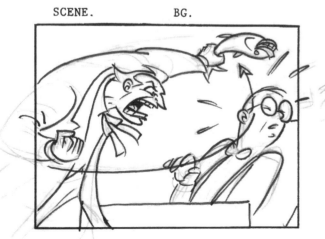

comic book; it's a street clothes superhero show. So when you translate that back into comics, enh, it's a bunch of people in street clothes. It's not as interesting, visually. I think Buffy is a concept that works better in live action than it does in an actual comic book.

Producing an animated show is a whole hell of a lot of work. I'm kind of a control freak, so I'm there from the beginning of the show to the very end of the show. I do delegate a lot of the work. Fortunately, I've got an immensely talented group of artists working for me, so obviously, I don't draw all the character designs and I don't storyboard everything and I don't write everything, but I try to keep my hand in and try to keep an eye on everything to make sure that it's going along the way I think is best. It's tough sometimes, because I have a pretty clear vision of how things should look, or how a sequence should be boarded, and when I look at the other guys' stuff, it's almost never as I saw it in my head. Then it becomes a matter of, "Well, it's not how I thought it should be, but the bottom line is, does it *work?*" Because, most of the time, even though it's different than what I expected, it works just as well as the way I would have done it, and often, *better.*

The way it's been working the last couple of years, especially on the *Justice League* [animated series], is I concentrate heavily at the beginning of the process and at the very end. I work with the writers very, very closely at the beginning to make sure that the elements that I think are going to make a successful cartoon are in place, and things that aren't working, I try to work with the writers and to come up with solutions that will fix those problems, so that when it goes to the artists, to the directors and the character designers and the story-

board artists, a lot of the potential problems have already been ironed out. It makes the director's and the board guys' jobs easier, if they don't have to spend their time trying to fix story problems, or filling plot holes, they can just concentrate on telling the story as clearly and as dramatically, as possible.

And then at the end, in post-production, I'm very, very heavily involved. So if there were problems that cropped up during the process, hopefully I can fix them in editing or with sound or with music. In animation, theoretically, you should have more control than, say, in live-action, because you're literally creating every visual element from scratch, but there are still things that are beyond your control. Especially because we're doing so many shows at the same time and we're on a really tight deadline. Yeah, in the best of all possible worlds, I would love to be able to sit down and storyboard an entire cartoon myself and control every single aspect of it so I could get it done exactly the way I wanted to. You're still going to send it off to be animated overseas. And they do a wonderful job over there. But sometimes you'll have a certain idea of the way a scene is going to play or even the timing of it or the acting of it, and it comes back kind of different. So you can't be too much of a control freak; certain things are still beyond your control. Whereas in comics, it's different, depending upon how involved you want to get into it. Especially me, the way I work precludes me from working with inkers, because I don't pencil very tightly. The system I've come up with is that my pencils are very, very loose, and I do most of the actual drawing in ink. So I have absolute control of what the artwork looks like. And if I have time, I'll even color it myself so that I can't complain about the

The storyboards animated in "The Laughing Fish." Joker TM & ©2004 DC Comics. Art ©2004 Warner Bros. Animation

coloring. So when I get the comic book in my hand, I go, "Ah, I made this. Me and a writer and a letterer, we made this comic." So it's not me and an army of people. So, to a degree, you have a little more control over the finished product in comics than in animation. But I'm satisfied in both mediums. I've been very lucky to be working with excellent collaborators all across the board.

The Batman episode, "The Laughing Fish" was a story that I actually had a lot of input on, for a variety of reason. I ended up story-boarding over two-thirds of that show myself just because there was a lack of artists who were available to work on it. I thought Paul did a great job on the story, and I saw a lot of possibilities for visuals. It was, at that point, one of the darker Joker stories that we had done. And we always kept wanting to make the Joker darker and scarier than we'd seen him in animation before. So I spent a lot of time really, really massaging that board, and trying to get as much mood and mystery and impact in it as possible. And when the animation came back, I thought it was soft. This is the problem: if you get too into something, you have these preconceived notions in your head as to how it's going to move. I thought this was going to be our big, scary Joker show, and it wasn't quite as scary and as intense as I'd hoped it would be.

So right around this same time, I was reading this book by Stephen Rebello about the making of *Psycho*, and there was a chapter on the music. And I had seen the movie many times, but had never quite realized that the entire score was done with strings. There's no woodwinds, there's no brass, there's no percussion. It's all strings. That was a really interesting notion. So when we were spotting the music for "The Laughing Fish", I brought that subject up as a possible way

of going with the music, to increase the mood and the creepiness of the show that was somewhat lacking in the animation. At the time, that's what I thought. Shirley Walker didn't really go all-strings with it, but she definitely gave a Psycho-esque, Bernard Hermann-esque score to that show. It's really downbeat and it's really off and it's not this big, grand, exciting Batman score, the kind of thing that we'd been doing at that time. It was very much almost like a horror movie score. And it helped immeasurably. It really helped that episode a lot. That is a good example of using the music to push the animation.

We've had other episodes that were okay, a good story with mediocre animation, or a mediocre story with good animation, and if you get a really good score on it, it will physically improve the look of the animation. It's the weirdest thing. The music will add an emotional resonance to the story that it doesn't actually already have. It's amazing. Actually, going back to "The Laughing Fish"… I watched it again a couple of years ago, and, y'know, it's fine; I think it's a fine show. At the time I was really disappointed just because, in my own head I saw how it was going to come out and it didn't match exactly what I wanted. But, in retrospect, I look at it now and it's like, no, it's really a good show. But in a way, it's still good that I was disappointed at the time, because it gave me the opportunity to push Shirley in another direction she might not otherwise have gone in, and it certainly helped the show overall.

Batman and the Joker in the climactic battle scene for "The Laughing Fish." Batman, Joker TM & ©2004 DC Comics. Art ©2004 Warner Bros. Animation

VISUAL LANGUAGE

Bruce Timm did not go to art school and was never classically trained. Nonetheless, he voraciously studies art and is drawn to an eclectic mix of visual styles and artists ranging from Art Deco to Russian constructivism. Batman: the Animated Series was inspired by the Max Fleischer Superman cartoons while Superman: the Animated Series finds roots in the work of Jack Kirby. Timm will hold animation meetings to show work by traditional and comic book artists for inspiration. Inspiration is the quickest way to a develop uniqueness, and Bruce Timm is never satisfied with the status quo.

BRUCE TIMM: Every show I do, I want to do something a little bit different than what I have done in the past because I don't want to get pigeon-holed. And I get bored. I don't want to just keep doing the same stuff that I've done in the past. Also, each show that we've done has been quite a bit different than the previous show, so they *should* all look a little bit different; they shouldn't all have the same look and feel. I mean, you can't get more different than Superman and Batman. Batman's all about being dark and scary and spooky, and Superman is the opposite of that–literally the opposite. There's as many things that are different about the two shows that are similar.

Then, when we did the revamp episodes, *The New Adventures of Batman*, my own personal style had evolved a little bit from Batman to Superman–from working with Glen Murakami and Shane Glines–where things had gotten a little bit more angular and graphic. So we pushed that a little bit further on those new Batman episodes and made it really graphic and really angular, and were pretty pleased

with the results on it. That was mostly just a way of keeping it interesting to me and to the crew, because we had done, like, eighty episodes of Batman up until that point. It was like, man, do we want to just go back and do what we did three years ago, four years ago? So changing the styling of the show was a way of keeping it fresh and interesting to us. Also, there were things about the original Batman show that, as good as it was, bugged me. With four more years' experience under my belt, I figured I could go back and restyle the show and apply things that I'd learned over that time to make the animation better.

And when we did *Batman Beyond*, we wanted to change the style a little bit *again*. We certainly changed the color styling a lot, and the background styling a lot. Still applying some of those graphic, really streamlined designs that we'd done for the first Batman show, we put a little bit more detail on it because it was a futuristic show; the costume design and the background design had a little bit more detail on it. Then when we went to do *Justice League*, in a way it was almost a throwback to the old Batman animated show, by putting the highlights back on Batman and changing his design a little bit. Trying to come up with a style that would work for a broad range of characters. On Batman, that real hard, aggressively graphic design worked for that show, because it was all so weird and kinky. You had all those weird villains, those really spooky villains. But *Justice League* is not a dark show, generally. And it wasn't all about Batman; it was about all of these other characters. So we needed to come up with a style that would include all those other characters as well. It was almost a halfway point between the Superman show and the real ultra-graphic, revamped Batman show. You try to adjust the stylization of the show to what you think the show needs.

For the Batman series, (left) Batman becomes the Dark Knight through use of shadow and atmosphere. For the Superman series, (middle) Timm goes for the opposite look. In *Batman Beyond*, (right) a streamlined, futuristic character design is developed. Batman, Superman TM & ©2004 DC Comics. Art ©2004 Warner Bros. Animation

FAVORITE CHILDREN

When asked to list his favorite projects, Bruce Timm is reflective: every project contains different challenges. In animation, he has produced numerous series for Warner Brothers, but ranking them is hard.

BRUCE TIMM: That's like asking which of your children is your favorite. I've liked all of the projects that I've worked on, for various reasons. Certainly, at the time, that first Batman show was a real charge for me, being that much in control of a show and having it come out that close to what my interior vision was, it was a real thrill. And again, the critical acclaim and the ratings success was almost gravy. I mean, it was very gratifying. I was very satisfied with the show at that point. Superman was a little bit tougher show, because I wasn't quite as in tune to the Superman character as I was to Batman. But, again, in retrospect, when I go back and look at some of those old Superman shows, they're pretty damned good. I mean, we did a really good job on that show. And obviously, some of the ones that I was really into at the time, like the Darkseid episodes, even back in the day I knew we had done something really special with those. And the pilot, too, I really liked the pilot show that we did, "The Last Son of Krypton." I thought especially the first half hour of it was dynamite.

I think we did a bunch of really great shows on *Batman Beyond*. I really liked the styling of the show; I like a lot of the character stuff that we did. I think we kind of petered out too early on that show. By the second season, I think we were all really burnt, because we'd been working non-stop on all these superhero shows for many

years already at that point. And as I've said before, when we first started *Batman Beyond*, we were doing the Superman and Batman revamp shows at the same time, so we were really burning the candle at both ends at that point. It's almost a miracle that the *Batman Beyond* show came out as good as it did, because we were all just running on fumes at that point. I think our inspiration started flagging by the second season. The first season was pretty solid, and by the second season we had way too many shows where the dad of one of Terry's friends couldn't make the car payment that month and so became a super-villain. There were a lot of really lame villains in the second season and not very interesting stories. And then there was a little bit of time off in between *Batman Beyond* and *Justice League*, so we got kind of ramped up again. Certainly by the second season of *Justice League*, I think we're firing on all cylinders again.

Clark Kent changes into the Man of Steel in "The Last Son of Krypton." Superman TM & ©2004 DC Comics. Art ©2004 Warner Bros. Animation

DRAW ALL THE BLOODY TIME

For artists breaking into the field of animation or comics, Bruce Timm always gives the same advice.

BRUCE TIMM: Just draw all the bloody time. I mean, that's the thing. I'll go through periods where I'm so busy doing the actual production of the show that I don't get a chance to draw, and I get really rusty. Whenever I actually have to sit down and actually draw something, I'm really, really rusty. It takes a long time to get back up to speed to actually churn the drawings out. So literally just draw all the damned time. There are people I know who don't draw for fun. There are artists that I've worked with who only draw when they're getting paid for it. And I can't even understand that. I could understand it if they're too tired at the end of the day to draw. But I've met a lot of artists who literally don't draw or have never drawn for fun, where they only draw just to make a living. And it's like, how can they even do that? If you don't love what you're doing, if you don't get any satisfaction or thrill from actually drawing, then why are you even doing it? Why aren't you working at K-Mart, y'know?

As for people trying to break into the business, there's no easy answer. Every place that you're going to apply to draw, they have their own yardstick of what they're looking for. Diversity is a good thing. As I said before, once you get in the business, diversify as much as you can so you don't get pigeonholed as "just a storyboard artist" or "just a background guy" or whatever. It's good to have lots of different talents and skills. Same thing goes for your portfolio. I'm all for people having their own individual style, but at the same time, when you're going out to look for work, when you're showing your work to somebody, you have no idea what they're looking for. If they're only looking for the next Adam Hughes, and you've only got Bruce Timm-style stuff in your portfolio, you're not going to get the job. There's this thing I call "the orange theory." If you're looking for work and the guy who's hiring is looking for somebody to draw an orange and you've got an orange in your portfolio, you're going to get the job, whether it's a good orange or not. I've seen that happen. Some art directors really have a real limited world view. They can't extrapolate. They can't see that if you've got a well-drawn apple, that you should be able to draw an orange. People looking for work, they should have as many different kinds of stuff in their portfolio as possible. They should be able to show that they can draw people *and* backgrounds. Okay, I realize this is a case of "don't do as I do, kids, do as I say." But it's true. Because you never know what the art director is looking for.

An example of Timm's drawing. By continuously drawing, an artist can achieve confident, dynamic lines. Few artists are more dynamic than Bruce Timm. Justice League TM & ©2004 DC Comics.

Comics & New Media

Three award-winning veterans of the animation industry joined forces to form a new media company, phuuz entertainment in North Hollywood, California. Co-founders of this new enterprise are Emmy Award-winning producer/director and former executive creative director at Film Roman, Eric Radomski, former VP/GM for LEVEL13.NET (Film Roman's Internet entertainment site), Jay Francis, and former production at Warner Brothers Animation, Ken Duer.

phuuz develops original properties for new media like video and computer games, wireless technologies, DVD, internet, and traditional media like television, film, comic books/graphic novels. They also develop for ancillary markets like toys, fashion, advertising, music and utilize new media platforms to maximize franchising and distribution opportunities. Eric Radomski (whose credits include: Xiaolin Showdown, Batman the Series, Mask of the Phantasm, Freakazoid, Spawn, and Spicy City) and Jay Francis (whose credits include: Level 13.Net, King of the Hill, Mission Hill, The Oblongs, X-men: Evolution and the Simpsons) share their thoughts on storytelling and its evolution and survival in the new media age:

JAY FRANCIS: Eric and I both started in the animation industry in 1985. Network and syndicated television animation was in its heyday and there really wasn't an Internet, DVD, or strong video game market in which to present new and unique independently produced ideas. Obviously, that's not the case in today's technology based entertainment industry. With the multitude of distribution platforms that exist today and the ability to produce content cost-effectively, we felt we could create a business that could take advantage of our project development and production experience. Thus *phuuz* entertainment was born.

Despite the bursting of the dot-com bubble, the Internet was and continues to be an eye-opening platform. Independent producers from around the world can effectively present concepts to a world-wide audience and receive immediate feedback. This is an incredible phenomenon, one that we feel will give the independent creator more opportunity and perhaps some leverage in dealing with the major entertainment corporations. The ability to distribute to even a grass roots level audience is gigantic to an independent producer.

ERIC RADOMSKI: Evolution of entertainment is the basis for *phuuz*. I was a creator and I wanted creative freedom instead of my work always being commercially driven. Comics are a great escape for someone to tell their own story freely; there's no budget for special effects and you use your own means. The Internet and our animation business is similar. On the Internet you can create your own material, you're responsible for it, and no one will tell you no. Artists have the chance to get back to the reason why they got in the business: to be free and not have their creativity squelched.

It starts with a story you want to tell, the ability to create it without the interference of a higher up, a limited budget, a deadline, or the worry of your weekly paycheck. *phuuz* is inspired by the Internet mentality—to keep a story as pure as possible without compromising your artistic value while still maintaining some commercial value. I want to free you up to express yourself and put your money where your mouth is. It's a great time to be in the business when the audience and delivery is changing.

Kids born after the 1980s are raised on video games and the Internet. These digital natives absorb content from numerous sources. How can creators adapt their storytelling in these new mediums while maintaining control?

FRANCIS: If by control you mean how an audience acquires the content, I'm not sure that creators ever had complete control *per sé*. The audience's ability to download music, films, and television shows without compensation is something that the entire entertainment industry has to figure out. If by control you mean the control of the content, then I think the new mediums are perfect for the independent artist. Good storytelling is good storytelling regardless of the medium. The ability to tell a story the way you want and let an audience decide whether or not it's compelling is all most creators have ever wanted. The Internet specifically and to a lesser extent video games and direct to video distribution have allowed the creator the final say in all creative aspects of the content.

Control is going back to creators: the creator brings the creation to the audience and the audience dictates if it's worthwhile—if you scrape off the surface, it's *still* about a story. Is it compelling enough to watch?

phuuz develops properties for new media, including computer games, DVDs, Internet, and traditional media. How can a story be best matched to its perfect medium?

RADOMSKI: This generation and the evolving audience is driven by personal statement. It helps to be aware of the things they like to be known for as individuals: the things they wear, the music they listen to. This helps decide which form and media would appeal to the potential audience. For example, people into extreme sports have a certain attitude and a presentation of themselves as to what they wear and with the attitude of having no fear. They consider themselves extreme even though like anyone else, they're cautious. They can't participate like these athletes do, but they admire people who break rules and wear the graphic images and clothes.

If I see an artist that has pushed the envelope and developed their own style and looks like they have something that would appeal to that particular audience, then that would be an apparel/branding graphics for that particular artist. If there's a character that's developed by the artist along the way, then it can be more than a graphic.

You figure out who the character is, how they tie into the whole skater/extreme sports culture, and you create a storyline for the character. And then you think of where the gap is for that particular character. Is there a comic book on this kind of character already? If so, how about a video game? Cartoon? Books? Is it a comedy or drama?

There is a bit of a contradiction when I said you want to go for the pure, creative freedom, but you still have to consider what a studio will finance into a movie. If skateboarding is out, what about motorcross? There is no perfect formula. Something I create that's original comes from the things that I like and my inspirations. If you're familiar with the arena, the creation is more believable to the audience.

FRANCIS: When we develop a property, we look at it upside down, right side up, left and right to make sure it fills more than one medium. The reality of our business is that a property has to have multiple lives. Can it be a feature, comic book, toy, video game, and a television series? That said, if a story and/or character is compelling enough to warrant development, we have to stay true to the original concept. Perhaps we might bend a bit here or there to attract a buyer but we feel it's important to stay consistent to the overall concept.

The reality of the business is that the story has to cross mediums. In adapting to different media, you can't lose what's initially compelling about the story by changing major parts of it. You stay true to the initial story, and we want the creator to stay true to that goal.

Most content developers can be heavy-handed, forcing ideas in the most unlikely matches. Few titles utilize a multiple mediums to their fullest potential. How can an idea be successful in multiple arenas?

RADOMSKI: We instinctively knew all along that the potential was there for ideas to cross-pollinate. Seeing all these possibilities out there like the Internet and computer games–it's endless. When I went back through my store of ideas that I jot down, I suddenly saw the possibilities for all of this because of this epiphany of new opportunity. Pure excitement. I have to curb myself because it's almost like the ideas are endless now and not all of them can see the light of day. Not everything can be as huge and successful as *The Matrix*, but I don't feel restricted in selling myself to one area. I can do whatever I want and throw it out there and have just as much chance as having something made as anyone. There's so many different things I want to do, I almost wish for a 48-hour day.

FRANCIS: I think you need to build an environment around a compelling story or character. Two examples that come to mind, The *Matrix* and *Gorillaz*. The *Matrix* isn't just a movie and a video game. It's

clothes, toys, accessories…in fact, it's a culture, a community, an environment. Similarly, the *Gorillaz* dvd is an exceptional example of melding animation, interactivity, merchandising, music, and games. Once immersed in the world of *Gorillaz*, it's hard to categorize it has just a cartoon or just a rock group.

RADOMSKI: Tapping into your audience is important.

In today's markets, audiences are much more difficult to identify. However, they also are the most critical. How does a creator win over an audience?

RADOMSKI: San Diego Comic-Con is a perfect example: it's gone way beyond comics…big Hollywood studios preview their materials there because they know this is their audience and the audience will soon be in online chat rooms and instant messaging their friends. And it's all free marketing. It's also showing respect for the audience's taste and opinion. If you can go directly to the source–like online sites–and test out the material, they'll ask for more if they like it. If you go directly to that one percent audience and hand out the free samples and ask them what they think, it's a lot more effective business-wise because you're not spending near as much as other forms of advertising. The audience will gravitate toward quality and their specific taste. And it's a true test of if you're your idea will even work. It's not a network telling you who they think the audience is and forcing you to compromise your idea.

FRANCIS: If I had the answer to how to definitively win over an audience I'd be retired in Hawaii right now. It certainly isn't a science; who really knows what will work, what doesn't? *Power Rangers* is a global phenomenon, why? *The Iron Giant* barely registered a blip. Put them side by side and tell me which should have been the winner. I think all any creator can really do is stay true to a vision. If you try to create a project with the idea of pleasing everyone, you're doomed.

What makes an idea attractive to phuuz?

RADOMSKI: We all have our individual tastes, but we do respect those differences and have some similarities. Speaking for myself, I see value in what other creators have even when it's not something that I may like completely. When I look for stories for *phuuz*, the first order of business is, unfortunately, business. I look at the concept first and think if it has the ability to branch out into many avenues. And second, look at the creator attached to the project and hope they are the type than can expand with the idea; that's not necessary, but it's important that creator be involved in the various concepts so they can be true to the original idea.

"Good storytelling is good storytelling regardless of the medium. The ability to tell a story the way you want and let an audience decide whether or not it's compelling is all most creators have ever wanted."

– JAY FRANCIS

As far as the ideas and the types of things we're looking for, I'd say a unique looking style is important and it no longer is restricted by hand-drawn 2-D, which I am still a huge fan of. Even just a written idea can be forward thinking. I don't mind being derivative or adapting basic story ideas like a writer's workshop as long we look at how the world has changed around us. For example, if I were producing a Bugs Bunny cartoon today, the setting and story around Bugs would reflect contemporary themes. Bugs' personality can cross generations, which is the same with a lot of the Warner Brothers characters; you can put them in the future or in gladiator times and they're the same personality. If you have that core idea and purity, you can build it out from there.

As long as you have an open-minded creator, it's a great starting point.

FRANCIS: I'm partial to stories and situations that make me laugh, characters I can care about, and are visually compelling. The old Warner Brothers characters had that appeal for me. I feel the best creators can so define the personality of a character in such a way that we feel that we know the character intimately. The stories and characters can come from anywhere, comic books, video games, short films, etc. Uniqueness is good, stories and characters that fit together perfectly is even better.

RADOMSKI: And it falls into that cliché of life imitating art or art imitating life; it's that scenario where you reflect your surroundings or environment. The creation of a character is the creator expressing their point of view whether it's serious or completely ridiculous.

I worked with Todd MacFarlane on the *Spawn* animated series. I didn't know the comic but when I did understand the character, I was very inspired by the kind of Faustian storytelling only hinted at reading the first of his books. [MacFarlane] created this thing and wasn't focusing on interesting parts of the characters, which made me uncomfortable. He only wanted to make it really violent and wanted Spawn to be a big guy that only beat up monsters. And I know HBO didn't pick up [the series] for that reason. HBO hired me to give the story some body. Todd got the basic concept, but it just wasn't the most important thing to him. And yet, how do you argue with someone who had such meteoric success [with the comic]? It's great he found his audience and figured out how to exploit it. When the high-budget *Spawn* movie came out, it was so off the mark from the concept that the series crew and I were embarrassed. It was so disappointing; they missed the mark of who the character was.

Like with the classic Warner's characters, you don't screw with the personalities or you lose the character. As soon as you limit the character to a few catchphrases, you lose the motivation and appeal and turn it into advertising instead of storytelling.

At *phuuz*, we want to create an environment where the creator can see their idea through and expand their idea into areas they may not have thought of without compromising their original idea. We offer and promise that to the creator.

That's been very attractive to the creative people we've talked to because that's all any creative person desires: to have a little play room and the tools to make their idea come to life. And that's just not available in the mainstream industry these days unless you have a small group that can respect the idea and the art form. Right now only the wealthy few can play and do what they want: Lucas, Spielberg; everyone else has to climb up the ladder, struggling, begging, and compromising. Sure Lucas and Spielberg made crap, but the fact that they did some great stuff is inspiration for everyone else coming up that they can do great stuff, too.

> *"If you have that core idea and purity, you can build it out from there."*
>
> — ERIC RADOMSKI